RED SEA PERIL

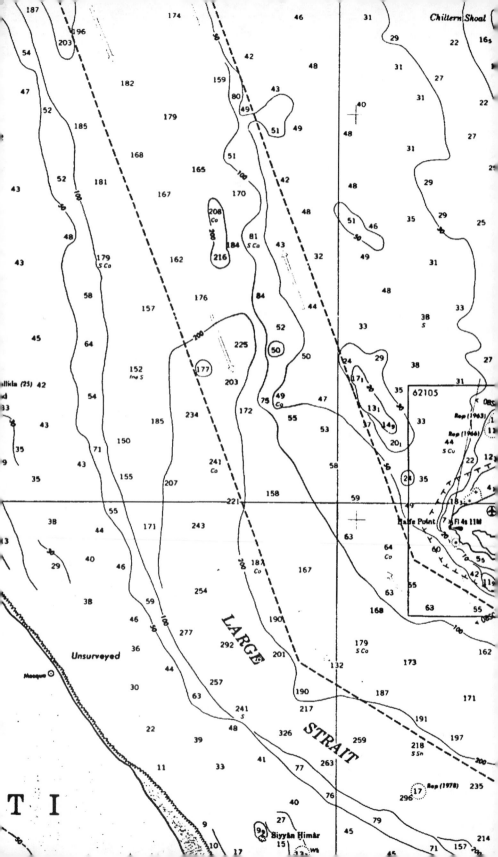

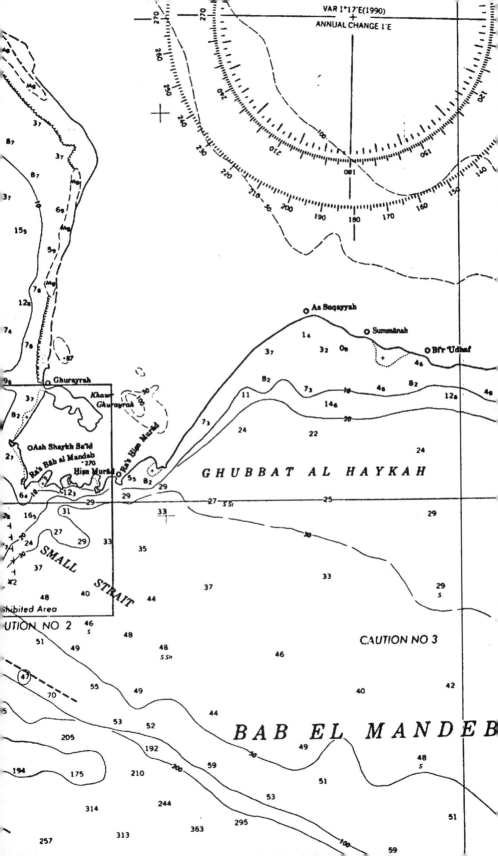

RED SEA PERIL

SHIRLEY BILLING

 SHERIDAN HOUSE

First published 2002 in the United States
by Sheridan House Inc.
145 Palisade Street
Dobbs Ferry, New York 10522
www.sheridanhouse.com

First published in Great Britain 1998
by Cruising Association

Library of Congress Cataloging-in-Publication Data

Billing, Shirley
    Red Sea peril/Shirley Billing.
        p. cm.
    Includes index.
    ISBN 1-57409-137-9 (alk. paper)
    1. Billing, Shirley – Journeys. 2. Billing, Peter – Journeys.
    3. Billing, Shirley – Captivity, – 1996.
    4. Billing, Peter – Captivity, – 1996. 5. Eritrea – Politics
    and government, – 1993-. 6. Seafaring life. I. Title.

    G540. B355 2001
    963.507'2'0922–dc21   2001031099
    [B]

Edited by Fred Barter

Printed in the United States of America

ISBN 1-57409-137-9

Contents

Foreword *by Basil d'Oliveira*
Author's Acknowledgements
Description and layout of ketch CLYPEUS

Chapter

Dedication

To Peter, my husband and my home.

To our family who generously let us go
and then worked so hard to get us back.

To Brian and Lorraine Raison
of MARA who stood by us.

To Linda and Don Bryce of GREEN DOLPHIN,
Bill and Karen Kneebone of KULAROO
and all the other international yachtsmen
who helped, and cared and sent donations
to the "Save CLYPEUS Fund."

"But if the while we think on thee, dear friends,
All losses are restored and sorrow ends."

Shakespeare sonnet

FOREWORD

Even though my good friends Peter and Shirley Billing
had always been keen sailors, nevertheless it came as quite
a surprise to everyone when they decided to sell up and
undertake a passage to Australia. It was a brave decision to
make. Little did any of us think they would still be
cruising in 1998.

Peter and Shirley left St Katharine's Dock in March 1983.
Over the subsequent years they have virtually circumnavigated
the world apart from the short 1500 mile sector between
Cyprus and Ibiza to link up with their original outbound
track. They plan to complete this final leg during 1999.
They have completed over 55,000 miles of ocean cruising
which is a considerable achievement in its own right.
They have kept family and friends in touch with their travels
and experiences by sending a regular series of highly
interesting and informative newsletters. You read the letters
over and over again - and waited for the next issue to arrive.
These letters have provided an excellent basis for this book.
One particular quote sticks in my mind - the Billings
definition of "togetherness" is "being seasick simultaneously
over the side holding hands".

When sailing up the Red Sea in 1996 they anchored in the
right place, but at the wrong time. The story of their arrest,
interrogation and transport across the desert to Assab for
further questioning is unusual. However, the ominous flight
to Asmara on one way tickets under false names is the stuff of
fiction and not the normal cruising story.

This book expresses the experiences, frustrations and
enjoyment involved in ocean cruising together with some
astute observations about the many places and peoples
visited.

Basil d'Oliveira

28 August, 1998

Author's Acknowledgements

To the caring international yachtsmen and women

To Rosemary and Noel who alerted Basil
and took the brunt of media enquiries and kept the whole
family informed, together with Andrea and Rupert, and
Sheila and Tony, who gave supportive back up.

Basil d'Oliveira for his knowledge, understanding
of the situation, and quick response in alerting the
authorities and the media.

Azib, the kindly proprietress of the
Khartoum Hotel, Asmara.

Dr. Rod Hicks, the Honorary British Consul in Asmara.

Monique and Etienne Forget, our French fellow detainees.

Alice and Paul who gave me the time to write
it all down in Wisconsin, USA.

My sisters, Hilary in Australia, who incisively edited out
anything not immediately relevant and Sheila, who has
given me constant encouragement.

Lois and James Barrell for their never ending
welcome to their home.

All those friends who have kept in touch and made it
worthwhile writing the letters and recording our feelings.

Brian and Lorraine Raison of MARA and
Don and Linda Bryce of GREEN DOLPHIN
for some of the photographs used in this book.

Fred Barter and Geoff Doggett who have taken
me under their wings and allowed my book to fly.

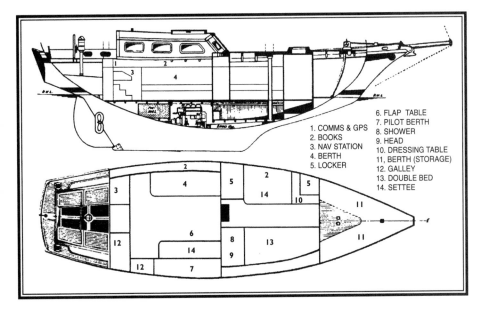

6. FLAP TABLE
7. PILOT BERTH
1. COMMS & GPS   8. SHOWER
2. BOOKS   9. HEAD
3. NAV STATION   10. DRESSING TABLE
4. BERTH   11. BERTH (STORAGE)
5. LOCKER   12. GALLEY
                        13. DOUBLE BED
                        14. SETTEE

Clypeus   35' ketch.   A ferro-cement Endurance 35.

CLYPEUS *has a conventional interior: from the aft cockpit you step down into the main dog-house cabin. The wide carpeted step is actually the lid of the small fridge/cooler. One more step takes you onto the wooden parquet floor under which is the Perkins 4108 diesel engine. On the left, the navigation desk has our radios and GPS (Global Positioning System) above it. A 6' red velour settee with storage under and a bookcase behind, reaches to the bulkhead. On the right, is the galley.*
A stainless steel sink and draining board are athwart the cockpit bulkhead and a Neptune calor gas cooker with an oven, adjoins along the side. The fiddled flap-down table sits to the right off-centre in front of another short settee, with a full sized pilot berth behind it.

Forward to port, is a hanging locker and wardrobe, opposite the bathroom which has a washbasin, toilet and shower. Further forward is the main bedroom cabin with a high double bed over lockers, and on the port side a small settee, dressing table and hanging locker. A door leads to a 'V' berth forward cabin, now piled high with stores, books, some of my shell collection, spare sails and paper files. The anchor chain rests in the forepeak.

(Clypeus is a Greek entomological term for part of the hard carapace of an insect).

Thailand Phuket •

CHAPTER ONE

*CLYPEUS, our
35' ketch.
A ferro-cement
Endurance 35.*

Lorraine and Brian Raison

*Peter said
"What are we
rushing back
to Europe for?"*

Andaman Sea and Indian Ocean

If we had carried on westwards with our Australian friends and not decided to spend a further year in Thailand and Malaysia, we would have missed one the most worrying, and possibly the most exciting, periods of our sailing life. As it was, the Eritrean Government, apart from locking us up in different places, flew us the length of their country, and showed us their capital city, all for free.

In 1995 we had sailed to Phuket from Singapore in company with MITHRA, SUNSHINE and SAOIRSE (pronounced Seersha), a fun-loving trio of yacht couples all from Fremantle Sailing Club. We had hoped to buddy boat with them through to the Mediterranean, keeping a safety net of regular radio schedules.

After a hectic Christmas and New Year party season, we four yachts started out to cross the Indian Ocean together. Sixty miles out of Phuket we all stopped in the Semilan Islands for a rest day. Indecisively, Peter and I sat on the dazzling white sand beach gazing at CLYPEUS, our 35' ketch, nodding in the turquoise sea.

Nuzzling our toes in the hot sand, Peter said "What are we rushing back to Europe for?"

"I don't know. To see the family I guess."

"Well, living will never be as cheap and easy as it has been sailing in Asia. I don't trust that cracked chain plate I found yesterday.

Let's go back, do more maintenance, explore more thoroughly, and cross the Indian Ocean next year.

"Yup, I'd like that. I could go to Oz and give Hilary another break. But what about our buddy boats?"

"They'll understand."

There and then we decided that neither we, nor our boat, were ready to embark on the hazards and dangers of the long voyage home to England.

Our friends did understand and promised to keep in touch by radio as long as they could. They would write and let us know about their experiences up the Red Sea. It was a sad goodbye; they had been such fun.

The extra year in Asia flew by. We explored fabulous Phang Nga Bay more thoroughly, revisited Langkawi, Penang and Pangkor. We anchored for four months up the Ding-Dings River in Malaysia. Peter replaced some chain plates and worked on CLYPEUS's hull. I flew down to Perth and cared for my bedridden father while my widowed sister Hilary went sailing on the three masted barquentine LEEUWIN.

We anchored for four months up the Ding-Dings River.

In December we once again prepared to leave for Europe.

January 11th 1996, Phuket, Thailand.

"Ready?" Peter asked, looking searchingly into my eyes.

"Well, yes. Let's go, go, go. There's enough food and drink on board to last us a month, and, as you say, it should only take ten days to Sri Lanka."

"Coffee first?" asked my procrastinating captain (assuming I have the title of admiral) - it takes us a bit of psyching-up to let go of land.

"No, let's get going. Otherwise MARA and KULAROO will be ahead of us all the time." This year's plan was to sail to Cyprus in the Mediterranean, keeping in radio contact with MARA and KULAROO, both cruising catamarans from Australia. Our ferro-cement Endurance 35 is no racing machine. We have to work hard to keep up with our larger, faster, friends.

Brian Raison

"Right." Peter said. "I'll start the motor. You pull down the Blue Peter".

As I pulled down the signal for imminent departure, I remembered last night's happy farewell party under the palm trees when Bob of LAZYBONES had recited "The man from Ironbark" and Patrick and Carolyn of COCKAIGNE had rendered a special "King of the Road".

"Right." Peter said. "I'll start the motor. You pull down the Blue Peter".

"Peter and Shirley awoke and the sun did shine,
Picked up the anchor and stowed all the line
Sailed 1,000 miles to a Sri Lankan Bay
And Shirley said "It's been a lovely day."
You sail a thousand miles and what do you get?
Another day older and deeper in debt
St. Neptune don't you call them
'Cos they can't go - They got to sail
Old Clypeus to a Cypriot shore."

Parting is so difficult. Will we ever see them again?

MITHRA, SUNSHINE and SAIORSE had kept us informed of their travels and the visits they had made up the Red Sea to Massawa in Eritrea, where they had been invited to a local wedding; to Suakin in Sudan; to Safaga in Egypt, from where they visited the Pyramids. The Red Sea hadn't been as daunting as anticipated; as long as you sailed early in the day and anchored before the strong northerlies commenced in the afternoon.

"No hurry, no worries," they said.

Peter slipped the yellow mooring buoy while I slowly motored forward sounding the fog horn to acknowledge the cheers of "Bon Voyage" and "See you" from neighbouring yachts. We were off, excited to be on our way over 1,000 miles across the Indian Ocean to Sri Lanka, but sorry to leave good friends and a delightful country.

We both felt seasick in spite of it being a fairly calm sunny day. Cream crackers and water were all we could stomach.

The white skyscrapers of Patong shimmered amongst green and grey hills and gradually faded away.

By 11am Peter had set the sails as he hoped they would be for the next ten days - full main and boomed out yankee. In the afternoon he hoisted the staysail as well. Then the sea became smooth and the wind disappeared. We watched frigate birds diving into the water and a few tidy white terns fluttered across the surface. Motoring all the way to Sri Lanka wasn't viable but we justified running the engine for a couple of hours to top up the batteries. The Perkins diesel engine performed steadily as it has done ever since Peter installed it in 1983.

CLYPEUS, our voyaging home, is a cutter-rigged ketch (two foresails, two masts) built in England in 1975 by Norman Bagshaw in Fareham. He had built her to sail around the world with his family, but by the time she was finished, his family had grown and gone. We had bought her in 1982 and now our sea-kindly, but overweight, home was over twenty years old. With three cabins she is an ideal cosy home in Northern Europe but not a cool boat for the tropics, as not enough wind can blow through her.

At 11pm Peter woke me. "Dolphins."

"Great!" I scrambled out of my bunk and up into the cockpit and could see their tubes of phosphorescence tunnelling, swooping and circling alongside. Suddenly they would sparkle up through the velvet blackness to snort and blow a fountain of stars. Cylinders of light swept to the surface exploding in a bouquet of shining phosphorescence.

Later on, during my three hour watch, we passed through our third patch of "poppling" water. It is always worrying when the sea pattern changes. Here the little wavelets couldn't decide which way to go and just slopped against each other continually colliding and bouncing away. A rainstorm calmed the sea down but it was still sloppy. Other boats had radioed back that they had experienced very rough seas around here 07°31N. 96°38E. We gradually left behind the popply sea and squid fishing boats glowing in the dark.

Each morning at 8.30 am on 4417kHz, all the yachts with radios crossing the Indian Ocean checked in and gave their positions and any news. This marine mobile net was hosted at first by Casey on SWEET SURRENDER until they anchored in Galle, then Maggie of WIRRAWAY kept control of the radio waves. It was pleasant to have a friendly greeting each morning and find out our position in relation to the other yachts. We also kept a 7.30am, noon, 6pm, and midnight schedule with MARA and KULAROO on VHF if within range, or 4417kHz if more than 20 miles separated us.

For dinner on our second day out we had roast pork and

roast potatoes, onions, carrots and green beans. We were obviously feeling better in spite of the boat rolling and the mainsail slamming when the light breeze died away. We let the main crash and bang for a few hours, then took it down, relaxed and waited for the wind. Gradually the breeze freshened and with a three-quarter moon behind us we could see both The Plough and The Southern Cross bright in the sky at the same time.

The wind stayed light but the sea became very disturbed. Next day's dinner was chicken cordon bleu in spite of the crazy rolling which didn't affect our appetites now. At sea, meals become the highlight of our day and a small cocktail beforehand made each evening a social occasion. We had made a pact before embarking on our voyage that this 3 hour watch would be our happy hour. All disputes forgotten, even if we reverted to not speaking again later.

We have never had to call our pact, not because we haven't quarrelled but because we both realise tolerance is essential when there is no respite from each other.

By the fourth night we had travelled 318 miles. Our thoughts were filled with the task of the finding the Sombrero Channel, which was less than a mile wide, through the unlit Nicobar Islands. CLYPEUS was speeding, at 6 knots, plus 2 knots of current, in the inky dark, towards our GPS waypoint at the entrance to the dreaded Channel.

"I wish we could have arrived here in daylight." I groaned, scared stiff, not being able to seeing anything, and having to just trust our planning, the GPS (Global Positioning System) and the compass.

The full mainsail was up and the yankee boomed out. Phosphorescent foam tumbled away from our hull as we rolled, rattled and swished through the water. Around us the wavetops were breaking shining white. Cascading foam ran down the face of the hills of water. We both sat in the cockpit, ready for any emergency. Peter finds it easy to rely on electronics and was reasonably relaxed - I would much rather see where we were going.

The GPS bleep told us it was time to change course. Peter went below and called out: "Change to 240°."

I undid the Aries self steering and stood holding the wheel peering into the dark distance and listened for waves crashing on rocks.

"How can you just sit down there so confidently marking our position on the chart?" I called out. "Don't you want to come and make sure all is well?"

"Nope. All is well. Just keep on course."

Half a terrifying hour, for me, passed. Not a light or a

Our thoughts were filled with the task of finding the less than a mile wide Sombrero Channel through the unlit Nicobar Islands. CLYPEUS was speeding, at 6 knots plus 2 knots of current, in the inky dark, towards our GPS waypoint at the entrance to the dreaded Channel.

darkening of the horizon showed the islands. Then he called out again "OK. We're through, change to 265° and I'll come and reset the Aries wind vane." Placidly he came up and took over. I went below, made us both a mug of Milo and collapsed into my bunk.

Three hours later I took over again and we carried on across the Indian Ocean averaging between 120 and 140 miles a day. I felt 'thick, thick, thick' as Violet Elizabeth used to say in 'Just William'. I noted 'Everyone else on the radio is very 'stiff upper lip' saying what a great passage we're having. We are - it's fast and safe but such unpredictable rolling in the cross swell. The sea isn't all going in the same direction and every so often suddenly tips the boat on its side - either way, you can't anticipate. So tummies are uptight and rigid,

By January 17th I had come to the conclusion that the Indian Ocean is an untidy, undisciplined, sea even on balmy days.

awaiting the next lurch and drop.'

MARAKI reported that while sailing at four-and-a-half knots they hit a sleeping whale. Their bow slid 18" up its back and cut it, sadly leaving a pool of blood behind. Other sperm whales, in the pod of about ten, gathered around it as MARAKI sailed on. They felt terribly guilty, but didn't know what they could do to help.

I felt queasy so lay on my bed and listened to music tapes and finished recording stories and songs for my grand-children. How I miss them. I wonder what they are doing?

By January 17th I had come to the conclusion that the Indian Ocean is an untidy, undisciplined, sea even on balmy days. Yes, we were having a wonderful sail as far as a warm wind under sunny skies; but the short swell and cross waves made it an uncomfortable ride. I wrote in my journal: 'CLYPEUS trembles like an excited puppy before she hurls herself forward down the next wave, then what a jarring and jerking as she is stopped short by ploughing into the next one.

Curling crests slap her from all sides. As she lurches so the main boom crashes against the rigging and twangs the shrouds and our nerves. The gunshot bang of a cross rogue wave suddenly lifts one side and drops her into a hole causing us to hang on and lift our mugs to keep the contents inside. It has to be endured to the end - like having a baby - you can't say "thank you, I have had enough now."'

The next day the sea motion was much better. The waves were still 1-2 metres but mostly going in the same direction. We had a lovely day, comfortable, easy, with relaxed tummies. I enjoyed reading "Ultimate Prizes" by Susan Howitch. Another lovely day followed and in the afternoon the coast of Sri Lanka was in sight.

The next day the sea motion was much better. The waves were still 1-2 metres but mostly going in the same direction.

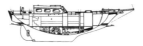

Sri Lanka
Galle Harbour

CHAPTER TWO

Sri Lanka   05°50'N Lat 80°22'E Long

O n our ninth day out from Phuket we sailed along the south coast of Sri Lanka. It looked like a beautiful island with yellow sand beaches, palm trees and distant mountains. An aromatic smell of tobacco drifted out across the water. Some fishing boats changed course towards us and we worried. Were they Tamil Tigers wanting money, arms or just cigarettes? Were they pirates? However the fishermen only waved and went on. MARA and KULAROO were now closing in behind us.   Dondra Light was a good mark all night and we entered Galle Harbour just after dawn. We had made 1030 miles in ten days having a good 1-2 knot current with us most of the time. Our best day's run was 140 miles.

We dropped the Bruce bow anchor and took a stern line to the buoy.

We dropped the Bruce bow anchor and took a stern line to the buoy in the centre of a circle of yachts. Amongst friends, we chatted on the VHF and were told to call Don Windsor Agency on Channel 69, who requested we wait on board for the Harbour Master. He arrived at 9.30, a pleasant substantial 35 year old Indian. We gave him a beer and he asked for a 'souvenir'. A packet of Benson & Hedges Gold satisfied him. I gave a packet to the crewmen holding the launch too.

With our ship's papers we rowed ashore through clean clear water. Don Windsor's office was nearby and was a pleasant rendezvous. Yachts' people sat sipping cold beer on the verandah. I read our mail while Peter filled in forms. An agent took us to Immigration, Customs and Police. They were all friendly and welcoming especially now we no longer carry guns. They had seemed a sensible precaution but had proved more trouble than they were worth. They had been left with the police in Singapore.

On the road from the harbour, visitors were accosted by a number of young men offering services: laundry, tours, and stores. Marlin seemed an honest cheerful young man who assured us he could fix anything we wanted. His long curls made him look like a cavalier - D'Artagnan could be just around the corner! He invited us to his house for fresh mango juice, information and fruit and vegetable price lists. Excusing ourselves, we then walked to Mike's Yacht Services, the most highly recommended of the agents, and compared prices and values.

On our return to the harbour via Don Windsor's a BBQ party with a band was in full swing. We chatted with other voyagers, swapped yarns and enjoyed the steak, sausages and fresh bread. However, we were really tired and excused ourselves, looking forward to an early night and a good sleep.

Suddenly, from a deep sleep, we were awakened by a loud BANG! which reverberated through the hull. We jumped up and went on deck. It occurred again and again every three or four hours throughout the night, in fact during our whole stay in Galle Harbour. We had been warned that the Sri Lankan Navy was dynamiting indiscriminately during darkness, but we hadn't expected it to be this loud or so worrying. Would the vibration frequency be exactly correct to make our concrete hull disintegrate? Peter assured me it wouldn't.

Two naval ships were anchored in the harbour, protected by netting to keep Tamil terrorist scuba divers away. The navy were taking the extra precaution of exploding charges to burst the eardrums of any divers who might be underwater.

When we awoke, silent fishermen in dug-out canoes alongside us were pulling in their nets. They weaved their primitive outriggers between the anchored yachts with never a word or sound. They smiled and waved when approached, but never intruded.

When we awoke, silent fishermen in dug-out canoes alongside us were pulling in their nets.

After taking our laundry to Marlin's home as arranged, he drove us into town and familiarised us with the old walled city of Galle.

Then he took us into the modern town, to the Craft Factory where lace, leather and batik

The Craft Factory where lace, leather and batik workers showed their skills.

workers showed their skills. The most interesting craft was the making of gold rings. After melting the gold in tiny crucibles it was poured into moulds carved into cuttlefish bones. We were then left to explore on our own; we hoped, but we just could not get rid of the touts who wasted our time offering to take us to places we didn't want to go. We gave in and walked for miles to find we were back at the factory we had already visited. The important church, we were assured MUST be seen, was locked when we arrived. Finally at the Post Office in the old walled town we firmly told our guides to please go away. We wanted to find our own way around.

Galle is a lovely little city of narrow streets. Some of the small houses were fronted with Doric columns. There were many Dutch style homes and a large white Catholic church. We walked right around the city wall stopping to sit on the grass below the lighthouse, to look on the beach for shells, and just view the peaceful scene. Once again the sellers of lace, semi-precious stones and coins just wouldn't leave us alone. We eventually became really annoyed and left. The sellers are so persistent. They just will not take "no thank you" for an answer. Having visited India previously, we decided then that we would not sail to Cochin after all. We just couldn't face India again and have the never-ending task of saying 'NO'. On a small boat you just don't have the space to take a souvenir from everywhere you land, even if you like what is being offered.

In the evening we joined Karen and Bill of KULAROO for dinner at the Closenberg Hotel on the headland. It was a charming old colonial hotel in a delightful setting. The cool ambiance was enhanced with much old wood and coral waterfall decorations. The sea lapped the rocks below the sweet scented frangipani trees, and we were left to order our meal quietly and with no hassle. Late, on the way home, allowing for the time difference, we called in at Don Windsor's to telephone our family to let them know we had arrived safe and sound. They were all well and happy.

With Brian and Lorraine of MARA and Karen and Bill of

KULAROO we booked a five day tour around Sri Lanka with Marlin. He invited us to his home so that his wife and mother-in-law could give us a cookery lesson. Asoka, Marlin's wife, and Karoona, his mother, showed us how to cook dahl, deviled potato, string houpas, fish emoutielle (clay-pot fish and coconut curry with tamarind), kancun (curried vine-leaves) and poppadums. There was no kitchen table, the maid crouched on her haunches and prepared the vegetables on a piece of sacking on the floor. They seemed a happy Hindu family with two children, a boy of five and a baby. Marlin told us that his mother still lived in the 300 year old Portuguese house his family had owned since it was built.

There was no kitchen table, the maid crouched on her haunches and prepared the vegetables on a piece of sacking on the floor.

We learnt a few words Hello - *aiwa*, G'day - *stootsi*.

Next day, in a Toyota minibus, we started our tour of the 2,500 year old rich cultural heritage of Sri Lanka. Our driver Fiat, was a slim, small, fifty-year-old Sri Lankan with reasonable English. He was an excellent, steady, driver and in the whole time, even on the tortuous mountain roads, we never had the slightest worry. Fiat set off to the east and our first stop was to see the stilt fishermen at Weligama. They perch on poles out in the surf, fishing with a rod and line. We felt duty bound to buy little handmade lace doilies from their wives as we took photographs. Fiat took us to a tourist restaurant, but it wasn't what we wanted.

Lorraine and Brian Raison

Our first stop was to see the stilt fishermen at Weligama. They perch on poles out in the surf, fishing with a rod and line.

The next stop was outside a wayside shack offering buffalo curd with palm syrup.

We wanted to eat where Sri Lankans ate and do our best to enjoy local food.

He took us at our word and the next stop was outside a wayside shack offering buffalo curd with palm syrup. Lorraine, Brian and I thought it delicious, but Karen, Bill and Peter weren't prepared to try. The buffalo curd came in hand-thrown terra cotta bowls and the palm honey is collected at a great height from the resin at the top of palm trees. Parallel lines are strung across from top to top of the palm trees and the men walk along the lower rope, one hand holding the top line. Resin is gathered and boiled like maple syrup. The dessert tasted like yogurt with honey. An hour later we stopped for lunch at an ethnic restaurant and all had curry and rice.

Our vehicle climbed up through verdant and colourful hill country to Ella Waterfall and on to Banderella. Sri Lanka seemed a lush and fertile Garden of Eden. Up in the tea country we stayed on a tea estate at the Himalie Guest House. Although the air was cool a pink mosquito net cascaded down above our bed. It seemed very romantic.

We walked around the plantation and garden and picked runner beans to be cooked for our dinner.

We walked around the plantation and garden and picked runner beans to be cooked for our dinner. After beers and a gossip we showered in cool (but meant to be hot) water and looked forward to our meal. The Kandy rice, brinjam (eggplant) curried runner beans and curried chicken were good and plentiful. We decided then to warn any of our friends contemplating a visit to Sri Lanka, not to bother if they didn't like curry.

We were all up by six the next morning to see the sun rise over the mountain tops tipping them with a rosy glow and pinking the puffs of mist rising from the valleys.

Frequently we stopped and investigated ancient temples and religious cave sites on our winding way up to Horton Plains. Tigers and deer still roam this area. We were hoping to look over the cliff edge at World's End, down into the abyss below, but the entrance fee to this natural site was 650 rupees ie. $US12. We decided it was a 'rip off' and it made us realise that soon many of the world's natural wonders will only be available to rich tourists. I spoke pleasantly to the National Park Warden and explained our point of view.

We decided to go for a walk on the plateau and then have lunch served in a clean, bright restaurant in the Government Guest House. However, when the bill was presented, it was far in excess of the meals ordered. Karen carries her pocket calculator and went through the account charmingly with the waiter.

"My goodness yes, it is 800 rupees too much." he said waggling his head. "So many little mistakes. We are very, very sorry, please accept our sincere apologies!"

We did not leave a tip.

After visiting the famous Newara Eliya tea plantation and factory we drove on to Kandy, the capital. The beautiful flower-filled capital city surrounding a serene lake has had a fascination for many years. In my school library in London, I had seen pictures of the Kandy Dancers in a National Geographic Magazine and was looking forward to seeing them. We found the Freedom Guest House that had three bed and breakfast vacancies, signed in, then hurried to book seats for the evening performance.

The dancing lived up to my expectations. It was splendid and vigorous in colourful costumes. The men were supreme in athletic ability and endurance. The whirling dervish dancing was exciting although I have no idea of the religious significance. Back at the Freedom Guest House with KULAROO and MARA we tossed a coin for the 'bridal suite'.

In my school library in London, I had seen pictures of the Kandy Dancers in a National Geographic Magazine and was looking forward to seeing them.

We won and carried our cases upstairs to an en suite hot shower and a good bed.

Another early start and an enjoyable morning was spent at a spice farm where we were shown many different spices growing and their uses explained. On to Polonnaruwa, the twelfth century capital of Ceylon. How little I knew of the history of these sophisticated ruins and temples and regarded with awe the Bhuddvistas carved from the standing rocks, There is nothing like travel to make me humble at my ignorance. We were advised not to go any further north to Trincomalee or the northern capital, because the Tamil terrorists were in control of some of the area.

Wild elephants and monkeys crossed the road in the sunset as we made our way to Dambuwella and booked into the Hotel Katapath Paura Dambulla, (the names were all so long and confusing). After dinner (the first meal which wasn't all curries), the waiter offered to take us to the cinema across the road. We were allowed to peep in and watch the last ten action-packed minutes of an Indian film during which a helicopter and a train crashed, nuns rescued women and children from a blazing inferno, and a girl who was chained to the railway track was snatched from beneath the grinding wheels by the swashbuckling hero. Hurrah!!

It was a 5.30am start to drive to the rock fortress of Sigirya - the Sri Lankan version of Ayers Rock in Australia. A 1,000 foot red rock stands proud in the centre of a vast plain with ancient castle ruins and the shell of an Olympic sized swimming pool at the top. Spread out below are the gardens of the old king's winter palace.

How little I knew of the history of these sophisticated ruins and temples and regarded the Bhuddvistas carved from the standing rocks, with awe.

The Dambulla Caves, where a reclining Buddha has lain and been worshipped since the first century BC, had a roof and wall paintings that were still colourful. The later Buddhas, stupas, bodegas and murals all had such involved and interesting histories, that I came away unable to remember much at all. Though I do remember watching papyrus being made and then having my name drawn on it in hieroglyphics with a stylus.

Back at the Freedom Guest House in Kandy, Lorraine and Brian won the bridal suite and we all left our bags there so that we could see the museum before it closed. As we walked back across the grounds of the Temple of the Tooth a young man introduced himself and took us to meet the abbot of the Temple. He blessed us - for a price! When Peter proffered an English Five Pound note, the abbott said "Is that all?"

Over supper we all decided we were ready to return to our boats via the Elephant Orphanage. When we arrived in the morning it seemed a sad place after the loving way we had seen Thai elephants treated. The Sri Lankan keepers didn't seem to touch the babies, who swayed from side to side, as though distressed, while waiting for their feeding bottles. Watching the large herd bathing in the river was unforgettable; they obviously enjoyed it so much, trumpeting water over themselves and their friends.

The Sri Lankan keepers didn't seem to touch the babies, who swayed from side to side, as though distressed, while waiting for their feeding bottles.

We all felt 'templed and curried out' and went straight back to Galle instead of going to Colombo. We didn't realise it was a wise decision, but the following day was when the devastating bomb went off in the bank at Colombo and 200 people were killed. We could easily have been in the vicinity.

Back on board, those eggs and bacon tasted so good. A gentle drizzle cooled the decks. We were so pleased to be home even when woken by underwater explosions.

The next few days in the harbour were spent sending mail and preparing for the next 1300 mile leg to Port Raysut in Oman. We enjoyed an evening of "Boggle" contest on LAZYBONES who had arrived from Thailand while we had been away. Rivalry at Boggle had been high all season and many a dastardly duel had taken place over Australian dictionary spellings. Bob had been king, but tonight the series was called a draw when, at last, Peter won.

The 'last night in port' celebration was a 'bangers and mash' (sausages and potatoes) supper on CLYPEUS.

Next day MARA, KULAROO, CLYPEUS and GREEN DOLPHIN with Linda and Don on board, all left with promises to keep regular radio schedules during our voyage to Oman.

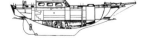

Maldives
Eleguma
Island

CHAPTER THREE

07°04'N Lat   72°55'E Long

Eleguma Island Maldives

The longest ocean leg of our homeward voyage started on Sunday February 4th when we sailed out of Galle Harbour into rough seas. We would have liked to turn back into the calm harbour, but the wind was from the SSE speeding us towards Oman, the Red Sea, and home - no complaints. On a broad reach, we headed towards the most northerly of the Maldivian atolls only 420 miles away. We hoped we would be allowed to anchor for a few days and see these pristine islands which may disappear if the sea rises just a few feet due to global warming. There is no official port of entry amongst the northerly islands, but yachts ahead had been allowed to stop for a few days if they had a reasonable reason.

On my watches, between making sure the Aries self steering was keeping us on course, looking for ships or half-sunk containers, and marking our position on the chart, I sat in the cockpit doodling some rhymes:

Eleguma Island Maldives.

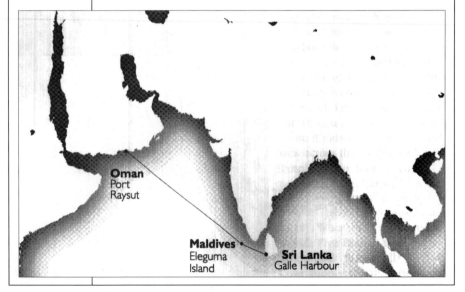

Oman
Port Raysut

Maldives
Eleguma Island

Sri Lanka
Galle Harbour

"Whistling wind, surging foam,
Still 6,000 miles to sail to home.
Slip-sliding down a watery hill
That wall of water could easily kill.

Wind-torn waves of sinister blue
Batter our boat and cowering crew.
Maldives ahead, only a few years more.
Before global warming swallows their shore
There palm trees bend, blue water plays
A respite earned before further days of chaos.

Encouraging voices on the radio sked
"We've just survived", "she's baked their bread."
Blue water cruisers do have more than a tinge
Of what most would call "The Lunatic Fringe."

On the third day I was still feeling seasick and slept on and off most of the day but it was worth it as we were making 6-7 knots on the lumpy sea. A cross swell bumped its way over the basic NE swell. Peter put a second reef in the main. He spoke on the VHF to a large tanker on a reciprocal course only two miles away.

"No." He hadn't seen us!

The estimated wind speed was now 30 knots. Two more merchant ships appeared up ahead on a parallel course with us. One to the south and one to the north: no problem.

At mid-day on the 6th the wind eased. Peter let out the reef and poled out the jib, wing and wing. As the wind died so CLYPEUS rolled, each side deck being awash alternately. As I marked the chart and wrote up the log, I noticed it was the 7th of February: our grand-daughter Emily's seventh birthday. I wonder what sort of party she will have this year?

Gradually the sea became calmer and the sailing good. We dried out a bit and discussed what our reason for stopping at

Gradually the sea became calmer and the sailing good.

Eleguma Island would be. Peter had an upset tummy so we decided a consultation with Dr. Don Bryce on GREEN DOLPHIN was necessary - on the radio, an appointment was made. Minor sail repairs were needed too.

At 6 am, it was only 67 miles to Eleguma Island in Ihavandiffulu Atoll. We could get there in daylight if we got

moving but we would have to motor. The engine wouldn't start and we ghosted along under sail for ten hours. Peter investigated every possibility and in the end decided that the following sea must have pushed water back up the exhaust pipe. It eventually started after he disconnected the exhaust pipe, started the motor, then pushed the exhaust pipe back on.

We approached the atoll just as the sun was setting behind a heavy cloud hovering over the island. I was afraid we wouldn't be able to find our way into the lagoon and would have to stay out at sea for another night. However, on the radio, Linda on GREEN DOLPHIN assured us it was a wide clear entrance and they would talk us safely in. They did. DE LA MER put all her lights on too and we anchored nearby in 60' on sand.

We sat in the peaceful cockpit and had a wee dram as the smell of blossom drifted across the water from the island. As we sat blissfully enjoying the stars and blessed peace, I thought of Masefield's line: "A quiet sleep and a sweet dream when the long trick is over." KULAROO sailed in, crossing the silver pathway from the moon. There are few pleasures in life as wonderful as sailing and there is nothing as pleasurable as when you stop!

In the morning, Don told us we could not go ashore until the 'Judge' and village Chief came out in their launch. Peter was studying the weather fax charts from Diego Garcia, Darwin, Rome, Cairo and Peking. I was sitting on deck sewing the numbers back on the sail when he called up to let me know "It is raining not in central China." We have Tony Hancock's classic comedy radio show tape on board of 'The Radio Ham', where, lost for conversation ideas, he repeats his Japanese contact's remark that "it is raining not in Tokyo."

An elegantly shaped local boat with a high bow.

It was so hot. I couldn't wait to snorkel. The coral looked so inviting I slipped over the side into the fantastically clear

water to explore. It was the most beautiful yet, complete and unspoiled. Yellow and black striped angel fish, smiling blue and black trigger fish, brown doctor and surgeon fish swivelled their eyes to watch me. A type of trumpet fish I had never seen before and little glistening guppies took no notice of me, nor did the garfish just under the shining surface.

Unfortunately, before I could get back on board, an elegantly shaped local boat with a high bow post and matching lower stern post, came alongside CLYPEUS. The Maldives are strictly Muslim and I knew I would offend if I appeared in a bathing costume so I stayed in the water, keeping my shoulders under and clinging to the stern ladder. The seaman holding the launch spoke quite good English. His name was Hassan and he had been to England. Like many Maldivians he had been a merchant seaman for seven years and had visited Liverpool, New York, Rotterdam, Greece and Italy. His wife's name was Safiga and he had two children. He invited us to his home.

The Judge and Chief spent half an hour on board examining our papers and accepted Peter's reason of 'sail repairs' as a legitimate reason for stopping. They left assuring us they would tell us when we would be allowed ashore.

We didn't have our VHF switched on, Peter was saving battery power and I didn't hear the other boats calling me:

"Come over, come now Shirley, we are swimming with huge manta rays."

Evidently the rays let them swim alongside them and were benign. The pod was of about six very large triangular fish with a ten foot wing span. I had swum with manta rays in Bora Bora and the Galapagos and just loved to watch their wing tips undulating as though gracefully flying through the water in slow motion. The next day I saw them in the distance and immediately tried to join them, but by the time I had donned mask and fins and swam to where I thought they were, I couldn't find them.

Small boys visited the yachts in little canoes and a plastic air-filled boat, given to them by a yachtsman, and gave us coconuts and papaya. We gave back apples and biscuits, pencils and balloons. MARA, INERTIA and WIRRAWAY arrived.

Small boys visited the yachts in little canoes and a plastic air-filled boat, given to them by a yachtsman, and gave us coconuts and papaya.

The ten yachts "resting" tried to organise a BBQ but the Chief would not give permission for us to land on the beach this day, perhaps tomorrow. After dinner Peter and I put on favourite audio tapes and waltzed and quick-stepped around our tiny cabin. In the cockpit the sky was clear, almost a full moon shone down on us sitting in our sarongs. A warm breeze gently wafted the scent of blossom across the lagoon.

The next morning was spent snorkelling, the water and air temperature were exactly right - I didn't even think of feeling cold. The hull didn't need any work - it was all play. Some boys brought over a few lambis shells and we went for afternoon tea on DOUBLE 'M' from Hull, England.

In the evening permission to land was granted, on a beach away from the village. Six boats joined together for a pot-luck supper on the sandy edge of the calm lagoon. After we had talked and eaten our fill, we laid on our backs on the sand and identified stars. It was a dark, dark, night until the moon came up. This was how I remembered our years exploring the South Pacific.

The next morning, boys brought us fish, and more papaya and coconuts. We gave them pencils, a set of dominoes and, the older ones some plastic safety-razors. They were thrilled. The manta rays came back but I didn't manage to get near them.

We were told we could go ashore and, dressed suitably with our elbows, knees and hair covered, Brian ferried Lorraine, Maggie of WIRRAWAY and me ashore. Peter didn't want to visit.

The babies had their slight little eyebrows heavily coated with black kohl.

Never have I seen such a clean and tidy village. Freshly swept white sand streets were lined with cream coral-block walls. Each wooden thatched house had a tidy fenced yard with wood and copra-string netting chairs in the shade of

mango or palm trees. Piles of coconut husks were tidily stacked for cooking fuel.

The public buildings consisted of a fish store, where tuna was stored frozen, until taken to the resort hotels on southern islands, a small concrete shed had 'CLINIC' and the opening times pasted to the door, also a school house and two mosques - a separate one for the ladies.

Hassan met us and invited us to his house for refreshment. His wife Safiga shyly offered us Tang orange

juice and insisted we sat down.
There were no chairs, but a raised
wooden platform a foot high,
covered in pillows. This was the
family bed at night, and all other
furniture during the day. We learnt
hello - *a salaam ale*, thank you -
sikurea, goodbye - *dani*. The Maldives
have been so isolated that their language and writing is completely
unique for a population of around
20,000 people. Grinning children
crowded round and peered in
through the windows. The babies
had their slight little eyebrows
heavily coated with black kohl. I
wasn't able to find the reason, but it
made them look like little old men.

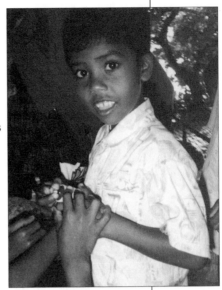

A nine year old proudly showed us how he could turn on and off a small bulb he had wired to a battery.

Safiga's parents, who lived next door, were introduced.
They were a handsome couple in their 50s who seemed active,
well and happy. We were also shown into a front room which
had a box shrouded in a white cloth in the corner. Hassan let
us peep underneath - a multi-system 21" TV! He had brought
it back from his sea travels. They could only watch videos at
the moment but were hoping for satellite TV sometime.

We sat in the shade in the main meeting area on wood
and copra-string latticed chairs arranged in a square around a
central arena. The children crowded around and tried to
teach us Maldivian and wrote their names. The girls were
very shy but the boys chatty. A nine year old proudly showed
us how he could turn on and off a small bulb he had wired to
a battery. Twelve year old Mohamad Samer who had some

The children crowded around and tried to teach us Maldivian.

English wrote the
alphabet and two little
girls called Nasheeda
and Agulima translat-
ed names of things we
could point to:
coconut - *kaashi*,
banana - *donkio*,
breadfruit - *bambookio*.
A chicken - *kookoolu* -
what a lovely sound-
ing word - we should
all use it!

On the way back
to MARA a fisherman

Lorraine and Brian Raison

in a dugout canoe held up a freshly caught sweetlip fish, offering it for sale. I had some dollar bills in my pocket expecting to buy some fruit or vegetables, but there had been no shop open on the island.

I offered two dollars for this splendid fish. He held up his hand gesturing too much, too much, so I gave him one dollar and he gave me two fish.

I felt so privileged to have visited and shared for just a few hours the simple life-style of Eleguma Island, a happy, clean, well-ordered community. Even though the girls (and ladies) were retiring and shy, they seemed happy and well looked after by their menfolk. No alcohol must lead to fewer domestic problems. There was much to think about over the next fifteen days as we sailed the 1300 miles to Salalah in Oman.

Before we sailed on Sunday February 11th I baked bread and set more mung bean seeds to sprout to supplement our potatoes, onions, pumpkins, rice, pasta and canned goods. Peter checked the batteries and topped up the gearbox oil. Later as we coped with sailing and navigating, both of us felt queasy. At around 8° 41' and 69° 44' we sighted five merchant vessels; a good lookout was necessary. The ships were sailing from the Red Sea to India through the Eight Degree Channel that passes through the Maldive Group.

Dolphins leapt before the bow to wish us a Happy Valentine's Day. We both felt fine and caught a small tuna. Porpoises played around us in the calm sea. They leapt and spun around before diving, whizzing beneath our bow and then bursting forth to leap and spin again. Some energetic ones leapt and slapped down with a huge splash. I sat on the bowsprit with my feet dangling in the water and sang while I

Under protest, Peter flew our green and yellow striped spinnaker.

videoed them, but of course, they never leapt when the camera was going. The wind was light and we couldn't make a hundred miles a day, even motor-sailing. A current from the north appeared to be setting us back. I made more bread and we had it warm with the last of our Sri Lankan cheddar cheese for lunch.

Under protest, Peter flew our spinnaker. When buying it we thought it would remind us of England's green meadows, and the buttercups and dandelions which flourish in the grass. It did. This would be the last ocean voyage of our circumnavigation, and I was determined to enjoy every moment we could.

Dolphins in the night, exchanging glances! Tubes of light and a line of iridescent bubbles of phosphorescence outlined their dorsal fins as they broke the surface. Leaping and splashing down into a cloud of green and silver stars.

Four hundred miles from the nearest land (the Laccadive Islands) we saw two shearwaters, one tropic bird and two flocks of terns as we motored on over a glassy sea.

Peter got around to doing a little job which has been on the list for thirteen years. On starboard tack the toilet seat lid has been a constant annoyance - always slapping me in the back and threatening the possibility of doing untold damage to Peter. He carved and fitted a wooden catch to hold it up: perfect!

Well over halfway, 750 miles behind us. Another night of amazing phosphorescence especially a 50 metre wide band of shimmering light running north to south. It was a dark night with no moon, but so eerie, with bright lights glowing from our bow wave, the curling wave crests, and our tumbling wake.

On day 11, we saw a very large school of porpoise. They stretched as far as the eye could see on either side of us. We caught more small tuna and tried to dry strips of the flesh, dipped in honey and soy sauce, on the cabin roof. It was reasonably successful but I didn't really like the taste and Peter didn't like the stickiness. In the afternoon when still 300 miles from Port Raysut, I counted 19 red crabs swimming sideways towards the east like lemmings; they had about 1,000 miles to go to land.

The next day a large shark took our lure, but we managed to unhook him and save our line. In the stiflingly hot cabin I baked bread and a pineapple crumble. Just before sunset more crabs were still swimming east, the sea was calm and a mist was rising. Did these signs portend some special event? This time I counted 50 crabs in five minutes. At midnight there was more fantastic phosphorescence, a blinding greenish light as our bow bucked into the swell and the bow wave formed. A brilliant milky way lit the sky.

The engine had been running constantly and at 0200 on Friday February 23rd we decided to turn it off. It was necessary to save a little diesel to ensure being able to enter harbour only 144 miles away. CLYPEUS slid to a standstill. However at dawn the wind came back with a vengeance, we reefed down and it was ROUGH. At 1400 the yankee foresail

blew out. We sailed on, flying just the main and staysail while we both stitched the yankee. On the 24th there was no wind and with little diesel, CLYPEUS just sat.

On the radio, STAR told us not to bother about hurrying into harbour as it was the 'end of Ramadan' holiday for four more days. Nobody was allowed to leave their boats as all customs and immigration officials were off duty. KULAROO, MARA and GREEN DOLPHIN were all safely in harbour but unable to go ashore.

It was frustrating to be only 40 miles away from port. Strong winds came for a few hours then died. Sails went up and down like yoyos. At last on February 25th we motor-sailed between the Arab dhows anchored inside the entrance to Port Raysut harbour.

The lascars on deck smiled and waved.

Blue and brown mountains shimmered above a sandy coastal plain. White, square, flat-topped buildings blazed in the harsh sun.

Blue and brown mountains shimmered above a sandy coastal plain. White, square, flat-topped buildings blazed in the harsh sun.

Through the binoculars we could make out brown camels cropping a brown landscape. Little whirlwinds of dust rose, swirled and disappeared. Cormorants, seagulls and herons strutted on the foreshore or stood on bollards drying their wings.

Our first aim was to buy telephone cards.

We spent seven hot, dusty, windy days in oil rich Oman and enjoyed the cool,

The fine new buildings in Salalah were impressive and elegant.

still, sparkling nights. It was a hot walk to the police post at the harbour entrance and although strict with paperwork they seemed incredibly inefficient. Each entrance or departure was preceded with an examination of every piece of paper in the office. Some names of crews and boat names were in English and some were in Arabic, depending on who had taken the initial information. Some pages were upside down, some

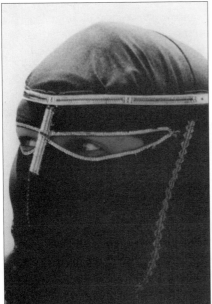

boats had left weeks ago but all their papers were still in the pile.

Our first attempt to go into town was frustrating. Peter had omitted to bring one of the papers the Immigration Officer had given him. No way could we be allowed into town without it. Passports were not enough. Peter had to walk in the searing heat back to the dinghy jetty, then row out to and back from CLYPEUS,

The few ladies that could be seen in the streets were all in full purdah.

Rifles were slung nonchalantly across shoulders.

then the long walk back to the Entrance Gate. He was furious. As he passed the sentry, probably looking like thunder, the sentry beckoned him over.

"What's the matter? he asked.

Peter explained.

"Calmly, calmly," the wizened sentry soothed. "Allah be praised. Just sit and wait. All will be well." Peter sat, he was too hot, fed up and flustered, to do anything else although he didn't know what he was waiting for.

Soon a lorry delivering boxes to the port stopped at the sentry box. A few words were exchanged with the sentry who then helped Peter up into the cab and the smiling driver agreed to drop him off where the dinghies were tied. It was only an hour before he arrived back at the office with the necessary papers and, with Lorraine and Brian, we walked towards town. Our first aim was to buy telephone cards to phone our families from the Lego-like castellated white telephone boxes. We got through to England, America and Australia easily and were delighted to learn that all was well.

In the vegetable shop it seemed extraordinary for an elegantly robed businessman to spend minutes choosing each potato,

During the week we were given lifts into Salalah by many local men - no ladies drove. As over 80% of the population own cars, there is no public transport. The fine new buildings in Salalah were impressive and elegant. On the quay was a sailing lugger, its planks sewn together. We bombarded the local photographic shop with film to be processed. The few ladies that could be seen in the streets were all in full purdah, enveloped in flowing black robes from head to toe. We noticed some slim ankles and elegant high heeled shoes. In the market large African ladies were in colourful robes with cloths over their heads, two gold rings through their nostrils, and gold earings. Muslim ladies serving in the stores had henna patterns on their hands.

Omani men are splendid and dashing in their flowing mauve robes. They wear little flat pill box hats, some patterned with pretty white and mauve designs to match their robes, which are charming. Rifles were slung nonchalantly across shoulders, and there were market stalls where gun belts and bandoliers with cartridge cases and bullet holders could be bought.

In the vegetable shop it seemed extraordinary for an elegantly robed businessman to spend minutes choosing each potato, onion or aubergine. What a waste of time for men, but wives were not allowed out of the home, even to go shopping.

One of the men who gave us a lift was Karam, a 28 year old, tall, dark and handsome Omani in a flowing robe of black simulated leather. Cool! I don't think it was really, he must have been very hot. He offered to take us to Mughsuyl to the beach to see the blow holes next day.

We met at the appointed time and drove west. On the road camels wandered hither and thither looking for something to eat. One or two cars sped the other way along the good beachside road.

One of the men who gave us a lift was Karam, a 28 year old, tall, dark and handsome.

Karam drove through the desolate landscape. On the beach a crowd of barefooted fishermen pulled in their net. Seagulls wheeled and screeched above them. At the cliff side we enjoyed the thump and whoosh as the water exploded up through the blowholes. Karam taught us thank you - *shukran*, good morning - *saba alkhar*, good evening - *masa alkhar*.

Next day he offered to take us to get our propane bottles refilled in a desolate industrial area. It took a long time because Peter wanted a different fitting put on our bottle, but the old one proved extremely difficult to get off. The Propane gas plant manager and three of his men spent an hour trying to change it. Eventually they succeeded and after refilling it with gas, charged only $1.50 for everything!

Peter bought some good bargains - a 10 kilo sack of perfect onions for $3.

In the meantime I wandered out of the car and watched some mother camels with their babies in a large fenced enclosure. After a while Karam joined me.

"I wish to say something. You may be very cross. Please promise not to tell your husband."

I was completely in the dark. "OK" I said, "go on," to this poor nervous young man.

"Could you be my special friend? You know, special person to me. Would your husband permit it?"

"No. He wouldn't," I laughed,

absolutely amazed. "In our country we are just one wife for one man. Besides, I am old enough to be your mother. Why haven't you a girl friend? You are handsome and clever."

He bowed his head. "I am sorry, you do not mind me asking?"

"No I don't mind you asking. It seems so ridiculous that actually I am flattered. But even if I were younger, I love my husband and have no wish to make love with any other man. Tell me why you have to ask such an old lady for love."

He sighed. "I have been married and have a son one year old. It was an arranged marriage. My wife and I did not get on. Soon we will be divorced, but I cannot speak to, or approach, a woman of my own age and religion. It is not allowed. The only way to talk to a girl is to approach her father and ask to marry her. There is no in between."

We strolled back to the car. "You will not tell your husband. He may be very angry."

"No. There is no problem."

Deep in thought Lorraine and I sat in the back of the car as we drove into town. "Did he ask you too?" she whispered.

I nodded. "Poor things! No wonder Arabs and Muslims are so often fanatical, their customs don't seem to allow any contact or relaxation with the opposite sex. To not allow men and women to even talk to each other seems unnatural."

While Karam and the men talked cars, we talked of the Maldives and of Malaysia where their relatively strict Muslim code seemed so much more sensible than this.

The new market was excellent. While Lorraine and I did grocery shopping, Peter bought some good bargains - a 10 kilo sack of perfect onions for $3. Five kilos of dates for about the same. I bought souvenir gifts of frankincense and myrrh together with charcoal tablets and little dishes on which to burn it, as well as Arafat type Arab head gear. The supermarkets were well stocked and clean. The little restaurant where we chose to have lunch had a small area sealed off for ladies. There were also some family rooms, where we all sat.

Karen of KULAROO organised a surprise celebration for Bill's 50th birthday.

In the taxi on the way home we pointed out to the driver some beautiful large homes with tiled facades, arched terraces and tall windows. We asked why so many were so big?

"If you have four wives and twenty children, you need a large home," he replied.

"How many wives do you have?" I asked.

He chuckled. "I am a poor man, I only have one wife, but I think I would only have one wife if I were a rich man. Many problems with many wives," he said sagely as he shook his head. He went on, "New houses still have a woman's room."

"What is that?" I asked, visualising a sewing room or even a harem.

"If a wife displeases her husband he has the right to lock her in the woman's room and she stays there alone until he gives permission for her to be released. It could be an hour, a week, or the rest of her life. It is up to the other wives to feed, look after her and plead her case. It is wise to be a good wife."

He also told us about popular Sultan Qaboose, the present ruler of Oman. He had deposed his old-fashioned father who was now enjoying retirement in the country with his many wives. Sultan Qaboose was using the country's vast oil income wisely. His people felt they were all getting their fair share and the roads, schools, hospitals, housing and sanitation were improving daily. Of course there was still a long way to go in this large barren land.

Karen of KULAROO organised a surprise celebration for Bill's 50th birthday. Five couples dinghied over to MARA, which was bedecked with balloons, and we all enjoyed a relaxed and happy evening.

One of the things in Oman I really appreciated was the excellent telephone service. Once you had purchased a phone card the calls were cheap and clear. We splashed out and phoned our families on arrival and before departure. Great!

Yemen
El Mukhalla

CHAPTER FOUR

12°47'N 44°59'E

Al Mukalla

On Sunday March 3rd loaded with frankincense and myrrh, spices, dates, sacks of onions and potatoes, and jars of little beetroots and cucumbers I had pickled, we sailed west in a fresh southerly breeze in the sunshine towards Yemen. With the binoculars we examined the interesting coastline of cliffs and beaches. The brown mountains were shrouded in mist which gradually revealed yellow desert sand sloping down smoothly, like a glacier, to the blue sea. Glittering flying fish flitted fast across the water. As night fell, domestic lights twinkled up in the mountains bright and high enough to be mistaken for stars. A perfect night for sleeping on deck.

Next morning, we were about ten miles offshore when a small fishing boat approached. The two lean men in raggedy clothes and rough turbans indicated that they were hungry. We gave them water, biscuits and cigarettes. They offered us fish in return, but I had already spent the morning dealing with the two small tuna we had caught and didn't want any more fish. This time I had bled the tuna then put them in boiling water for one minute, then filleted them. They were much more appetising - like tinned tuna.

On the third morning we watched the full moon sinking as the sun was rising. I sketched, then painted, two flying fish, *Coetus Voluntaris*, which had landed on deck. A pleasant hour was spent composing a rhyme to go with them in GREEN DOLPHIN's visitors' book:

> *"Flying fish GREEN DOLPHIN chased*
> *To the Arabian Coast in undue haste.*
> *"We're slow and heavy," Don had called*
> *But iron sail, it never stalled.*
>
> *Fresh and rested, but full of cheer*
> *Linda would ask "Are you near?"*
> *How good it was to know she cared*

And made us feel a voyage shared.
Although their sails we never saw
Once they had left a foreign shore."

Visitors' books on blue water yachts are often works of art and lovely reminders of friends and times spent together.

In the light wind, the cruising chute was hauled up and down a few times. The engine was turned on and off a few times too. At mid-day I wanted the cruising chute up, Peter didn't. He eventually hauled it up for me "for the last time" and I enjoyed standing at the steering wheel, playing it. For six hours we were doing over six knots in the calm sea. The breeze filled CLYPEUS's billowing green and gold foresail and she picked up her skirts and danced for me, like a staid crinolined matron after too much sherry. It reminded me of Joyce Grenfell's 'Stately as a Galleeeon'.

There was no wind the next day, and when MARA caught us up we took photographs of each other almost sailing. They motor sailed ahead and got into Al Mukalla before dark. We decided to sail, and at 5pm still had 15 miles to go so we just gilled around offshore all night, not wanting to enter a strange harbour in the dark. Actually we could easily have gone in with the full moon but "discretion is the better ..... and all that."

At 4am we started our sail towards this ancient city of tall white buildings wedged on a narrow strip of level ground between steep brown mountains and the sea. Menacing great boulders looked ready to roll and crush the houses and minarets below. Four small forts dominated the cliff top above the town. The three other yachts in our little fleet had organised for Alexander, the local taxi driver and 'fix-it' man, to take them (and us) to buy diesel at 6 cents US a litre. While we waited for his taxi to appear on the quay Peter prepared our diesel canisters and I put our washing to soak.

When I looked into the clear aquamarine water, voracious brown leather-jacket fish were attacking the bread like one imagines piranha fish feed on fresh meat.

Anticipating fresh bread as soon as we got ashore, I threw some stale slices of bread over the side and was suprised to hear splashing. When I looked into the clear

aquamarine water, voracious brown leather-jacket fish were attacking the bread like one imagines piranha fish feed on fresh meat. They fought so hard the bread was moving around in circles in the middle of thrashing brown bodies. I had been looking forward to swimming, but now?

Ashore we booked into Customs and Immigration who issued passes to allow us past the soldier with a rifle guarding the dock gate. While the men went off to get diesel, Linda and Karen, and Lorraine and I, in couples wandered the streets. This was different, really different.

The land was so dry; not a tree or a flower could be seen. The tall sun-bleached, flat-roof houses with blue shuttered windows, clung to individual terraces, and were dominated by the domes of tall mosques and the towering brown mountain that intruded right down to the water front. Narrow alleys, which only humans, donkeys and goats could climb, wound up between the houses, rocks and menacing boulders.

Ladies in flowing full black purdah, even with veils over their eyes, walked freely around. Most of the men in turbans, shirts and sarong skirts, had evil looking curved daggers stuck into their belts. On their dusty feet they wore sandals or thongs. There were many small, hooked-nosed Bedouin types and many African looking people - but no Chinese. Many men had round lumps above their jawbone, their brown cheeks bulged. Was it a physical characteristic of the race or did they have gumboils?

Apart from a few cars, this was a city from a bygone age of donkeys and carts. You could see men smoking gurgling hubble-bubbles in the cafes and abject poverty was everywhere. Bare footed children played between white sunbaked crumbling terraces and boulders. The girls under twelve wore flouncy, shiny, bridesmaid type dresses. The school girls wore black robes with white head veils and some had uncovered faces. Goats wandered between the blue-shuttered houses perched on the hillside. They nibbled at everything, even plastic bags. Have the Yemenis invented a new way of disposing of plastic garbage?

We bought a yashmak each - two-layered, black modern ones, with velcro fastening at the back of the head. I tried to wear mine on board but it made my face and neck so hot. I couldn't imagine wearing one every time I went out. There was a great choice of kohl eye makeup and ornate silver tiny flagons in which to keep it. The shop-keepers were very friendly.

Rice, pita bread, good vegetables, goat and chicken meat, dates and spices, were readily available.

A shy young man approached and introduced himself as

He furtively looked around and said it wasn't safe to talk.

an English student. Did we have time to talk to him? Lorraine and I sat at a little cafe table and had Coca-colas. Mohammet told us he was training to be a teacher in the English Department of the Mukalla Teacher Training College. He had finished school at 18, done a year's Military Service and was now on a four year course. Newly qualified teachers and doctors only earned around $100 US a month. As soon as they qualify, he and his colleagues would try and get jobs in Saudi Arabia or Oman.

He wouldn't talk about unification with North Yemen. He furtively looked around and said it wasn't safe to talk. The young men seem so lonely. Another student joined us. They were interested in many things but mainly about how boy meets girl in the west. There is no way they can even talk to a girl unless they marry her. No contact whatever is allowed as in Oman.

Many male couples walked along the streets hand in hand. Husbands have the right to beat their wife to death if she opposes or annoys him! Divorce consists of the man saying to his wife "Go away".

We asked with concern about the bulge in the mens' cheeks. They rocked with laughter. "No problem, they are chewing "Qat" (*catha edulis*) a narcotic leaf. With no alcohol the men must have something to comfort themselves."

We met an English/Lebanese artist, travelling on her own, who had just spent two weeks living in a Yemeni home. She said the women didn't read, write, embroider or knit. They chatted, painted henna designs on their hands and feet, ate, slept and got fat. She thought they did their housework in a most impractical and time-consuming way, and spent hours cooking. They made such a mess as they cooked and ate, they had to clear up the house three times a day. (Like Indians they use their right hand fingers only for eating.) It sounded as though the ladies had lost all incentive to try and be efficient.

Lorraine and I climbed up through the back alleys and the women talked to us through the bars of their glassless windows. They were smiley and friendly and we exchanged our names, ages, and those of our children and grandchildren.

With henna-painted hands they passed us cold fruit drinks through the bars, which would seem to us like prison bars. Children called down from upper windows and women hid behind the curtains if we looked up.

Frequently men approached us trying to sell Maria Theresa silver coins. They said they were imported from the Austro-Hungarian Empire around the 1700s. We didn't know how authentic they were and have no particular interest in old coins, so disappointed them. Peter had hoped that we could buy some cans of beer, but no alcohol was sold to anybody, anywhere. However, we were able to buy 'Fosters Australian non-alcoholic beer.'

Alexander had organised two cars for our day tour. He led the way and we were in the rear taxi with Jack the fifteen

year old driver. Only five minutes out of Mukalla - bumpety-bumpety-bump, we had a flat. He rolled a spare tyre out of the boot, but there were no tools for the repair. A passing motorist took a message to Alexander who was driving somewhere ahead. He came back with some tools and helped repair our tyre. It was a long hour standing in the hot sun. We were warned not to use cameras or videos as there were soldiers posted on the cliff top to our left, and no, we couldn't look for sea shells on the beach because it was mined.

We drove inland through a landscape of barren hills and

Grazing for cattle.

mountains, stony and sandy plains, a few straggly dusty date palms and some biblical looking low thorn bushes. What a Godforsaken country Yemen is. How they can have such faith in Allah when he has given them such a rotten deal. How lucky we are to have been born in green and fertile countries. Between the few lonely small towns young barefooted girls with wild hair herded goats along the desolate roadside. Unfortunately the women and girls don't want to be photographed, but the men do.

For lunch our guide led us into a concrete garage with a roller shutter door near the old town of Shehar. Hard-eyed, hooked-nosed Bedouins sat eating and drinking, their ornate curved daggers glinting from their waists. Our table was laden with dishes of goat meat and mounds of fresh pita bread. The goat stew was very tasty and tender and we enjoyed the crispy pita bread washed down with Canada Dry cola.

Hard-eyed, hooked-nosed Bedouins sat eating and drinking.

In the afternoon we visited the former Sultan's elegant small palace, which was completely gutted only last year by the North Yemenis because a resistance group had held out in it. The courtyard

The former Sultan's elegant small palace.

Linda Bryce

We managed to talk to them and photographed them.

pool was still full of freshish water and families had come to picnic in the grounds. We managed to talk to them and photographed them. They were as curious about us as we were about them.

   In the middle of the desert a deep cavern revealed a blue water-filled grotto. Young men were swimming in the deep water. Nearby there were a few fields of maize and tobacco

In the middle of the desert a deep cavern revealed a blue water-filled grotto. Young men were swimming in the deep water.

watered through narrow plastic irrigation pipes from the grotto. The landscape was very dramatic; bare mountains, cliffs and hills of cream crumbling rock.

We were delivered safe and sound back to the harbour for a cost of only $20 a couple. Peter went to Alexander's little shop and told him how much we had enjoyed our day, and also to buy some gear box fluid. Alexander gave him some little gifts, incense sticks, a bracelet and a gilt necklace for me.

The next evening we ate out at an open air restaurant where chickens were spit-roasted in the forecourt. The chickens were so good we bought some for our voyage to Aden and in the morning followed KULAROO and GREEN DOLPHIN out of Mukalla.

When we arrived in Aden I wrote to our grown children Paul, Noel and Andrea and their families telling them not to worry if they didn't hear from us for a month or so as communications would be poor travelling up the Red Sea.

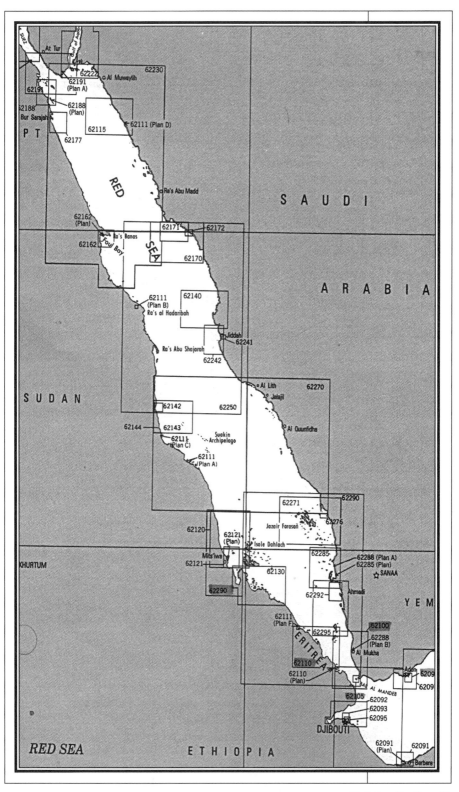

Yemen Aden

CHAPTER FIVE

Aden   12°47' N Lat   44°59'Long

Aden Harbour shimmered as the heat of the March sun intensified, scorching the decks of yachts nodding at their moorings. Every day one or two of the dozen international cruising yachts, stocked with water, fuel and fresh food, set their sails and headed out into the Indian Ocean. Lines of white plastic mooring buoys nodded in solitary idleness to bob back and forth in the tideway as yachts hurried north up the Red Sea before northerly winds of later months blew against them. GREEN DOLPHIN and KULAROO had left the day before and reported on their daily radio sked of fair winds and reasonable seas as they sped west towards the Red Sea.

We had hoped to leave this morning with MARA, but our grey Avon inflatable dinghy had broken adrift from their stern the previous evening as we enjoyed a farewell dinner to say goodbye to new Canadian friends on KAIEN who were heading south to the Seychelles. It had been a happy evening exchanging their experiences in the Mediterranean and Red Sea, and our travels from Singapore. At midnight, standing chatting on the wide stern deck as we prepared to return to our boats, we realised that our dinghy had gone walkabout.

The men had immediately climbed down into the remaining tenders and zoomed around the harbour searching for the grey rubber dinghy in a black night. The Marine Police had confronted them, instructing them to return to their yachts:

"It is our job to find your boat. Not yours. Come to the office in the morning at nine."

Brian had kindly taken on the job of ferryman and duly landed Peter ashore. They stood together expectantly in the Marine Police Office at the correct time, but were studiously ignored.

Eventually they were told "Come back at ten."

On re-presenting themselves at ten they were told: "Come back at eleven", then "two", then "five" and still no dinghy.

"Well, if you're sure you will get your dinghy back from the Aden police today, we'll go on,'" Brian said in his

Australian twang as he rowed away; his oars dripping oil and water as they rose and dipped into the dirty harbour. Like us, he realised that without a dinghy and unable to get ashore; we would be completely at the mercy of the Aden authorities. However, we didn't think we needed to go ashore again. All our stores were on board and we had obtained our Egyptian visas ready to visit Cairo and the Pyramids.

"Yes, go on," we both chorused confidently, "we'll be following you in just a couple of hours. Switch your radio to 4417 at 6 o'clock as usual and we'll let you know what happened."

"Well, if you are sure," he hesitated.

"Yes GO. Now." Peter insisted as, standing on deck, I curled my hand supportively into his. "Another day wasted is another you are likely to have to fight northerly head winds."

We watched Brian row back to Lorraine who was standing on the deck. They exchanged words, waved, and prepared to set sail.

We went below for a cup of coffee. Peter brought me up to date on what had happened ashore. "They found our dinghy and it's in the Naval Dockyard waiting to be collected, but they say it can't be released immediately because the Officer in Charge isn't on duty. It was my stupidity," he confessed. "I only tied it loosely as the painter was covered in oil. It was filthy," he sighed.

Peter hates getting his fingers sticky; to the extent that he would rather go without an orange than tackle peeling it.

Hearing the grinding of an anchor chain being raised, we clambered up on deck to see MARA stow her anchor and sail out of the harbour towards the Red Sea and Europe.

As they came past we called, "Bye, bon voyage. See you later today or tomorrow. We'll catch up, don't you worry." Holding hands and wondering if we'd been over-confident about the return of our inflatable, we watched until they were out of sight, longing to be sailing alongside them.

We retired below out of the searing sun and pulled off our clothes. It was hot, so hot. Perspiration dripped from our noses and elbows as we resumed our chores. Peter, now in his early sixties, looked fit as he pulled on his little red and black Tahitian skirt, and replaced the sweat band around his high forehead. He sat on the settee re-stitching the jib, as now after more than 50,000 miles our second set of sails were beginning to come apart at the seams. It made me smile. This was my conventional English husband: a collar, tie and socks man. It had taken three years of sailing in the tropics for him to actually discard socks when wearing sandals. Now he resembled a Polynesian pirate, slim and tanned. I loved and

With no dinghy, we couldn't get ashore; but neither of us wanted to re-visit poor dilapidated Aden.

appreciated him more than at any time during our 42 years of marriage. Now he is not only my husband, he is my home. We have lived in so many places over the last few years that he is the only constant in my life. Wherever he is, is home.

I sat in my sarong, on the starboard settee behind the table, turning the wheel of the sewing machine, making an Eritrean courtesy flag, ready to fly at the crosstrees, when we booked into Massawa, our next port of entry. The pattern for the flag had been drawn for us last night by KAIEN as no reference books yet showed a flag for the three year old nation of Eritrea.

With no dinghy, we couldn't get ashore; but neither of us wanted to re-visit poor dilapidated Aden. It was impossible to get through the dock gates without some semi-official asking for baksheesh. What had once been a major British port was now a litter of semi-derelict concrete offices and shops resting on a pile of cinders.

In Aden market, friendly traders had asked our nationality. When, with a little trepidation we replied "British", they would smile and say "Welcome. Please come back." One little old man passing by in the street, hugged and kissed me, his bristly beard scratching my cheek. "Come back," he said. "Come back, We need you British to put us right again."

In Aden market, friendly traders had asked our nationality. With a little trepidation we replied "British".

What a surprise! At the start of our voyage thirteen years ago, we had been a little ashamed, rather than proud, of our country's history overseas. But, as we visit former British Colonies we see the remains of our democratic system and infra-structure, which are helping the local people.

Recently North Yemen had invaded South Yemen and bombed and strafed its major asset - Aden. The strict Muslim North Yemenis had cracked down on the smart, as well as the sleazy, entertainment that had helped Aden's reputation as an 'interesting' tourist city. The Russians hadn't managed to keep the port busy and prosperous, now it looked as though a giant had upturned an ashcan and broken buildings had tumbled down with the black and dusty cinders. A few rusty Russian merchant ships anchored in the magnificent harbour gave a melancholy echo of proud days of the bustling port. The battered face of the clock tower frowned down at us with the hands forever balanced at four - forty. Forlorn robed Somali refugees wandered the streets, too proud to put their hand out for help, but with desperation in their eyes.

By 10pm the police and dinghy still hadn't appeared.

"We may as well go to bed," Peter suggested. "They will probably bring the dinghy first thing in the morning."

At 2am we were awakened by someone shouting "Mr. Peter. Mr. Peter."

Peter crawled out of bed. From the cockpit he saw four men in a launch. "What do you want?" he shouted.

A cultured voice called in English: "Is this CLYPEUS? Are you the gentleman who lost his dinghy?"

"Yes, I am," Peter said looking at his watch.

"Good, Please come with us."

"What now?"

"Yes, now."

"OK. Hang on while I get a flashlight and shoes," my patient, imperturbable husband replied.

I stood in my nightie, hidden by the cabin door, and handed them up to him.

He climbed into the launch and ... vroom, vroom... they had sped off into the black night. The throb of the powerful motors faded into the distance.

Suddenly left alone I thought, 'Who are they? Where have they taken him?' Nobody had given any identification. He hadn't explained. I could only assume he had recognised somebody and knew who they were and where they were going.

I dressed and put the kettle on for a cup of tea and worried while sewing the finishing touches to the Eritrean flag. Our circumnavigation across the Atlantic and Pacific to New Zealand, and Australia through Indonesia to Singapore, had involved us in many scary situations, but this was different yet again.

At 3am vroom, vroom, and they were back. As the launch came alongside, Peter handed up our familiar oars and climbed aboard. Another man wearing an old shirt, cotton trousers and dusty sandals climbed up and sat on the cabin top assuming an authoritative pose. We recognised him as one of the semi-officials who had tried to make us pay a landing charge.

Then the grey Avon inflatable dinghy was lifted up on deck together with our Mercury 2.2 outboard.

"Fifty US. dollars." The man sitting on the cabin top said.

"Fifty dollars? That's a lot of money, I will need a receipt" Peter replied.

"Thirty dollars then."

"OK, thirty dollars for the time and effort you have made. Hang on."

Peter went below and found the bills which he handed over.

The man climbed down into the launch.

"What about a receipt?" was lost in the roar of the engines as the smiling Yemenis raced away with their baksheesh.

"Ah well, cheap at the price!" Peter sighed as we went back to bed.

At first light on Saturday morning we up-anchored and motored out of the harbour calling Harbour Control on the VHF radio and thanking them for their courtesy.

"Creep!" I whispered with a grin at Peter as he held the microphone. "Imagine thanking them for all that hassle and a wasted day."

"It doesn't hurt to be polite," he admonished and then said, "I can be as two-faced as they are. Let's go, go, go."

We hoisted all sail to catch MARA, and hopefully the other friends in our small fleet with whom we were keeping in radio contact each day at 8am and 6pm on the 4417 kHz SSB marine frequency.

In hot sunshine over a sparkling sea, the Yemen desert landscape to our north rushed by, as we enjoyed sailing free in the south easterly breeze. The twang of the fishing line, as it pulled the bungy cord tight, brought us both into the cockpit. Carefully Peter rolled in the line.

"Whatever it is, it's big and strong. You hold it while I put the gloves on."

We keep a pair of industrial work gloves in the cockpit to protect our fingers from the straining line, and the teeth of large fish we haul up. During thirty years of cruising we have both had deep cuts from fishing line pulling through our hands.

"Let's hope it's a mahi mahi. I'd love some good white fish." I said as I handed the jerking reel back.

A streak of white, with a triangular dorsal fin, shot off to port breaking through the waves.

"Oh no! It looks like another shark. We can't eat enough before the flesh smells too strong. I don't want it."

"Neither do I. Yes, I think it is a shark. A big one." Peter gasped.

Now we could see it was over a metre long, with a light grey back and darker fin. As it was hauled up, its white underneath rasped against the hull. The hook was through the bottom lip of its ten inch wide lower jaw. It flipped and struggled and banged against the side of the boat as we sped on through the water.

"I can't lift it over the lifelines, and I don't want all those teeth in the cockpit. How can we let it go without losing another hook and line?"

"I'll get the kitchen scissors and try and cut the hook out". I fled down into the galley.

Emerging with my kitchen gloves on and the orange-handled kitchen scissors, I attempted to cut the shark's lip.

"Hold it still, hold it still". The shark rolled and turned and thrashed to free itself.

"I'll have to have a rest." Peter lowered the line a little so that the weight was taken by the sea. The shark twisted and turned and fought.

"OK. Let's have another go." He lifted the white belly towards me.

It jerked and swung.

"No, that won't work. Get the boat hook quick. It's killing my arms."

I passed him the boat hook from the cabin top and he hooked it inside the shark's upper jaw taking the weight off the fishing line. It stayed still for a moment and I managed to snip through its lip to free the hook. One shake and it was free. It flopped back into the water and for a second, laid still.

"Oh! I do hope it's OK." I murmured sympathetically.

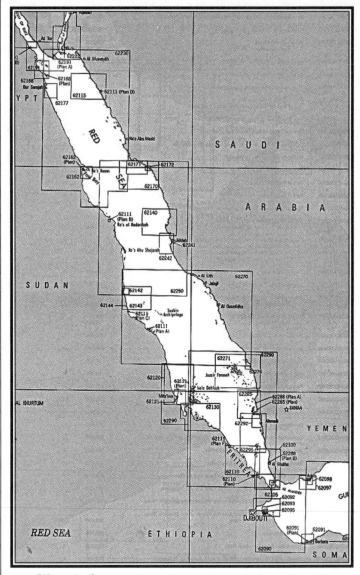

We waited.

"Yes, there it goes." The school shark recovered and sped away at top speed.

CLYPEUS raced on towards the hazards of the Red Sea. We were excited and scared about facing the challenges of dust storms; burning winds blowing off the desert; and finding our way into reef strewn anchorages. What would a 'marsa' look like? We had read about the keyhole breaks in the off-shore reefs, where, with caution and the sun overhead, it was possible to shelter from rough seas, but not from the wind. Would we be able to cross the busy shipping lanes safely as

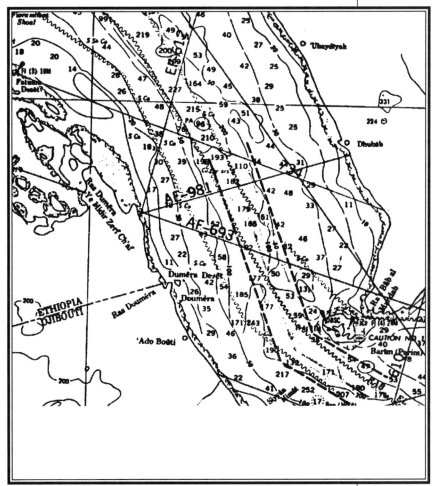

The Bab El Mandeb Straits.

we tacked through short steep seas kicked up by sudden squalls and winds from the north? CLYPEUS doesn't go well to windward, particularly against steep waves which tend to stop her dead.

Would we be holed up for days, hiding in marsas until the strong winds dropped and allowed us to continue north? Would we have days to read and write, sort photographs, and try to get some order into the thoughts and remembrances of this year's voyage? We also wanted to swot up on the new places we would visit, Eritrea, Sudan, Egypt, Suez, and at last the Med! We were almost home to England.

I was looking forward to adding to my large shell collection by beach-combing the lonely shores, wading in the warm water over white sand. This would be our last chance to swim and snorkel over coral. A final opportunity to enjoy the different colours of the tropical seas, from deepest cobalt through the spectrum of light blues and aquamarines to white froth as the ripples stroked the sand. We had been told to expect some of the clearest, least-disturbed, waters, corals and sea-life that remained in our ever-more polluted world.

As night fell, we reduced sail as usual by putting a reef in the mainsail and exchanging the genoa for the high cut yankee. Strong tail winds and high seas thrust us north-wards towards the narrow channel into the Red Sea, from time immemorial a place dreaded by sailors; The Bab El Mandeb Straits, which in Arabic means 'The Gate of Tears'. What would they mean for us?

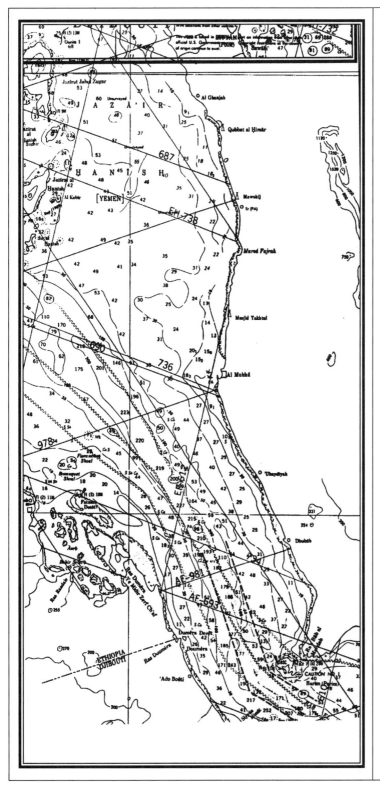

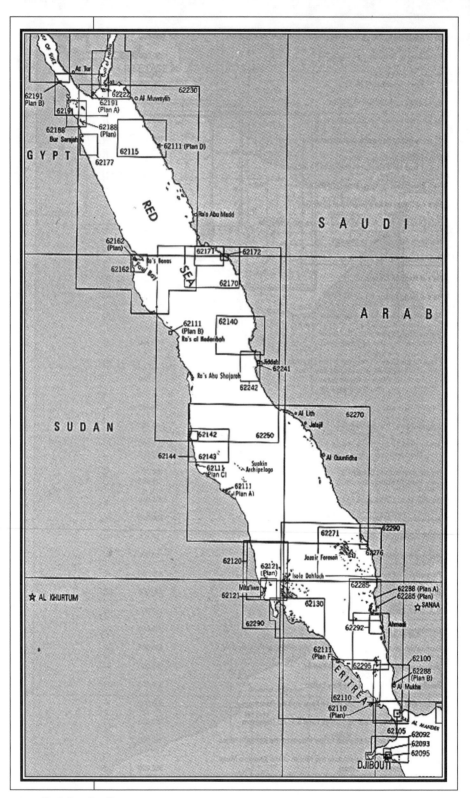

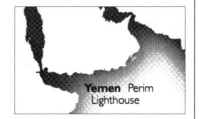

Yemen Perim Lighthouse

CHAPTER SIX

Perim Lighthouse   12°36'N 43°26'E

During December, stories had been relayed on the marine radio of yachts that had been stopped for some hours by the Yemeni military as they sailed up the inner passage into the Red Sea between Perim Island and the Yemen mainland. To avoid any similar hassle we passed by the inner passage and headed further west towards the main channel and the busy international shipping lanes.

In rough seas and with a fierce wind blasting up behind us, the flash of Perim Island lighthouse passed to starboard and gradually faded astern. Checking behind every few moments to see when there was a space to cross the shipping lane, we watched twinkling lights gradually become great shining tankers and merchant ships as they neared. Sometimes I found it difficult to decide whether we were in a direct line with their course, often calling Peter up on deck during his off watch to advise me which way we should head to avoid being run down. In high seas, from the pilot house of a tanker,

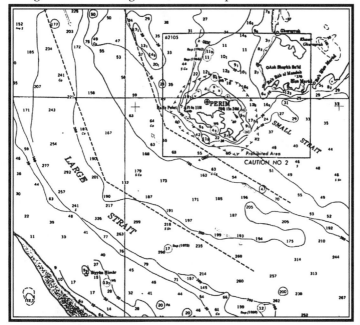

In rough seas and with a fierce wind blasting up behind us, the flash of Perim Island light-house passed to starboard and gradually faded astern.

the officer on watch, whose line of sight doesn't allow him to see less than two miles ahead, cannot see a small yacht. He often doesn't even know we exist.

Blazing lights illumined high decks loaded with multitudes of steel containers, or an extravagant mass of pipework on the leviathan tankers. The throb of mighty engines rose above the sound of the wind moaning in our rigging. Huge propellers churned the sea, leaving a high wake fanning out behind them. We would turn our bows to meet the wakes head-on. As the natural waves smashed into the offending wakes and combined to form an uneven mountain of water CLYPEUS would buck, dip and twist and quiver under the weight of water that invariably crashed over our foredeck.

Eventually there was a suitable gap between the lights of merchant vessels heading up the northbound shipping lane,

The chart showed a sheltered anchorage behind a headland.

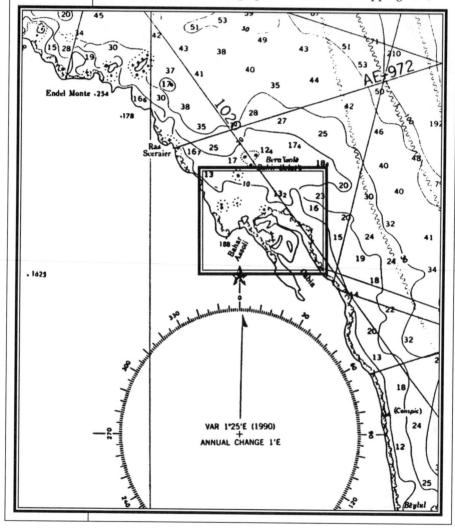

so we heaved in the sails, turned west on to a port tack and skimmed across the channel parallel with the waves. Within the separation zone, with the sails eased, we sailed north until there was another longish gap between the oncoming lights of south bound vessels and hurried across. We wanted to get to the western shore as quickly as we could and actively avoided going anywhere near the Hanish Islands which we knew were in dispute between the Eritreans and the Yemenis. We had heard only positive reports from the yachts ahead about conditions on the Eritrean coast.

Our normal watch routine of three hours on, three hours off, didn't work well that night as weaving between the ships needed two pairs of eyes and hands. When daylight came we took turns to try and sleep, but with continuing hot strong winds and seas towering up and curling, sometimes crashing almost on our stern, we didn't get much rest. However, the rough weather seemed a small price to pay for the joy of travelling north with the wind behind us.

The sun sank in a pink and purple glow behind a ridge of black craggy mountains. The foreshore looked dark and menacing. We sat in the cockpit appreciating a desert sunset and looking for signs of any change in the weather. Did that purple sky portend a dust storm which would sand blast the paint from the hull?

A million bright stars twinkled and shone overhead but the relentless hot wind continued to drive us north. Our Phillips G.P.S. allowed us to track our course accurately and keep safely between the shipping lanes and the coral reef-strewn Eritrean coast.

On the 8am radio schedule MARA reported they would make Marsa Dudo that night, anchor, and wait for us. We raced along under the hot sun at six knots but realised as we studied the chart at 3pm, that with 23 miles still to go, we wouldn't make Marsa Dudo before the light was too poor to con our way through the coral to their anchorage. In this region darkness falls about 6pm and as the sun gets lower it reflects off the water and the coral becomes invisible. The British Admiralty chart showed a sheltered anchorage behind a headland, about five miles to the west, on the Eritrean mainland. We made for it and put the anchor down in twelve feet of clear water into hard sand, sat back, and caught our breath.

The sandy peninsula had a peak of grey rock at the tip that deflected much of the wind. Hills of white sand with scrub, and others of black volcanic boulders stretched away to the south. What looked like remains of little black stone houses with no roofs were dotted around. (We later realised

The sandy peninsula had a peak of grey rock at the tip that deflected much of the wind.

they could have been gun emplacements.) The crescent of the calm aquamarine bay was wondrously quiet. Eagles soared overhead and shearwaters swooped out beyond the headland over the grey and white rolling hills of water.

Peace at last!

An hour later, at 5pm a grey open launch approached, powered by two large outboard motors at the stern and a large machine gun, covered in sacking, mounted amidships. Men in assorted clothing, carrying automatic rifles sat uneasily on either side. The boat nudged up astern. We stood in the cockpit apprehensively.

On the bow, a tall mature man dressed in traditional African robes called to us,

"Good afternoon. No worries. No problem. We just wish to see your passports and papers. I am not army. I am interpreter."

"OK." Peter said. "Welcome aboard. I'll go and get them."

Two unsmiling young black men in cotton camouflage trousers and shirts, carrying rifles, clambered aboard. The interpreter followed.

"Please come down into the cabin. Would you like tea? Some dates?" I offered as we usually do to officials.

One soldier stayed in the cockpit, his rifle at the ready.

Seated at the cabin table the interpreter took a date and popped it into his mouth, with thanks. The soldier unsmilingly refused and was obviously suspicious and nervous.

So were we; the atmosphere was charged with distrust.

Peter presented our passports and the ship's papers.

They scrutinised them carefully, looked around the boat, examined the forward cabins, then left.

"No problems really. A normal efficient, coast guard type inspection of a foreign boat," we reported to our friends on the radio.

We settled down to dinner and then bed.

At 10 o'clock shouts awoke us and we quickly pulled some clothes on.

The launch and the armed soldiers were back.

"Your passports, we must have them now." A soldier in the bow shouted across the breaking seas.

"No, certainly not. We don't give our passports to anybody. Where is your authority to take them?"

Silence.

"We want your passports now."

"No. Our passports are the property of the British Government. We do not wish to give them to you. You saw them this afternoon and they were in order. Where are YOUR papers to tell us who YOU are?"

The launch banged and scraped up and down CLYPEUS's transom.

"Keep away," Peter shouted. "You'll break the self steering gear."

The launch backed off. Two soldiers huddled and talked for a minute.

"OK. You follow us to our base and we do not take your passports."

"What?" I asked incredulously. "Now? It is much too dangerous to take up the anchor and follow you in the dark in shallow water between coral. We draw two metres."

"No problem. You not give us passports, you must follow us."

Restlessly the soldiers shifted and threateningly caressed their rifles.

"But we cannot see, there is no moon."

"Follow our torch light."

Peter shrugged and muttered. "Six soldiers with rifles and a machine gun - we can't argue."

Engine on, anchor up; cautiously we followed their blinking flashlight for a mile or so between islands towards the mainland.

After a tortuous half an hour in the dim light, we could see the outline of another yacht.

"Anchor near this boat."

Peter went forward, the chain rumbled out and CLYPEUS settled again.

"Now your passports."

"But you said, if we followed you, you wouldn't need them."

"Your passports.... Your passports. Give them to me now."

The water was a little calmer inside the bay. Even so the gunwales of their boat ground against our hull. We looked at each other in despair.

"OK. OK. Stay back and I'll get them." Peter went below and fetched our passports. He handed over our precious identity and the launch rushed off into the night.

Sleeping was difficult. We whispered to each other lying on top of the sheets in our double bunk. Our passports had never been taken before. What was going to happen? When would they bring them back? Peter decided to sleep up in the main saloon where he would be nearer any action. I stayed below and listened to the wind howling. Gradually the boat dipping and bobbing in the two foot scend lulled me to sleep.

We awoke early to see white water still all around and CLYPEUS a quarter of a mile further from the shore. She had dragged her anchor - the twenty kilo Bruce. Turning the engine on, Peter went forward to raise the anchor, straining back and forth as he worked the manual winch. When he raised his hand, I motored her closer to the lee of the little island, watching the depth meter with great care. We re-anchored in twelve feet. As he returned aft, his hands supporting his aching back, he asked, "How deep?"

"Twelve feet."

"What's the rise and fall of tide here? Is twelve feet enough to keep her keel from the seabed? What's the state of the tide now?"

We peered at the shore line. There was too much spray and whitewater movement to tell where the high water tide mark was.

"Let's get the computer and tidal programme out."

We went below and while I prepared breakfast, just coffee, bread and butter and a selection of additives, he booted up the Toshiba laptop. PC TIDE worked out the tidal predictions.

"We will be OK," he confirmed, slicing the hard ethnic

bread we had bought in Aden. He spread it with butter and his beloved Marmite, then peanut butter on top of the thick wedge. I cut an almost transparent slice hoping it was thick enough to hold the marmalade with cheddar cheese which is my favourite breakfast. Every five minutes one of us put our head out to check that we hadn't moved again.

On the 8 am radio schedule we contacted our friends and told them of our predicament, but not to worry, we were sure our passports would be returned during the day.

At 9 am a spume of spray approaching from the shore heralded the launch. Soldiers climbed onto their bobbing bow and pointed rifles at us.

"Come ashore now." They shouted.

"No we cannot, it is too rough and our boat is not safe. We cannot leave her in thirty knots of wind." Peter yelled at them.

And indeed it was impossible for them to get onto CLYPEUS. Their launch was crashing up and down and as they approached, it banged against a stanchion, broke it off and gouged a lump out of our hull.

"Stay away, stay away," Peter shouted, "we're not going anywhere. It's too rough. Where are our passports? Please bring them back. You said if we followed you here you would not take them."

The helmsman at the stern shouted a warning to the soldiers on the bow and backed the launch away in the turbulence. The soldiers conferred with him. The launch circled CLYPEUS and then returned to the shore. They disembarked and walked to a hut on the beach which had a slim radio aerial tower alongside.

We spent the day on anchor watch, sheltered from the searing sun by the cockpit awning and solar panels. Gulls, terns and boobies hovered on the rushing wind and swept down over the whitecaps topping the restless blue-grey water. Eagles screamed high above as they circled their nests on the small island. Odd sticks protruded from rough nests on the craggy rock summits, and juvenile squeaks and squeals could be heard, but we couldn't see the chicks even with the binoculars.

However, we could see on the mainland: camels, large and small, roaming between small square huts. Dilapidated boats and the ruins of a stone house were scattered along the desert foreshore. Shimmering black volcanic mountains and yellow sand dunes stretched away to high purple mountains in the pale misty distance.

In the cabin I decided to make bread. Kneading the wholemeal dough in the ninety-five degree cabin was hot work, but it would be easier here at anchor than when the boat was tossing around in the sea tomorrow. Peter sat in the shade on deck and spliced a new anchor warp to the C.Q.R. anchor.

At mid-day after a cool non-alcoholic beer (no beer or spirits are available in Muslim Aden any more, not even any duty-free) we enjoyed oven-warm crisp-crusted wholemeal bread, butter, cheese, pickle and tomatoes. In the afternoon we carried on with our chores; sorting vegetables and fruit, turning the vaselined eggs (the vaseline preserves them by excluding fresh air), writing up the log and journals, checking the water in the batteries, reading about Abyssinia, Sudan and Egypt so that we had a smattering of background knowledge before we arrived. We didn't bother to put the mainsail cover on as we expected to leave at dawn.

We kept our radio schedule at 6pm and told our friends on MARA, GREEN DOLPHIN and KULAROO what had happened.

"Give me your passport numbers," demanded Linda on GREEN DOLPHIN. She is one of the clear-voiced efficient American ladies who sometimes seem to dominate the radio waves. We were lucky to have her as a friend.

"No, I'm sure there isn't really a problem. I will give them to you tomorrow morning if we think we are in trouble," Peter replied. "By the way, there is a French yacht called PEEWIT anchored nearby. We have been trying to call them on VHF but nobody seems to be on board. Their red inflatable dinghy is trailing astern though."

"OK. I'll make a note of that.   Let's call each other a little earlier than usual tomorrow. How about 7 o'clock," suggested Linda.

"That's-a-roger. OK, 7 o'clock. How are you doing?" Peter enquired.

"We have problems too. Our transmission has failed, but KULAROO is going to tow us into Massawa for repairs."

"Bad luck. Let me speak to Don as we have similar engines."

A technical conversation ensued which finished with Peter saying:

"It sounds as though my spare drive-plate will fit your engine. I'll help you put it in when we get to Massawa in a couple of days. Hope all goes well. Have a good night. CLYPEUS clear", and he signed off.

I couldn't help saying "You always procrastinate. You know our passport numbers off by heart. Why didn't you give them to her?"

"It seemed a bit over the top. Making a mountain out of a molehill. What's for dinner?"

After an early meal we went to bed feeling depressed, aware that with no passport you are nobody. Why hadn't they been brought back?

At midnight the wind had died a little, and the sea was calmer. The roar of the launch nearby woke us.

"You come now. Come ashore and speak to our chief." A soldier shouted from their bucking bow.

"What now? Can't it wait until morning?"

"No, come now."

"Is he there now? Does he wish to speak to us at this time of night?"

"Yes, now. Come."

"Wait until we dress."

They climbed onto our pitching deck. Two intimidating soldiers, both with automatic rifles came down into the cabin. They were wearing long green cotton trousers. The one we assumed was senior had on a yellow and green camouflage short-sleeved shirt and the other, a scruffy tee shirt. The interpreter, clad in long trousers and loose shirt, followed them down.

We prepared to leave, my mind racing as to what we should take, Peter's mind racing as to what he needed to do to the boat if we were going to leave it for a couple of hours. I collected a cotton head scarf and sandals; a sun hat for Peter and his sandals.

Back in the main cabin I said "This is ridiculous," and reached towards the VHF short range marine radio. "I'm just going to tell our friends what is happening."

As I picked up the VHF microphone both ebony-skinned soldiers sprang forward. One grabbed my shoulder and threw me back onto the settee, the other grasped my wrist in a vice-like grip and forced the microphone from my hand.

"No. No." he shouted.

"Let go! Let me go!" I shouted back.

"I say," said Peter, shocked at the roughness and speed with which they had responded.

"No radio," ordered the senior soldier.

"Now, now, no problem," soothed the interpreter. "But you cannot use your radio."

The rough soldier let go my wrist and I rubbed it.

"It is just like Bosnia," I accused him. "Just like Bosnia. You take elderly people from their beds in the night and whisk them to where they do not know."

He looked suitably chagrined. "Not like Bosnia," he said; hurt that I could think such a thing.

"Come. Now. Bring blankets." The senior soldier commanded.

"Blankets?" I echoed, astonished.

"Put in a couple of books too," Peter suggested, "it looks as though this could take a few hours."

I was shivering with fear and shock, as nobody had touched me roughly since my father had shaken me by the shoulder for some misdemeanour in my teens. Blundering into the forepeak, tears welling up in my eyes I dug deep down for a sleeping bag. Thinking to myself, don't panic, don't panic. Now blanket? blanket ? We haven't used a blanket in years. Can't remember where they are. Where did I store them? Never mind, this zip-up sleeping bag will do. What else do we need? How long will they keep us, surely only until morning? Better take my high blood pressure pills and HRT tablets. I'd better take a roll of toilet paper if Eritrea is anything like the other countries we have been visiting, tissues too. Good job I put on trousers and a loose top, I'll be dressed suitably even if they are Moslems.

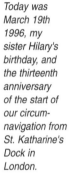

Today was March 19th 1996, my sister Hilary's birthday, and the thirteenth anniversary of the start of our circumnavigation from St. Katharine's Dock in London.

'No, I won't bother to put in our toilet bags, we'll be back to wash and clean our teeth'. Foolishly I didn't bother to put them into the large plastic bag with the sleeping-bag and bits and pieces. We were bound to be back on board in the morning.

"Come. Come now," the soldier urgently hassled me, waving his rifle in my direction.

I could hear Peter saying "I wish to check the anchor and put the sail cover on."

"Check anchor. Yes. Sail cover, no time. Come now."

Peter locked the cabin door behind us and we climbed into the launch. Three nervous young soldiers clutching their rifles climbed onto CLYPEUS.

"They guard your boat. Make sure it not drag anchor."

"Thank you," Peter muttered, wondering what they would do if it did drag.

Huddled beneath a mounted machine gun on the pitching deck of the small Eritrean gunboat, Peter and I regarded each other in disbelief. Ten minutes ago we had been fast asleep on CLYPEUS. Now, in the pitch black, we were being forced ashore by ill-clad Eritrean soldiers. These war-torn young men regarded us suspiciously as they nonchalantly leaned against the gunwales, their backs to the wind, cradling their rifles to protect them from the spray.

It was impossible to think of a sensible reason why two sixty-plus year olds should be taken from their well-worn yacht in the middle of the night. Today was March 19th 1996, my sister Hilary's birthday, and the thirteenth anniversary of the start of our circumnavigation from St. Katharine's Dock in London. After sailing over 54,000 miles and visiting forty-nine countries we thought we had experienced most types of reception. Never had we been treated as spies? criminals? drug dealers? gun runners? What did they want? What were they looking for? Were we hostages? For what? Some international incident we didn't know anything about? This must be a silly mistake.

Warm sea-spray spattered our faces and clothes as the launch plunged towards the beach.

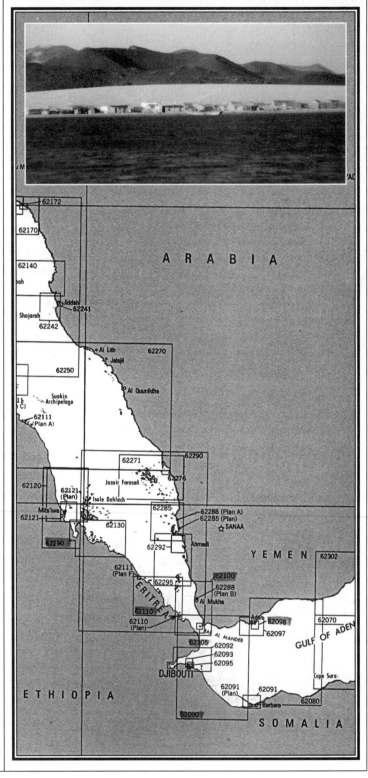

ARABIA

62172

62170

62140

62241
Jiddah
Shajarah
62242

Al Lith
Jalajil
62270
62250

Al Quunfidha

Suakin
Archipelago

62111
(Plan A)

62271

62290

62120

Jazair Farasañ

62276

62121
(Plan)

Isole Dahlach

62285
Mits'iwa

62288 (Plan A)
62285 (Plan)
SANAA

62121

62130

62290

62292
Ahmadi

YEMEN
62302

62111
(Plan F)

62295

62100

ERITREA

62288
(Plan B)
Al Mukha

62110

62110
(Plan)

Aden
62098

62097

62070

GULF OF ADEN

BAB EL MANDEB

62105

62092
62093
62095

DJIBOUTI

Cape Sura

62091
(Plan)

62091

ETHIOPIA

62090

Berbera

62080

SOMALIA

CHAPTER SEVEN

Eritrea
Baraisole Bay •

Baraisole Bay - Day 1   13°39'N Lat 42°10'E Long

The military launch slammed through the waves. Warm sea-spray spattered our faces and clothes as it plunged towards the beach.   Where could they be taking us? There wasn't a town for miles as far as we could see, just the plaited huts of the fishing village and a shed. Peter had his protective arm around me as I clutched the top of our bag, a plastic dustbin-liner containing our few belongings. I huddled up to him, aware of his comforting strength.

"Love you," I whispered "and I've no regrets."
"Love you too and feel the same."
He squeezed my shoulder.

"I wonder if the crew of PEEWIT are ashore and can explain what this is all about?" It did seem odd that their red rubber dinghy had been left tied from the stern to bounce up and down in the rough sea. Hopefully its painter wasn't chafing. Perhaps they had plenty of money and decided to take a safari trip into the desert? It seemed a peculiar place to start.

No warnings had been posted in Aden last week about any trouble in Eritrea. Nothing had been mentioned at the Egyptian Embassy in Aden. We had been twice to apply for

Baraisole Bay

and collect our visas. The friendly staff had chatted to us about our voyage but no warning had been given. We had heard on our ham radio in December and January that yachts had been shot at by Yemenis near the Hanish Islands. We had made sure we were nowhere near them by sailing close to the western shore of the Red Sea and had anchored to rest at an anchorage marked on the British Admiralty Chart. Letters from friends who had day-sailed this way during the past two years had told of the friendly people of Eritrea, trying hard to extract themselves from the debris of thirty years of war. Tales of invitations into homes and offers of traditional coffee; even taking part in a wedding celebration, had encouraged us to look forward to visiting Eritrea, although we had been dreading the hazardous Red Sea.

As the military launch approached the beach we could dimly make out soldiers, camels, donkeys and goats on the foreshore. An anchor was thrown over the bow and the stern swung around pushed by the waves towards the beach. The helmsman tipped the powerful outboard motor propellers out of the surf. The soldiers indicated with their guns that we jump ashore. Timing our jumps between waves, we landed in ankle deep warm water and took our first steps in Africa. This wasn't the way I had envisaged it, under armed guard!

Strong hands helped us through the surf. Suddenly the wind was much hotter, a shrill scream turned into the first notes of a donkey's heeee-haw as he brayed at the excitement. The hot wind swirled warm sand around our wet legs and stung our faces.

As the military launch approached the beach we could dimly make out soldiers, camels, donkeys and goats on the foreshore. An anchor was thrown over the bow and the stern swung around pushed by the waves towards the beach.

Heads down, eager, armed soldiers on either side escorted us up the beach to a baking wind-blown hut. Off-duty men, lying on their beds in the open under the wide eaves, peered out of their wraps with interest like bug eyes from cocoons.

Inside, out of the wind, the sand-floored hut was lit by a flickering wick emerging from the neck of an old bottle half-filled with kerosene, pushed down into the sand. Apart from feeble flashlights, this appeared to be the only light in the camp. Mice skittered away from under a bed as we entered. The leader indicated to two camp beds with dirty mattresses, and none too clean blankets, which were still warm and had obviously just been vacated. Nobody wore uniforms or stripes or badges. The only way to tell who was in charge was by the tone of voice and the way the others did as he commanded. Were they even actually army? They could be a well-organised pirate band. The only clothing they all had in common was their brown plastic sandals.

"Sit."

We sat; together; side by side; holding hands; on one bed.

"Where is your officer?" Peter asked.

"You wait," they turned to go.

"Please don't shut the door and lock us in," I pleaded.

"OK, no problem," the tall man who had acted as interpreter answered, and he chatted to the leader who nodded OK, but spoke to the armed soldiers sitting outside the door.

A few minutes later they came back with a plastic detergent bottle bound with wet sacking and poured out two glasses of water for us. The leader and the interpreter faced us.

"My name is Safaii," said the mature soft-eyed interpreter. "Don't worry. I'm not a soldier, I work for the Marine Research Department." He nodded to the water, "It's OK to drink. Comes by truck from Assab." He was a different type of African, tall and handsome with broad shoulders and a charming smile; perhaps a Nubian? The soldiers were small, but strong, fine-featured men with sharp eyes and quick movements. Their late Emperor, Haile Salaisse, whom I had seen at Queen Elizabeth's coronation, was a benign and older reminder of Abyssinian stature.

The leader looked at us piercingly and spoke sharply in what we assumed was Eritrean.

"Why did you come to Baraisole Bay?" was translated in a gentler tone.

Peter replied evenly. "We didn't know we had come to Baraisole Bay. We didn't enter any bay. We just anchored behind the nearest headland to sleep. You made us come two miles further into the bay last night." He continued. "We anchored where the British Admiralty Chart shows an anchorage. Under international law, ships can anchor for forty-eight hours for rest or repairs, as long as they do not go ashore. We have not been ashore and have done nothing wrong. Why have you taken our passports?"

"What is your mission?"

"What do you mean mission?" Peter replied, startled at such an assumption.

"Don't you know this is a War Zone?"

"What do you mean War Zone? No warnings have been given. We knew there was a dispute about the Hanish Islands so we didn't go there. Where is your officer? When can we have our passports back?"

"Our chief will come from Assab in the morning."

"In the morning! Why bring us ashore now, in the dark, if he isn't coming until morning?"

"Don't worry. No problem." Safaii tried to soothe.

"Yes, there is a problem. We are here and not on our boat. What do you want us for? How can we trust you? Everything you have told us so far has been lies. First you said that if we followed you, you wouldn't take our passports, and then you did. Then that your chief was waiting on shore to talk to us. Now he isn't here."

I regarded Peter with awe. He was being so strong and sensible. My mild, shy husband? I had never seen him act this way before.

"Sleep now." They turned and left us.

The wavering light cast weird shadows on the wall. Mice scampered in and out of the corners. I opened the sleeping bag we had brought with us and spread it on one bed and laid down. The hot, howling wind echoed our despair.

Peter refused to lie down and was prepared to sit up all night on the edge of the bed to demonstrate his disapproval. After half an hour, nobody came. Nobody was going to come, so I gently suggested he lie down beside me and I curled around him. It was too hot to need a cover, in fact I would have liked to take some of my clothes off but with the open door and soldiers outside...

We laid close, trying to sleep but with a thousand thoughts rushing through our brains. With my arms around his chest I whispered in his ear how well he had done. How he had been calm and forceful, strong without being rude.

"Please God don't let them separate us," I prayed.

Camels and goats snuffled around outside. Waves crashed against the shore. Was CLYPEUS dragging her anchor? How was our uninsured home, our all, surviving with three armed soldiers sitting on guard in the cockpit? Would the gunboat damage her when they took the soldiers off in the morning? When would they take us back out? When would the officer come? What could he possibly think we had done?

I tried to think things out clearly. Had we done anything wrong since we had anchored yesterday afternoon?
No, nothing I could think of. How was I going to go to the bathroom?

This was really happening to us. It wasn't a sick dream. I lay curled around my dear husband thinking about how we had abandoned a normal happy, if stressful, life in Wokingham, Berkshire, about thirty miles west of London, in 1982, to sail around the world in our own boat. We wanted to spend more time together, to travel and have adventures. Well, now we were achieving that on all points!

*How would we cope,
how would I cope?*

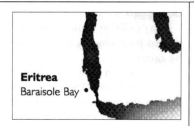

Eritrea
Baraisole Bay •

CHAPTER EIGHT

Baraisole Bay - Day 2

I dozed fitfully, fearfully. What if we were separated? How would we cope? How would I cope? Could I withstand interrogation, harsh words, brutality? Thank God the soldiers didn't seem interested in me as a woman only as a prisoner. I was more fearful of being shot than being raped. Would we turn out to be an expendable embarrassment when they realised their mistake: shot and quietly dumped in a ditch to save face?

My father used to say 'I wore my heart on my sleeve.' I know I do. I'm a softie and I like being one, but during our voyage I have frequently exhorted myself to 'toughen up'. Well now I would have another opportunity to show I wasn't a prissy girl with no guts. I must try and be calm and strong like Peter and support him, not be a drag. But I mustn't speak out of line again, like I did trying to call on the VHF. The way the soldiers reacted had really frightened me.

The buzz of flies and the braying of the donkey awakened us to a brilliant pink and orange dawn which we could see through the open door. The sea to the east was a mass of white water. CLYPEUS was still there, in the same place, occasionally burying her bow in the waves. The sun reflected from her gold anodised masts and blinked reassuringly from her stainless steel mast steps.

"Are you OK?" I whispered to Peter who still had his eyes shut, not wanting to recognise the day and its problems. "CLYPEUS looks alright and is in the same place."

As I put my feet on the sand I heard the scurrying of mice under the bed. Quick as a flash, I pulled my feet back, picked up my sandal and banged it on the ground. Little grey creatures ran into low crevices under the shed walls. I went to the plywood west wall and raised the window shutter. Through the glass-less hole I could see a line of camels plodding away over the yellow sand hills. From the village came three totally black-clad ladies walking towards the north accompanying a train of donkeys laden with barrels. The black figures flicked sticks and prodded the animals along the path until they disappeared out of sight across the desert into the haze.

Safaii came in and asked if we had slept well. He apologised for taking us from our usual beds, but they had their orders by radio.

When I asked "Where are the donkeys being taken"?

He said "They are being taken to get water for the village as they do every day, four hours to the well and four hours back".

He organised a glass of hot sweetened black tea (shahi) for us. Later we were given the soldiers' breakfast - a large tin plate covered by a thick grey spongy flat pancake (injerra) with a tasty bean (foul pronounced fool) mix in the centre. It didn't look very appetising but we were hungry. Safaii showed us how to tear the pancake and use it to scoop up the beans. They had no cutlery.

It was indicated that there were no toilets except for the beach. We were allowed to hunker down out of view, with just our heads showing. We accepted the situation with difficulty, thankful that the roll of toilet paper had survived the wet ride ashore.

The morning dragged on. No dust rose across the desert to indicate the arrival of a vehicle. I sketched how we felt in my notebook.

How had we got ourselves into this mess?

We were allowed to sit on a bed outside the hut and keep an eye on CLYPEUS bucking at her anchor. We tried to read the books I had hastily stuffed in with our sleeping bag: "Requiem" by Claire Francis, "The Man Who Made Husbands Jealous" by Jilly Cooper, but the pages swam before our eyes and we couldn't concentrate. Having left my camera on board, I tried to sketch the scene in front of us.

No officer appeared, but the senior soldier made us re-enter the hut and questioned us some more. His name, we now knew, was Mahamir, and Safaii was the interpreter. Mahamir's questions seemed harsh and long but Safaii obviously shortened them and made them more gentle.

"Why did you come to Baraisole Bay?" he translated.

"To shelter from the strong wind and sleep. We didn't know it was Baraisole Bay. There is an anchorage marked behind the headland on the British Admiralty Chart. By international law ships are allowed to anchor for 48 hours for rest and repairs as long as the crew do not go ashore." Peter answered patiently.

"What was your last port?"

"Aden."

"Why didn't you book in at Assab?"

"Because it has a difficult entrance between islands and reefs and we wanted to get as far north as we could while the southerly wind was with us. Also on the marine radio we heard that the crews of yachts that called at Assab had to pay $US30 each for a seven day visa which did not give them time to get to Massawa and visit Asmara. At Massawa they had to pay another $US25 each, for a further seven day visa."

"Why were you going to Massawa?"

"Friends who stopped there in their yachts last year and the year before, wrote very positive reports. They said it was a pleasant place, the people were friendly and Asmara, up in the mountains, was a cool and beautiful cathedral city with fine boulevards and restaurants."

"Where were you going after Massawa?"

"Sudan. Suakin; the interesting ruined city which was the last slave trading town and also we will be able to buy more diesel."

"Then where?"

"To Egypt, Safaga, to visit the Valley of Kings, to Cairo to see the Pyramids and then through the Suez Canal to the Mediterranean."

They regarded us with disbelief.

"More than fifty yachts have already sailed up the Eritrean coast this year." Peter continued. "Why have you picked on us?"

Our interrogators walked out.

Half an hour later, having watched the daily round of the soldiers: washing, combing their hair and cleaning their teeth with small sticks, and chatting to each other, I cautiously got up and walked to the door.

"OK if I go see the cook?" I asked the guarding soldier squatting outside. Shouldering his rifle from across his knees he went into the radio shack where his superior sat with the radio transmitter.

"OK," he agreed as he walked back and sat outside our hut door again.

I went to see the cook and discover how she made such large dustbin-lid size pancakes. Although she had no English, by gesture and a few words, it was explained that Worku was the young government cook from Addis Ababa. She showed me how she cooked the slightly bitter-tasting pancakes 'injerra' and 'kicha' on a wide tin plate (the top of an oil drum) on a drift wood fire. She lifted the lids of two large blue plastic tubs and we peered inside at the grey fermenting batter.

"Three days," Worku gestured. "Then cook."

I didn't manage to find out what type of grain was used. A kettle boiled on a rusty biscuit-tin-cooker filled with charcoal. Worku was about 20, petite, bird-like and dainty and had a welcoming smile and the understanding empathy that women are lucky enough to share.

It was a lonely and hard life for her, the only girl amongst the twenty men. She appeared to rule the kitchen with a rod of iron when soldiers were sent to assist her. She was busy so I retreated back to our hut.

At 11 o'clock Safaii returned and offered to take us for a walk around the village. Peter stayed in the hut - surely their chief would come at any moment and he wanted to be around when he arrived.

The village was a collection of drab brown huts made of palm leaf matting, flattened cigarette cartons, beaten out oil drums, and a few pieces of drift wood. Smaller plaited fences surrounded the huts and little shelters had been made which enabled goats to lie down in the shade. Some goats wandered around with dirty pieces of cloth tied beneath their udders; I assume to stop their kids feeding and reserve the milk for children.

Safaii was greeted with enthusiasm, because as an official, responsible for distribution of international aid for various projects like outboard motors and a health clinic, he was well known and respected. He introduced me around. Everyone smiled and shook hands. The small children hid behind skirts and the toddlers I approached and tried to talk to, cried in terror at my white face and blonde hair even though it was mostly covered by my headscarf tied back at the nape of my neck.

The little wood and matting school had sixteen children between the ages of seven and twelve. A total of twelve boys and four girls. Safaii explained it was a Muslim village and many parents did not approve of girls being educated. The boys sat in three rows of benches in front, with the four girls dressed in long robes at the back. A young male teacher, a blackboard, and a small table completed the school. Thirty-two big brown eyes in shining eager faces regarded me with interest. The teacher asked them to count to a hundred in English and then, along the benches, take turns for the next letter of our alphabet.

I shook hands with them all, told them my name and asked theirs.

"Good morning, my name is Shirley. What's your name?"

Giggle giggle, "My name is Abrahim."

"Good morning Abrahim. How are you today?"

"Very well thank you." Giggle giggle. A brown hand came up to hide shining white teeth.

"How old are you Abrahim?"

"I am eleven years old."

"My grand-daughter is eleven years old. Her name is Laura."

They were interested in my six grandchildren so I wrote on the blackboard their names and ages and that some lived in England and some in the U.S.A. Then the class sang well and in tune without any accompaniment, after the teacher had hummed the first note. What enthusiasm! It was a joy to hear their loud young voices bursting with pride as they sang their Eritrean song.

Thinking I had interrupted their lessons long enough we said our goodbyes and walked further along the shore to where young camels were hobbled in the shade of plaited walls. A few scrubby pandanus palms bent to the wind.

An old woman crouching on the foreshore was breaking volute shells between two lumps of rock. She picked out the inside and, with a toothless grin, offered me a two inch long twitching sample. The raw white flesh was sweet and delicious. Peter wouldn't have tried it, but tasting the food the local people eat, and are generous enough to offer when they have so little, doesn't worry me. I don't always like it, but I know they are not trying to poison me.

I smiled at her and said "Thank you. Very good," and gave the 'thumbs up' sign that seems to be an international sign of approval.

"See the claw," Saffai said. "A kilo of those will sell for $US100. They are used in making perfume. We keep trying to tell the old people that if they just pulled the claw off and put the shells back in the sea, another claw would grow and they could harvest them commercially." He shrugged. "But this is a traditional food and this is the way their parents harvested them and this is the way they are going to eat them."

We strolled back to the army hut. Nobody had arrived but it was time for more questioning. Peter and I sat holding hands on the edge of one bed and, facing us, Safaii and Mahamir perched on the other.

"Why had we come to this Bay?" We replied as last time to all the same questions.

What was our last port?

Why hadn't we booked in at Assab?

Why were we going to Massawa?

Where were we going after Massawa?"

Safaii apologised that he had to repeat the same questions again. He argued with Mahamir and then told us that some of the questions were so stupid he wasn't even going to ask them.

After lunch - injerra and foul - Peter was told he must bring all our cameras, including our video camera, and charts ashore. He refused and said he would gladly take their chief to examine them on board when he came.

"No. Must get now."

"But there are hundreds of charts", Peter explained "and they will get wet and be spoilt if we try to bring them ashore in this weather."

"No. Now."

"I'm sorry NO. I will not bring them ashore. You will have to shoot me first," Peter said very firmly.

I was about to panic. "Don't even suggest things like that," I whispered fiercely.

He continued "We cannot trust you. Everything you have said so far has been untrue. First you said you would not take our passports, but you did. Then you said your chief was waiting here to question us, but he wasn't." He sat down looking very determined.

The leader, Mahamir, was very upset. He couldn't fulfil his orders. He stalked off, and shouted to all and sundry that nobody, but nobody, was to talk to us or look at us. Hostile looks and backs turned towards us all around. It was very upsetting.

However Peter was adamant. He was determined not to give in easily to their demands and assured me, "We are in the right; they have no legal authority to take anything from our boat."

We sat in our lonely shed slapping at the persistent flies as we tried to keep our chins up and read our books. Every so often looking longingly at CLYPEUS still riding the waves out there. When they examined our cameras and film, as they were obviously going to do, what would they see? Had we, by accident, videoed or taken photographs of anything military? We hadn't noticed anything. What if? It didn't bear thinking about. Yes, we had taken odd photos of the shoreline, and the eagles. Yes, I had videoed the eagles and the island, and the peninsula and mountains when we first anchored, before the launch came. Oh dear!

In the late afternoon we were brought more sweet black tea and Mahamir and another young interpreter came and asked questions. The aristocratic, handsome young national serviceman nervously introduced himself as Semir. He explained that he was taking the place of Safaii who had refused to ask us any more stupid questions and had been dismissed. Semir apologised for his bad English and for us being taken from our boat. He said he was ashamed; it was like taking his mother and father into custody. Peter was still adamant about not bringing ashore our cameras and charts.

Mahamir left and came back a few minutes later with our passports. He gave them to Peter and spoke earnestly.

"We promise we will not rip out the film or touch the

charts until our chief comes. Maybe tomorrow."

Peter argued, but finally agreed we would bring all the Red Sea charts and cameras ashore. The launch took us out to our dear home. Watched by two soldiers, Peter unhanked and stowed the foresail, then assembled the still cameras and Red Sea charts. I took the opportunity to use the bathroom and surreptitiously wipe the video film we had taken of the shoreline yesterday, as we had no idea whether there was anything that could be incriminating on it. Then I packed up some clean underwear and our toilet necessities.

Ashore everyone was happier because they had been able to carry out all their orders.

Petite Worku performed the special Eritrean coffee ceremony for us. She had changed into a pretty satin printed dress with puffed sleeves and looked charming. She brought various bits and pieces into the shed including a biscuit tin filled with already burning red hot wood, and sat on a log beside it, fanning it with a little rush mat. In an old pineapple tin with a wire handle the grey/green coffee beans were roasted over the fire until they were dark brown. The appetising aroma filled the shed. Her hollow log seat was turned upside down, the roasted coffee beans poured into it and using an old metal axle shaft, she ground the beans with this makeshift

We sat in our lonely shed slapping at the persistent flies as we tried to keep our chins up and read our books.

pestle and mortar. Finally, she boiled the coffee in a traditional jabena coffee pot. It was delicious with plenty of sugar
and we sat around making polite conversation. Worku
 insisted I kept the terra cotta jabena as a gift. It had
"KEREN", printed on it in white glaze. I was delighted at her
kindness and generosity. She must have so few possessions
tucked away in her little lean-to room attached to the kitchen.

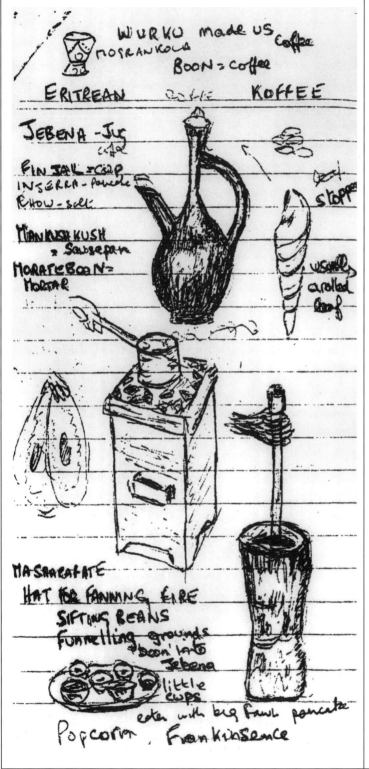

WURKU made US Coffee
NOSRANKOLA
BOON = Coffee

ERITREAN ~~coffee~~ KOFFEE

JEBENA - Jug

FIN JAL = CUP
INSERRA - pancake
RHOW - salt

TIAN KUSH KUSH
= Saucepan

MORATEBOON =
MORTAR

stopper

usually
a rolled
leaf

MA SHARAFATE
HAT FOR FANNING FIRE
SIFTING BEANS
Funnelling grounds
+ boon into
Jebena
little
cups

eaten with big fawl pancake

Popcorn, Frankincense

Petite Worku performed the special Eritrean coffee ceremony for us. She had changed into a pretty satin printed dress with puffed sleeves and looked charming. She brought various bits and pieces into the shed including a biscuit tin filled with already burning red hot wood, and sat on a log beside it, fanning it with a little rush mat.

Eritrea
Baraisole Bay •

CHAPTER NINE

Baraisole Bay - Day 3

T he day wore on, but still no officer. That evening a truck came and took Safaii away. We were very sorry to see him go. He was a solid, mature and sensible 38 year old man who obviously used his own judgement. He was worldly and had his reputation to retain amongst the local Eritreans. We had a confidence in him that we didn't have in these other excitable, over-armed and over-enthusiastic young black national servicemen. When he left we sat on our bed holding hands, I held back my tears but we both felt very miserable and apprehensive. It was just the army and us now, no steadying outside influence.

We tried to encourage each other and asked Mahamir if we could walk along the shore and look for shells to add to my large collection. After discussion, and producing the roll of toilet paper, this was allowed, although two 'minders' strolled discreetly in parallel half a mile away. The sun sank behind the hills and darkness fell quickly.

Now we had our passports; of course we thought of escaping and discussed the possibilities. But CLYPEUS was such a long way offshore, we could never swim to her in the rough

There was no way we could get the charts back on board without help, and we certainly couldn't sail over 1,000 miles without them.

sea and no way could we get the charts back on board without help, and we certainly couldn't sail over 1,000 miles without them.

When we returned to the hut, two soldiers, sitting on their beds outside, were taking turns to play traditional music on a home-made lyre (a dulcimer?), which looked as though it had been made from sun-bleached drift wood. They twanged the strings in a rhythmic discord. When other soldiers gently sang the melody it was a pleasing noise.

After dinner, injerra and beans again, the musicians carried on playing and in the dark I could make out a few young men dancing in a circle. However, Peter was distraught and not interested. All he could think of was another day wasted in our race to sail north before the wind headed us. Would our friends have realised what had happened to us? What could they do about it if they had?

That night we asked if we may sleep in the open under the corrugated-iron eaves; perhaps it would be cooler than in the hot shed.

It was a mistake. The sand was blowing everywhere. We were given a sheet each to wrap around our heads and bodies, but gritty sand swirled around and managed to find its way into our eyes, ears, our hair and up our noses. It grit-blasted our legs if they escaped the sheet. No wonder the off duty soldiers had looked like moth pupae peeping out of their cocoons when we arrived last night.

The goats wandered around the hut looking for scraps, donkeys brayed and the camels made that excruciating scream as though they were being tortured. Peter assumed a foetal position with his sheet wrapped around him. It was still only eight o'clock. I couldn't sleep.

Eritrean music was still being softly played in the corner so I walked closer to listen and sat on an oil drum. The dancers gesticulated that I join them, so I stepped into their circle and walked and turned and beat the floor with the odd heel/toe in time with them. They were delighted and Worku came and joined in as well. It was all very soft, low key and pleasant. Music and dance are a wonderful bridge between all nationalities. It has brought me close to many Pacific Islanders, Chinese, Australians, Indonesians and Malays. I have learnt their dances, and they have attempted Scottish jigs and Greek grapevines that were part of my repertoire as a Keep Fit Leader. However on this occasion there was too much tension to try and do more than a few steps. I retired sadly to wrap myself in my cocoon beside restless Peter.

"We must write an official request to contact the British Consul," he said.

He stayed awake most of the night composing a letter.

As daylight emerged above the eastern horizon I watched Worku pick out sticks and logs from the pile of driftwood to light the breakfast fire in her corrugated-iron kitchen. Quietly, not to disturb the sleeping soldiers, she filled the huge kettle from the cylindrical water tank, pushing the goats out of the way to get to the tap. She must be a very independent young

As soon as it was light Peter printed his letter on the back of an old crew list from our boat's paper.

WE, PETER AND SHIRLEY BILLING ARE BRITISH SUBJECTS AND OWNERS OF THE BRITISH REGISTERED YACHT 'CLYPEUS'.

WE HAVE COMMITTED NO OFFENCE IN ERITREA BUT YOU HAVE KEPT US HERE AGAINST OUR WILL FOR THREE DAYS. THIS IS AGAINST INTERNATIONAL LAW. WE WISH ONLY TO CONTINUE OUR VOYAGE TO MASSAWA TO OBTAIN ERITREAN VISAS.

YOU HAVE ALSO:

FORCED US TO MOVE OUR YACHT IN THE DARK TO AN UNSAFE ANCHORAGE AND DAMAGED OUR BOAT IN THE PROCESS.

FORCED US TO HAND OVER OUR PASSPORTS AND ESSENTIAL YACHT EQUIPMENT WHICH IS AGAINST INTERNATIONAL LAW.

FORCED US TO LEAVE OUR YACHT AND STAY IN YOUR MILITARY BASE.

STOPPED US BY FORCE FROM USING OUR RADIO TO TELL OTHERS OF OUR PROBLEMS.

AS WE HAVE 'DISAPPEARED' AND ARE NOW BEHIND SCHEDULE, THE CAPTAINS OF OTHER YACHTS WILL HAVE REPORTED OUR DISAPPEARANCE TO THE BRITISH GOVERNMENT REPRESENTATIVE IN ASMARA.

WE ASK THAT YOU RETURN US TO OUR YACHT, TOGETHER WITH ALL OF OUR POSSESSIONS SO THAT WE MAY CONTINUE OUR LAWFUL JOURNEY.

SIGNED P Billing
22nd MARCH 1996 Shirley Billing

woman to manage such a hard job with no female company.

As soon as it was light Peter printed his letter on the back of an old crew list from our boat's papers. We signed and stamped it with the red seal of CLYPEUS.

He handed it to Mahamir early in the morning and requested he transmit it to his officer in Assab. Mahamir grudgingly accepted the paper with no comment and studied it carefully. Then he shrugged and walked into the radio cabin. We didn't realise he couldn't read it and that now Safaii had gone, perhaps nobody in the small camp could read English well enough for it to be transmitted.

"Perhaps your officer will come today? Perhaps tomorrow?" Peter called after him. Mahamir just shook his head as he walked on.

We retired, despondent, to our bed in the hut. Peter sorted through the ship's papers and handed me bits of paper that were no longer needed so that I could write down what was happening to us.

After breakfast - injerra and foul and a long glass of shahi- Semir, the National Service interpreter, came and sat beside me and showed me some small photograph albums of his friends, family and home in Asmara. Pictures of hand-some young people under beach umbrellas; graduates of Asmara University, which he had attended, enjoying a day out at Massawa's seaside resort. His parents' home in Asmara was a modern detached house with a scarlet bougainvillea - covered high wall around it. His sister and her children in their modern home looked well-dressed and charming. Her husband owned a sandal factory. They were all Coptic Christians.

Semir showed me photos of groups of young men posing, looking smart, or fooling around making informal human pyramids. He wanted to look like Michael Jackson and certainly did when posing with wisps of his black curly hair brought forward around his face in some of the photos. Campus pictures showed pretty girlfriends and, to our western eyes, normal groups of relaxed young people togeth-er. It was refreshing to see them mixing after visiting Oman and Yemen where the boys and girls were not allowed to even talk or meet before their own wedding. I had been astounded to learn that even guests at Muslim wedding parties were segregated and men and women celebrated in separate rooms.

The day dragged on, still no officer and no answer to our request for contact with the British Consul.

I sat outside sorting and cleaning the sea shells (strombus) I had found on the beach last night. Slowly, one by one the bored young soldiers shyly gathered round and, with their noticeably delicate and long-fingered hands, sat under the awning and helped to clean the shells. They were eager to practise their minimal English. With extensive hand gestures I told them I had sons their ages, but they hadn't had to do national service. They told me their names:

"Vittorio",
"Pedros",
"Unas",
"Jacob".

I shook hands with each one and repeated my name as they had taught me:

My name is Shirley, "She me Shirley".
Your name is: "She me ken?"

In fractured English, with Semir's help, we talked of families and home towns. and I learnt a few Eritrean words:

Good morning - *kamar hadak koom* (*ka* for males - similar to Thai grammar)
Please - *Besaka* (sounded like Malay)
Thank you - *yo fo nelli*
Beautiful - *sembati*
Very good - *patami subor*
Water - *mai*
Coffee - *Koffee*
Sugar - *shuka* - now those two I could remember!

According to the soldiers, the most important towns in Africa were Cairo, Capetown and Asmara. They told me about the war between Eritrea and Ethiopia, "although we are brothers now." Ethiopia had crushed Eritrea and taken away all industry. They had sold the telegraph infrastructure to India. The railway engines, lines and signals had been removed - the lines had been pulled up to make defence barriers. Elevators and escalators had been taken out of buildings and transported to Addis Ababa. They had even removed the traffic lights and sold them off.

Mahamir was approached and I was allowed to visit the kitchen and watch Worku preparing lunch - her kitchen was so hot she hardly needed an oven! With Semir's help she told me that she came from the north of Eritrea, a town called Keren, 100km. north of Asmara towards Barka.

"The jabena you gave me," I gesticulated, "from your home?"

"Yes," she smiled shyly.

"Thank you very much. *Yo fo neli. Yo fo neli*"

Huge smiles all round. I obviously hadn't got it quite right, but they understood.

No, she hadn't been to University but to college in Addis Ababa to the government school for a cookery course. Yes, she enjoyed her job, it was seldom quite as lonely as this, often there were girl soldiers.

I didn't manage to find out how old she was, but would guess at 22 and not married.

In a cauldron over the wood fire lunch was progressing. Great hunks of shark meat, with the skin still on, protruded through a bubbling grey scum. It would take a miracle to make it look attractive.

A soldier was sitting on a log of wood helping. He scraped the cooked shark flesh into shreds with their only fork until a huge mound of white meat tumbled over the edges of the flattened piece of tin. All the shreds were tipped into a large saucepan holding a tomato type sauce.

At lunchtime it was served in the centre of two huge injerras as usual. The soldiers sat around their 'kitchas' in two groups and carefully, with their right hands, pulled off the edge of pancake and scooped up the now tasty looking shark and tomato sauce.

I waited expectantly for our smaller pancake, but Worku had obtained a few plaice-like little fish from the village fishermen and fried them for our lunch. They were pleasant and tasty. No fruit or vegetables were provided. It is difficult to know how they all stayed healthy on a diet which appeared to be completely lacking in Vitamin 'C'.

We laid on our bed outside under the wide eaves of the shed and tried to catch up on some sleep, but the insidious sand swirled everywhere. The scorching wind whined and huffed and puffed - master of all. White wave-tops raced across the pale milky aquamarine sea and a white hot sky burnt down on the black cinder mountains and yellow sand dunes.

In the early afternoon a truck arrived. Great celebrations and greetings. Eritrean men greet each other by clasping right hands and then banging their right shoulders together. Three times for an acquaintance, five times for a good friend, seven times for a joyous reunion. Most of these lads received seven bangs. They had been away on leave.

However, the superior, smart, but unsmiling, driver of the truck regarded us with displeasure and disappeared into the radio shack with Mahamir. Half an hour later Mahamir approached us and with Semir translating, told us it wasn't possible for their chief to come and see us. We would be driven to Assab for questioning by him. We must take all our cameras and ALL our charts, not just the Red Sea area.

"When?"

"Now."

We were bundled into the launch, with an escort of four

armed, but now smiling, soldiers and taken out to CLYPEUS.

I asked that the sharp-faced, meticulously dressed, driver come too. I wanted him to see how difficult things were and what our boat was like, and perhaps make him a friend, so that he would be sympathetic to our situation. However, he was much more worried about getting his smart polished shoes wet and was not a happy sailor.

When he was on board I wished I hadn't invited him, as he snooped around. He picked up our books and magazines and examined them, peeped under the floor, looked in cupboards, scrutinised our electronics, the long distance radio, and the VHF. Quite spy-like!

Feigning clearing-up, I gathered our logbook and Red Sea Pilot and hid them amongst magazines and papers in the forward cabin. Peter took out all the charts from Singapore to Cyprus, which were stored separately from the charts of the rest of the world, and wrapped them in a thick orange garbage bag. While he set another anchor, I packed a bag of clothes.

What to take? Would there be a tribunal? Would we be charged? If so what with? Would we be in prison? In front of a firing squad? It just wasn't bearable to think too far ahead. Keep sensible I scolded myself and mundanely asked the driver, "Will it be cold?"

"It could be. Take jackets," was the answer.

Jackets? What for? I thought. We were close to the hottest place on earth - the Danibole Basin.

I packed smart clothes and included a blazer and tie for Peter, and my smart black trouser suit, in case we had to appear in a court. Pondering while packing on why he had said "take jackets", Assab was one of the hottest towns in the world.

"Hurry." the driver admonished. "Best if we get to Assab before dark."

One and a half beautiful brown crusty loaves lay waiting to be eaten. Was it only the day before yesterday I baked that bread? I pushed one in a plastic bag for Worku, hoping she would know how to eat it. Because they certainly wouldn't have any butter or jam in their stores.

The cabin door was locked again and we thought we had done everything we could to protect CLYPEUS, except put the cover on the mainsail. There just wasn't time.

Ashore we were hustled to pick up all our bags. The soldiers stood around. I wanted to say goodbye to Worku but she was off duty and somewhere in the village. While on board, I had found a little gilt necklace I had been given, and wrapped in it a $US 5 note as gift for her and put it in an unsealed envelope. I gave it to Mahamir and asked him to give it to her, "You look inside and see. No problem." He seemed very pleased as he looked at the little gift. "Tell Worku, my cooking, my bread, I bake." I offered the plastic bag and opened it for him to look. He peered inside and grunted.

Most of the dozen soldiers shook our hands and said goodbye and not to worry. A few special young men were not embarrassed by my motherly kisses on their cheeks. We had all softened considerably. Semir took a group photograph. As we walked toward the truck he sidled up to me and said quietly,

"My friend, who has just come back from Assab, said the French people were not put in good accommodation, they complained, and were put into a hotel for the next night. You make sure you stay in hotel." It was the first we had heard of what had happened to the French couple, we had been too frightened to ask.

"Thank you." I was almost in tears. These gentle young men with their beautiful hands and good manners and obvious affection for each other, had impressed and pleased me. Their mothers would be proud of them.

In a mixture of suppressed excitement and trepidation, we climbed up into the Toyota Land cruiser cab. We were actually going on an inland trip into Africa. Apprehensive, but ...Wow !

Three soldiers with rifles settled in the open back. The truck jolted over the stones, up the sandy track and around the back of the first black cinder hill. How long would it take to get to Assab? What would it be like? Was this really Africa? What would they do to us? Would CLYPEUS still be afloat when we returned? What could they possibly want to know that we hadn't already told them? The hot wind whined over the vast windswept plain as we raced 120 kilometres south across the primeval desert and its spine jarring waddies, to the naval establishment at Assab.

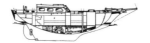

CHAPTER TEN

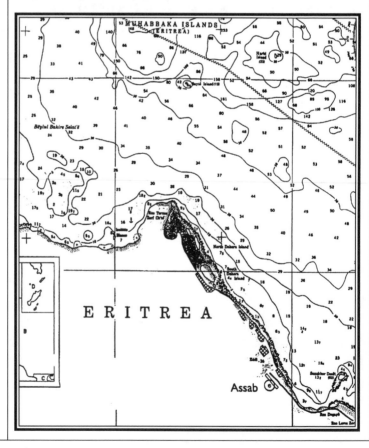

Eritrea
Baraisole Bay •
Assab •

Assab - Day 4

The drive to Assab was fascinating, a landscape completely new to us. Far to our right, to the west, high jagged mountains disappeared into the purple haze. Closer, hills of broken black lava flowed down across the track and sand flats towards the shore. Squashed between Peter and the driver, three abreast in the high cab, I could see on our left the heavily salt-laden sea parading never-ending lines of white horses towards the beach.

"We would still have this glorious wind behind us if we were sailing," Peter muttered.

Flat miles of sand, stones and a million shells, stretched forward as far as the eye could see; obviously this flat plain had been below sea level not so long ago. A few camels grazed midst the grey scrub and pale flat-topped trees growing in the now dry wadis. An ostrich galloped away as we approached, his bare white legs a surprising contrast to his black feathered body. Flamingoes stood on one leg in the shallow milky water beside the salt flats. Their red stick legs supporting pink bodies and snaking necks as, with their strong beaks underwater, they guzzled in the white sediment.

The truck twisted and dipped then slowly wobbled across the dry wadis with extreme caution; there would be no passing traffic to render assistance. We flew over the hard-packed sand, twisting between potholes leaving a cloud of muddy yellow dust behind us.

The thin-lipped, chain-smoking, driver's name was Ibrahim and there conversation ended. He pushed an audio tape into the tapedeck and turned it up loud. A hard rhythmic twanging filled the cab, basically the same sound as the young soldiers had played on their homemade lyre for five or six hours last night. When a melody was sung over the twanging, it was quite pleasant.

In the middle of nowhere, a robed young man stood at the roadside, obviously wanting a lift. For many miles we hadn't seen any homes, huts, tents, or even caves. Where had he come from? Where was he going? The desert stretched ahead as far as the eye could see.

Unconcerned, Ibrahim didn't take his foot off the throttle.

"Are you not allowed to give lifts in army vehicles?" I asked. "He must have many miles to walk."

"This is a navy vehicle," was his curt reply as he leaned forward pressing the throttle harder and turning the tape louder. We bounced and jarred along without conversation.

A few dusty pandanus trees heralded a village. Goatherders quickly gathered their flock out of our path. Girls cradled large dusty gourds on their hips, their thin brown arms carrying them comfortably as they walked from the well towards the village. Nobody waved or smiled. Matting box houses dotted the sandy brown earth, with smaller shacks alongside for the goats.

Another dirt road joined from the interior. At the junction, there was a primitive wayside cafe but we didn't stop. Camels and donkeys were tethered outside the insubstantial pandanus matting and cardboard structure. The village itself appeared to be on a mound surrounded by a high wooden paling fence. Wells were scattered around the outskirts of the village with people, camels, donkeys and goats taking refreshment. The scene seemed as old as time. It could have been one of the oldest inhabited places on earth.

At dusk, as we neared civilisation, partly demolished army tanks and armoured carriers littered the roadside, relics of the recent war. Dusty and decrepit Russian military jets heralded Assab's new airport. We reached a tarmac road and sped over the last few miles into the town. Not many people were out on the streets. Crumbling old colonial houses and warehouses lined the approach to the port.

The truck pulled up outside a substantial but war-torn house near the dock gates. We were led into a high ceilinged room with broken windows, bathroom-green walls and a Turkish looking boxed arch with white icing around its decorative edge. A dusty 21" TV dominated one part of the room, which had brown shiny lounge chairs and a coffee table. Various men in civilian clothes were lounging around but, ignoring us, gradually disappeared when we sat down. A stone-faced aproned woman gave us a glass of water each and then some sweet black tea.

Ibrahim silently handed the papers, including Peter's written request to be allowed to see the British Consul or continue on our lawful way, to a relaxed lean man who stayed sitting. This casually attired man sat up, read our formal letter, put his head in his hands and thought. Another gentleman dressed in a short sleeved shirt and slacks, but with well polished new black shoes, came in and softly introduced himself as the Commander of the Eritrean Navy. Speaking in good English he suggested we may like to wash and brush up before he asked his questions.

At the time I thought the small bathroom we were shown was awful - tatty, and not too clean. However, later I appreciated that actually the toilet flushed, it had a seat, and water came out of the washbasin taps.

Back in the main room, full of trepidation, we nervously sat on the edge of the brown plastic material covered settee and awaited questioning. It was non-aggressive and benign. The commander asked all the questions we had answered before but also wrote down a complete list of our family, jobs, our route over the last thirteen years and how we had spent the time. He particularly questioned us on coming through the Bab Al Mandeb Straits and the timings. He told us that no anchoring was allowed unless we had booked into Assab.

We answered everything truthfully, even telling him that we had $US1,000 plus travellers' cheques with us. Gradually we began to relax and trust this meticulous gentle man, Mr. Achmed.

Everybody we met in Assab was polite and soft spoken.

They are fine-boned people with delightful manners, and elegant hands with long tapering fingers. What a pity we were in such a worrying situation, otherwise we would have enjoyed the experience.

At last, he stood and said. "Now we will take you to your hotel and have dinner together." At the hotel we were shown to a bedroom with two double beds and an ensuite shower and toilet. The door had no handles only a lock.

For dinner we chose local food. It turned out to be injerra pancake and chicken in a chilli black bean sauce. The chicken had extraordinarily long legs and only a little brown meat.

Before Mr. Achmed and his colleague Mr. Goullard left, they gave us a telephone number in case of problems and suggested we meet in the hotel foyer at seven in the morning.

After a shower, we both settled down to enjoy a good night's sleep, thinking an early start would mean we would be back on CLYPEUS before it got dark. We were excited and less worried about our future and, facing each other with our noses close, I whispered about which groceries I would buy in the morning. Peter thought he would probably have to go through our route on the charts with Mr. Achmed. We comfortably held hands and prepared to sleep.

However, the air conditioning didn't work and there were no mosquito screens. We spent an uncomfortable night under the fan with the windows shut tight. The whine of mosquitoes reminded me of our home on the 19th floor of a smart apartment complex in Singapore, where we had been 'up in the world' for a few years - what a contrast!!

I thought about the pleasures we had enjoyed sailing across the Pacific visiting small remote islands on our way to New Zealand.....

So many unexpected opportunities had occurred since we dropped out of the rat race in 1982. I lay clean and comfortable and remembered some good times - happy childhood days, our own three children now happily married with families of their own, and my dear sisters in Wales and Australia. I thought about the pleasures we had enjoyed sailing across the Pacific visiting small remote islands on our way to New Zealand, sunny Australia, and the years ashore in Taiwan and Singapore.

As the fan blew hot air around the room, I eventually fell asleep thinking of the two wonderful years we had just spent homeward bound. We had meandered between Malaysia and Thailand and had time to make some good friends to keep contact with as we voyaged towards Europe. Where were our dear friends now? Would they be able to help us? What were they doing? Had they managed to alert the authorities of our capture?

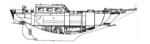

......and the
years ashore
in Taiwan and
Singapore.

Eritrea

Assab

CHAPTER ELEVEN

Assab - Day 5

We awoke after a hot sticky night in the Assab hotel room. With luck we could be back on board today and sailing north tomorrow. All the commander's questions had been answered truthfully and we felt we had established a good relationship.

Downstairs we ordered coffee as we didn't know if our 'hosts' would be breakfasting with us. We didn't know who would be paying the bill either. At seven o'clock Mr. Achmed and Mr. Goullard joined us for orange juice. As we chatted, they explained that the Eritrean military had no titular ranks or official uniforms. The freedom fighters wanted to eliminate titles and class distinctions.

I asked if we could buy fresh vegetables and bread before being returned to our boat. A non-committal reply was given.

They drove us back to the house where they had questioned us the previous night.

"We wish to ask a few more questions," Mr. Achmed started, when we were once again side by side on the settee, sitting further back now, more relaxed.

He again asked us about coming through the Bab El Mandeb Strait and the timings. At no time did he suggest looking at our log (which was on board anyway), which would have been proof of all the times, distances and places. To all long distance yachtsmen reading this, it must seem extraordinary that our log, our at-sea diary, was never even mentioned.

He looked at his watch, and then at Peter. "We would like you to fly to Asmara."

"When?"

"Now. Here are your tickets. Security and the British Consul wish to meet you." He wrapped up the announcement with, "you should also visit the Museum and Cathedral while you are there."

We looked at each other in surprise. My heart thumped with excitement, not altogether worried. After all, we wanted to visit Asmara and now we were being flown there.

These men had been so polite and friendly we didn't feel as threatened as we had been by the soldiers.

"I didn't realise I was married to '007'" I whispered to Peter as he put the Eritrean Airways tickets into his inside pocket.

ERITREAN AIRLINES

passenger ticket & baggage check

ISSUED BY: ERITREAN AIRLINES, P.O. BOX 222 ASMARA - ERITREA

L-CH № 35259

"You must take

Issued by **ERITREAN AIRLINES**	PASSENGER TICKET AND BAGGAGE CHECK Subject to Conditions of Contract In This Ticket	ORIGIN / DESTINATION A&A /ASM	BOOKING REFERENCE	DATE AND PLACE OF ISSUE ERITREAN AIRLINES

ENDORSEMENTS / RESTRICTIONS (CARBON)

NAME OF PASSENGER   KIRESTINA   NOT TRANSFERABLE   DOTTON MR.

PASSENGER COPUON   ASSAB ERITREA   DATE 28-03-16

ISSUED IN EXCHANGE FOR

CONJUNCTION TICKET (S)   ORIGINAL AIRLINE FORM SERIAL No. PLACE DATE   Agents Numeric Code   AGENT

X/O GOOD FOR PASSAGE BETWEEN POINTS OUTLINED	CARRIER	FLIGHT / CLASS	DATE	TIME	STATUS	FARE BASIS	NOT VALID BEFORE	NOT VALID AFTER	ALLOW	BAGGAGE CK/UNCK
FROM ASSAB	ET	562	28		OK	1			20	PCS WT
TO ASMARA					VOID					PCS WT
TO VOID										

TOUR CODE

ADDTIONAL ENDORSEMENTS / RESTRICTIONS (CARBON)

EQUIV. FARE PD.   TAX 4.05   TAX   TAX   FORM OF PAYMENT   CASH + R-U# 5147

L-CH № 35259

your cameras, but the charts will stay here." Mr Achmed ordered.

Immediately our bags and cameras were picked up, we were hurried to the car and driven to the airport.

Assab airport is still being built. Not many planes take off or land. Dilapidated MIG fighters were scattered around the perimeter. We were pushed into the line awaiting the body search procedures, next to a wedding party and were included in the shower of rice scattered towards the departing couple. Boarding passes were thrust into Peter's hand as we were being pushed into the already full airport bus. It drove across the tarmac and we were hustled into the Eritrean Airlines ATR 42 plane.

We settled into our seats and Peter examined our tickets. We saw that they were only for a one way journey and made out in false names: "Petter Ge Mes Ame and 'Kirestina Dotton Mr.'"

We settled into our seats and Peter examined our tickets. We saw that they were only for a one way journey and made out in false names: "Petter Ge Mes Ame and Kirestina Dotton Mr."

Suddenly our flight took on a more sinister outlook. Nobody would ever be able to trace us. We prayed that our sailing friends had informed somebody in authority of our disappearance by now.

During the three hour flight, along with the other passengers, we were offered a glass of orange juice and a lump of dry madeira-type cake. Below us the landscape was of sharp bare mountain peaks and volcanoes. No rivers or trees or settlements could be seen.

Our hearts thumped with apprehension. Were we being taken to Asmara to be formally charged with a crime? or to go before a tribunal perhaps?

The plane landed in the cool air on the 6,000 foot plateau. An inconspicuous gentleman in a grey woollen sweater and slacks escorted us from the plane and through the officials at Asmara airport, to where another Toyota Land Cruiser awaited.

We were driven for half an hour to a modern office block, led up three flights of stairs, and left with a desk official who obviously didn't know what to do with us. It was Saturday lunch time, we sat and waited. After looking at our passports, asking a few questions, thoughtfully tapping the desk with his pencil, then making many inconclusive telephone calls, he shrugged his shoulders and led us down to his own decrepit Fiat. It was an ancient family car full of old paper, broken toys and sweet wrappers.

Through the dusty car windows, we saw a city of blue jacarandas and pleasant tree-lined avenues. Donkey carts clip-clopped down the road and robed people walked and chatted on the sidewalks. There was rubble, and a few ruined buildings, but a peaceful and relaxed ambience pervaded the town. The gracious main street was edged with royal palms and pavement cafes. The Fiat drew to a halt outside the Khartoum Hotel. The driver led us up marble stairs to Reception on the first floor which was a bar/lounge area. Our footsteps clacked on the bare tiled floors and echoed through the corridors. He introduced us to an unsmiling Eritrean receptionist sitting behind a high cash till. She was wearing a red sleeveless tunic over a neat skirt and blouse. He chatted with her for a little then departed saying that somebody would come and see us tomorrow.

The receptionist indicated we follow her along a tiled corridor to a pleasant room with big windows looking out over the street and left us to unpack. Just as I was putting the last few clothes in a drawer she returned and indicated that we would not have this particular room. Hurriedly, she picked up a pile of our clothes and almost ran to a larger room with private shower and toilet, and smaller windows, at the back of the building. We scuttled along after her, clutching the rest of our things and wondering what the panic was. After she left, we wandered around the room, looked in all the drawers, unpacked a little and looked out of the window. Royal palms could just be seen, so we were not far from the main street. A knock on the door, a young waiter appeared, smiled and indicated we follow him. Where to now?

He led us to the dining room that had just two long tables with chairs around them. A patterned plastic cloth covered the tables and a knife, fork, spoon and paper napkin were laid out where we should sit. A pleasant lunch was served of spaghetti bolognaise and salad (the Italian influence in Asmara is strong).

We were escorted back to our room and discovered that the bathroom did have towels but no hot water, no toilet paper and the toilet wouldn't flush. Peter fiddled with the ballcock and made it work. Fortunately we had had the forethought to bring our toilet paper with us. Later in the week, after many requests, another roll of toilet paper was eventually extracted from another receptionist behind the bar. Gradually we settled into our new abode. I sat at the little card table and wrote down what had happened to us so far. We attempted to read our books.

Why had they taken the trouble and expense to fly us here? and why under false names? The air tickets were actually dated yesterday, so Mr. Achmed had known all the time that we would be flying to Asmara. So we couldn't actually trust him either.

At 7pm. no one had spoken to us, so I asked Peter "Do you think we can go to the dining room for dinner?"

"Nobody said we couldn't. Let's try it."

We clattered along the marble-floored passage to the reception and bar area, where a group of men were talking while watching TV. Conversation stopped and we were stared at. A huge new TV dominated the room. CNN news from America was on in English. Hooray! News of what was happening in the world may shed light on our position. We quickly sat down on a wood and leather-thonged settee and tried to be inconspicuous.

Click, an aerial dish whirred somewhere overhead. The screen went black, white numbers and declinations flew past on the screen.

"It's a satellite system," Peter whispered.

An Indian film with ladies in saris flashed by, then white numbers on a black screen again. Alternately and in quick succession, we saw spasms of black and numbers interspersed with a Muslim prayer from the Koran, an Egyptian newscaster, French news from Djibouti, an Ethiopian traditional dance, "Oh I wish he would stop it there," I whispered but the button-clicker kept clicking and the numbers kept changing. BBC news, cricket from where? Two seconds at the most were spent on each station. Football. At last, the screen was still while brown men rushed around the green screen kicking a football.

A small fifty year old man with dark hair in a city suit, sat tense and upright holding the remote control. "He must be the owner of the hotel," we agreed. Clustered close to the TV the five or six young men wearing leisure clothes looked fit and trim with short hair as they bent towards the set.

"Look like military." I observed.

A smiling waitress came and indicated towards the dining room. We followed and sat down at one of the two long tables which stretched the length of the room.

"A drink?" she enquired.

"Can we have a beer?" Peter asked hesitantly.

She nodded and, lo and behold, in a few minutes, two beers were set before us, followed by spaghetti bolognaise and then two thin over-cooked beef-steaks and salad and a fresh white bread roll each. Wow! This wasn't bad at all. However, we pocketed the rolls, not sure when we would be eating again. We tried watching the TV after our meal, but couldn't keep up with the continuous programme changing. We nodded goodnight and retired to bed.

Was CLYPEUS surviving? Where was the British Consul we were supposed to see?

Asmara - Day 6.

By eight o'clock we were up and ready for questioning. Nobody came to the room so we went to the dining room for breakfast. Hot rolls, butter, jam and shahi.

The TV wasn't on. The bar was deserted; so we returned to our room.

I sat by the window and watched some pre-school barefooted children below in the dusty yard. They were playing in, on and over, an abandoned wrecked truck parked in front of some mean concrete apartments. A little girl, with dark tightly plaited hair, polished the green painted truck bonnet and doors with a rag; a boy seated in the driver's seat firmly gripped the wheel and wrestled the truck from side to side along his imaginary road. Another boy climbed up and sat on the roof and shouted orders to the driver. They caught sight of me smiling at them and waved and smiled back. The outside two climbed up into the cab and the three animated children continued their play journey.

At 10.30, there was a knock on the door and a man dressed in grey flannels, an open neck shirt and sports jacket, introduced himself and said he was from the Ministry of Defence. He asked if we had enough warm clothes and money. We said that we had.

He told us not to get into contact with anyone (which we assumed meant not to make phone calls) and not to leave the hotel. Somebody would come and see us tomorrow. He left.

At lunchtime in the dining room we were sitting eating, (spaghetti bolognaise again, we didn't know how to ask for anything else and there was no menu), when a young man came in and sat at the other table. He said "Hi" and introduced himself as David, an Irishman selling financial services in Eritrea. He mentioned that he was going to see the British Consul tomorrow.

We quietly and quickly introduced ourselves and explained we were yachtsmen being held under suspicion of spying. Could he let the Consul know? Then we continued chatting nonchalantly, asking him questions about his business.

The waitress entered looking stone-faced and handed the young man a note. He read it then said unsmilingly "I must not speak to you," and abruptly turned his back on us and continued to eat his lunch.

We were devastated. Were we criminals? I pushed the food around my plate, I couldn't eat any more, it just wouldn't go down my throat. David's back loomed large. How could he do that? Ignore us and carry on eating?

As he finished his meal and prepared to leave, he whispered "Write out your names and passport numbers." Peter scribbled them on the paper table napkin and David picked it up as he left.

Humiliated, we returned to our room, and decided to eat in our room in future, we didn't want anything like that to happen again. If they didn't want us to talk to anybody why did they let us use the dining room? Why couldn't we chat to anybody? We weren't criminals, just being made to feel like it. Why hadn't the British Consul come to see us? The crews of the other yachts in our group, GREEN DOLPHIN, KULAROO and MARA must have been in touch with him by now. Why no word from anyone? We tried to read our books but couldn't concentrate.

The stern waitress indicated that our evening meal would be in our room. We asked for a glass of beer each, to raise our spirits.

I wrote up my journal and we went to bed early, totally dispirited. We laid with our arms about each other discussing some of the possibilities as to what might happen to us. If they really thought we were spies, why were they so inept? Sometimes generous, sometimes mean? Perhaps we were hostages?

If only the soldiers had said that first night "Go away, you can't anchor here," none of this would have happened. If we had realised that we were going to create such a problem we could have endured being so tired and carried on north through another night.

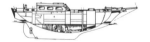

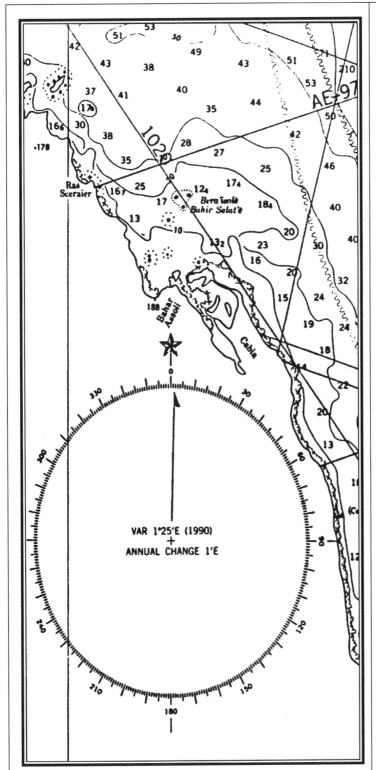

*If we had
realised that
we were going
to create such
a problem we
could have
endured being
so tired and
carried on
north through
another night.*

Eritrea

Asmara •

CHAPTER TWELVE

Asmara - Day 7

It seemed a very long day confined to our room. Breakfast of rolls, honey, and black tea, was eaten at the little card table against the wall which was covered by a large printed paper mural of a formal European garden. We had to buzz room service for everything. We picked up our books and looked at the pages. I asked for and was brought some hotel paper and tried to write letters to my sisters Sheila and Hilary. I couldn't write to my children, I didn't want them to know and worry about us until it was all over and we could play the whole thing down.

Still no hot water. We couldn't shower it was too cold. My hands froze washing out our underwear in the hand basin.

Peter searched for something to read and in the bottom of the wardrobe he found the drawer was lined with a New York Herald Tribune - a year old - but great! It had the crossword almost intact. It helped to take our minds off our predicament and together we almost solved it.

We waited for someone to come and question us. Nobody did.

Our imaginations ran riot. Why were they keeping us? Were they cooking up some plot to incriminate us?

To keep busy we made ourselves a competitive word game of the alphabet cut into little squares, with extra 'e's 'a's 'o's, etc. as in Boggle or Scrabble. Taking turns, we picked nine letters out of my purse, lay them on the table, and saw how many words we could make. Scoring one point for a three or four letter word, two points for five letters and three points for six. No points if we both had the same word.

The day wore on. We had now finished both books.

A sweet Abyssinian maid, in a bright yellow dress with a white apron and yellow scarf tied over her hair, brought our lunch in with a smile, That was nice. Lunch was spaghetti bolognaise again because we still didn't know how to ask for anything else.

A young woman, perhaps the manageress, knocked on the door. She offered to bring us some English novels. She came back later with Stephen King's "Needful Things."

Peter started to read it but I didn't want to know about anybody else's problems.

I had enjoyed reading 'Requiem', a novel by Claire Francis involving the dangers of crop spraying with chemical fertilisers. Trying to write articles and books myself I thought it would be nice for her to hear from a reader. I suddenly decided to write and thank her. It seemed odd that mentally, I could write to a stranger, but not to my family.

The anticipation of not knowing what would happen to us, or even why we were being held, was very stressfull.

Dinner didn't come until 8.30. It was tasty when we got it: "hungry chicken and herbs with carrots and potato" the waitress recited. We tried to exchange names, but hers was too difficult for me to echo or remember. I gestured that I wanted to wash and shower but no hot water. She nodded.

As she came to take our trays away a young waiter arrived with a bucket of hot water. I had a good wash in the cold bathroom. Peter followed. Another early night to lie and worry, and remember some of the incidents which had led us here.

———

We had started our carefully planned three year circumnavigation from London on March 19th 1983 but decided in New Zealand in 1985 that it was all happening too fast. It now didn't seem likely that Peter, in his mid fifties would get another job so what were we hurrying back to England for? We had sold our home, given up company pensions and cashed assurance policies to sail away. A third of our amassed capital had bought CLYPEUS and the other two-thirds were invested for our income.

While in Townsville Marina in 1989, his former American employers found him and offered a two year contract in Taiwan, to manage the design and training aspects of a new joint venture, manufacturing industrial electronics. After looking at the atlas and seeing Taiwan was on the same

While in Townsville Marina in 1989, Peter's former American employers found him and offered a two year contract in Taiwan, to manage the design and training aspects of a new joint venture, manufacturing industrial electronics.

latitude as Hawaii we decided another job would refurbish our cruising kitty after the stockmarket crash of 1987. A number of other reasons encouraged us to stop sailing for a time: Peter didn't like to think he had forever finished being a useful member of society and looked forward to going to work again. My parents, who lived in Western Australia, were now 84 and staying on the same side of the world meant I could visit them more often. Also we felt we had only scratched the surface of so many cultures in the 40,000 odd miles we had sailed, this would be a good opportunity to be part of a society again. The company also provided annual air flights home so we would be able to visit our parents, children and catch up on our new grandchildren. I had started writing and had several articles published in international sailing magazines and wanted to settle down to write a series of sailing adventures for children.

Singapore was on our route back to England and the company had an office there, so after joining the Darwin to Ambon Yacht Race and exploring Indonesia, CLYPEUS was hauled out in Singapore and propped up on the hard.

Two frantic weeks were spent packing up the boat and installing small fans to run from the solar panels to keep her sweet and dry in the hot humid climate. We had to buy warm clothes, Peter had a business suit made. We aquired new passports, visas and international driving licences. We were whisked from a small hot boat near the Equator, by what seemed deliciously decadent and extravagant Raffles Class on Singapore Airlines to Taipei. It was exciting to suddenly be living in ridiculously expensive air-conditioned five star hotels where our beds for one night cost more than a month's housekeeping on CLYPEUS. The cost of breakfast alone would have provided food for three days.

Peter said "Who is mad? Them or us?" He pointed out that we had spent more money and consumed more power, water, food and clothes in one month that we usually did on the boat in six months.

Taiwan was a culture shock. Although I had been trying to learn Mandarin from BBC tapes, we were aliens. The Chinese don't think the way westerners do. Foolishly, I decided we wouldn't join the American expat society based around Taipei American School but live amongst the real Taiwanese people outside the city.

I found a charming hacienda-type modern house high in the hills, from which we could just see the sea, close to where Peter would be working. The rented four bedroom, three bathroom home was in a compound with a robed Chinaman guarding the high iron gates which clanged shut behind us as we entered or left. I found the village shops sold no bread, butter, milk, cheese or other dairy products. We had to learn to live with chopsticks, rice, noodles and vegetables. I gradually achieved culinary prowess with a chopper and wok but never managed to buy and slaughter the live animals that were for sale in Danshui market: chickens, ducks, guinea pigs, puppies and even python. Most homes didn't have refrigerators.

The buses into town were OK, I could read the characters for Taipei, but coming home was via a variety of routes and destinations. Even the bus numbers were in Chinese characters. I learned to always carry my address written in Chinese, as telling a taxi driver in Chinese would bring a blank stare of amazement and disbelief.

In winter our house was above the cloud line and perpetually shrouded in cold mist, so the marble floors and concrete walls were always damp with condensation. The charming neighbours spoke Taiwanese, Hunanese, a little Mandarin and Japanese but no English. Life was lonely and cool. The only time we had the opportunity to speak in English was at the International Church which met in the American School.

It was also quite scarey with frequent typhoons and earthquakes. We got used to the indoor plants trembling and dancing to the earth tremors. Our valley was beautiful and I could walk for miles between rice paddies, over bridges and along lanes listening to the bamboo stands rustling and creaking in the breeze. Isolated farmhouses with curling gables and decorative tiled roofs dotted the terraced land and were reached only by a narrow footpath between the flooded rice paddies. An unused creaking iron suspension bridge over a deep gorge reminded us of the Japanese occupation as we handed ourselves across the vine covered broken wooden slats.

We also visited boatyards to watch yachts being built, in case we could find a bargain. It was a shock to see fibreglass hulls being laid in widely varying temperatures with wind and rain blowing through torn plastic sheeting. Three Frenchmen were living at one yard where their 60' sloop was being built. They each took an eight hour watch to make sure the specification was adhered to. "Turn your head and a mild steel screw has been slipped in instead of a stainless steel one," they said. "Go to the loo and you will come back to see sandwich foam filled with all sorts of rubbish." I'm sure owners who attended the building of their yachts finished up with a good deal, but those built on spec had no guarantee.

There was no sailing as such. Delivery skippers sailed boats to Hong Kong and if a major problem occurred and they tried to re-enter Taiwan they were chased away or shot at. Paperwork and procedures hadn't been invented for leisure craft to re-enter the country.

In 1990 Taiwan was paranoid about mainland China invading and every major crossroad had smart watchful soldiers standing beside their sentry boxes. Efficient well-trained soldiers marched or jogged up the village hill regularly; the rumble of tanks and armoured cars could often be heard during the night. The guards around Chang Kai Shek's tomb were veritable automatons from their glistening toecaps, up the knife edge crease of their trousers to their spotless white gloves and shining white helmets. They and the military police patrolled, goose-stepping, expressionless, with their eyes straight ahead. People scattered before them.

The Taiwanese still practise a colourful amalgamation of old Chinese customs. Fire crackers would suddenly explode in the street for no apparent reason. A funeral fleet of flower-decorated vans and cars would pass by in a cacophony of sound; trumpets, bugles, gongs and drums being blown and banged to scare the demons away by white hooded mourners. From the back of pick-up trucks, temple teams would bang their drums to encourage energetic lion dancers to prance in and out of shops to bring the proprietors good luck.

Saturday afternoons were often spent exploring the city. Walking though Snake Alley we stopped to watch snakes' blood cocktail being prepared and drunk. The vendor milked the venom from one snake (he annoyed it until it struck) into a small tumbler, then he killed and peeled the skin from another snake to drip blood into the glass of venom. Men crowded around, fingering their money. Would this gory drink really make a difference to their performance?

Chinese temples, their roofs surmounted by colourful dragons, were smoky inside with burning incense, dark and mysterious. Every factory shop, office and home had a shrine to various gods of good luck, wealth, good health or longevity. Peter found it disconcerting to come across his Managing Director burning 'pretend money' before the factory shrine to appease his ancestors so that they would look down kindly on the business!

Peter was given a new company car, and relished the road conditions, but I never did pluck up courage to drive in Taipei's undisciplined traffic. Martial law had only finished three years before our arrival and there were no vehicle driving tests. With over 18,000,000 people and a booming economy, millions of cars, and ten times that number of scooters were on the road, all fighting for space. The Taiwanese don't drive their vehicles, they wear them like roller skates, weaving from lane to lane, turning, filtering.

Scooter drivers choked in exhaust fumes or wore masks, girls rode sidesaddle on the back. Swarms of scooters buzzed around each car at traffic lights. They raced ahead and across, weaving and wobbling. Traffic lights only applied to those going straight on; U turns occurred anywhere and everywhere. Car wrecks were left beside the road as a dramatic warning.

I found a job as a secretary at Taipei American School and enjoyed working with the multi-cultural dedicated students. A brand new campus with good teaching staff, a swimming pool (where I taught aqua-aerobics), theatre, wonderful library and varied activities, kept me busy and happy while Peter travelled.

However, for him life was difficult. As the only natural English speaker in the company, every word had to be considered, spoken slowly and usually illustrated. Everyday the management and workers sat in a kitchen between the factory area and the smelly toilets to eat a good Chinese lunch cooked by an efficient and jolly wife of one the workers. Eating with chopsticks everyday, under the scrutiny of five or six secretaries, draughtsmen and accountants, all of whom watched every one of the gwailo's (long nose's) movements was totally embarrasing for him. They were fascinated by his big nose, the hair in his ears and on his arms, his white skin, what he chose to eat. Sometimes a thoughtful girl would kindly place the fish eyes, a much sought after delicacy, on his plate for him, or perhaps a juicy piece of pig's innards.

Life for me was very pleasant with tennis and squash courts and fine swimming pool included in the apartment complex.

The industrial pollution in Taiwan, and where he worked in Bangkok, Korea and China took its toll, and he finished up in hospital with a severe chest infection.

The hospital in Taipei. How different it proved to be from England's health care. Every consultation, x-ray, dressing or prescription had to be paid for beforehand. Money first, treatment later. Peter shared a two-bedded ward in the Adventist Hospital with an elderly Taiwanese gentleman who was

fed, washed and looked after by his wife and daughter taking turns to care for him. They lived and slept on a low camp bed against the wall. The nurses only gave injections, medicines and dressings. They thought me an inconsiderate wife, who went off to work and left her sick husband in the care of the hospital. It took him a long time to fully recover.

After two years Peter was transferred to clean, green Singapore and I enjoyed a busy expat life, studying then teaching English as a second language while he travelled between Malaysia, Korea, Thailand, India and New Zealand. Life for me was very pleasant with tennis and squash courts and a fine swimming pool included in the apartment complex. Many friends visited. Eating out was good and cheap and most people spoke some English. I could travel anywhere on my own, day or night, and not feel threatened. Driving the car was simple - drivers obeyed the rules - everybody obeyed all the rules, and after Taiwan it was a refreshing change and I loved it.

We joined Changi Sailing Club and gradually prepared CLYPEUS for sea again. We were able entertain many new cruising friends as they passed from Indonesia to Malaysia and helped them re-stock and get repairs made. We made friends with happy Australian couples on SAIORSE, MITHRA and SUNSHINE who were also preparing to sail to Europe. It was a happy time of hard work and anticipation.

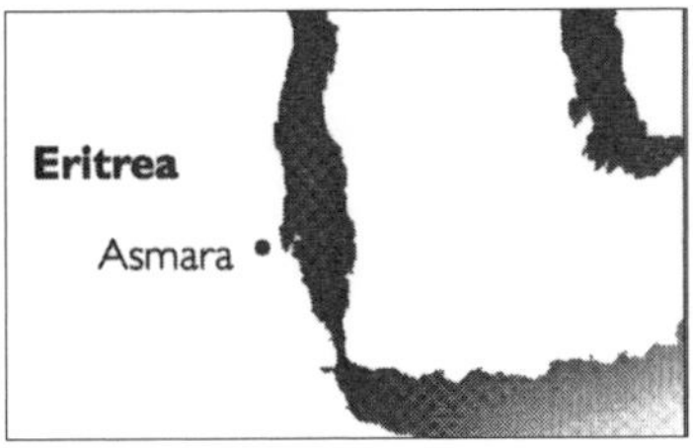

Eritrea

Asmara ·

CHAPTER THIRTEEN

Asmara - Day 8

At the Khartoum Hotel in Asmara minor problems were beginning to dominate our lives. No toilet paper; no hot water, the toilet wouldn't flush. Peter successfully played plumber again. The cold shower was in the centre of the bathroom wall with no screens or curtains. Taking a shower inundated the whole bathroom. The light switch box was dangling on its wires from the wall. Not a safe environment!

I sketched the cover of the Ethiopian Airways inflight magazine which was an illustration of an Ethiopian Funery head, and noticed an Asante proverb "All dwelling places are not alike." They can say that again! It reminded me of my children and how they used to tease me. Our small town in Berkshire did not have a great mix of population and at home when I commented with disapproval on some rough happening in the outside world they would admonish me with "Not everyone lives in Wokingham, mother!" - a personalised version of "All dwelling places are not alike." It brought a wan smile from Peter.

At 10am a Mr. Immanuel from Immigration came and interrogated us for three hours. A small precise, thin-lipped man with gimlet eyes and good English. With great concentration he questioned us incisively and quietly and wrote

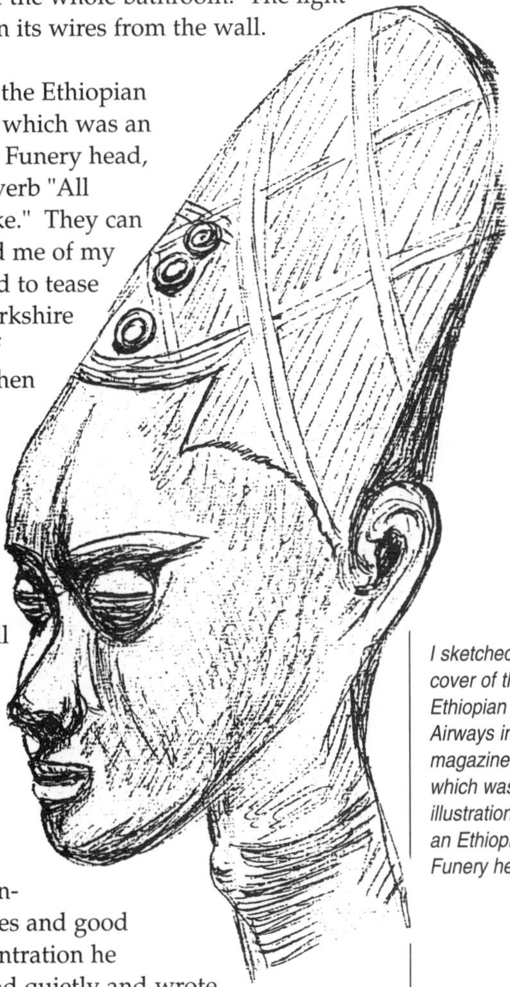

I sketched the cover of the Ethiopian Airways inflight magazine which was an illustration of an Ethiopian Funery head.

down our replies. It was easy to imagine a spotlight burning into our eyes from over his shoulder. Once again we told our complete life histories, about our parents, our children, our jobs, our homes and our voyage. He didn't smile and was curt and sharp. When he left at 1.00pm lunch was immediately brought in.

Over lunch we quietly discussed what he had asked. Peter worried that there may be some anomalies in the telling of our voyage, as recalling exact dates and places over thirteen years was difficult. We whispered about trying to escape. Was the room bugged? How had they known when he had finished questioning us and was about to leave? Lunch had been brought in at precisely the right time.

"We could climb down the gutter pipe close to the window." I whispered. "Then climb over the gate out of the yard belonging to the apartments and somehow get to Massawa."

"But we can't ask anyone to risk their boat and their lives to take us to CLYPEUS", Peter mumbled.

"No, of course, and it would take at least three or four days to motor sail to her against the wind, by which time the army would be out looking and waiting for us," I sighed.

"Don't forget there are three armed soldiers on board guarding as well. There isn't a hope of an escape succeeding."

We sank into individual thought and despondency. The Eritrean Authorities must release us soon. They couldn't really think we were spies, it was too ridiculous. We must just be patient and let diplomatic negotiations take their course, assuming they had started. Why hadn't the British Consul come to see us or sent us a note?

At three o'clock Mr. Immanuel returned and questioned us closely for another three hours. Once again he wanted to know our life histories, parents, children, jobs, homes, and our voyage. His questioning became more brusque as we came to the present time:

Why were we in Baraisole Bay? Didn't we know it was a War Zone?

He didn't believe that we knew very little about the Eritrean conflict with the Yemenis. He didn't believe no warnings had been given in Aden of a War Zone in the Red Sea or that other yachts were sailing through Eritrean waters.

I let Peter do most of the talking, but I did say gently, "we were in the Egyptian Embassy in Aden only last week to get our Egyptian visas and they gave no warnings of any problems reaching Egypt. They knew we were sailing to Safaga. If Eritrea had a Consulate in Aden we would have gone there for Eritrean visas."

Peter patiently explained that we listened to the BBC World Service and to other yachts on the VHF radio, but nobody had mentioned problems except not to go near the Hanish Islands. Other yachts had been anchoring to rest and recuperate on their way through Eritrean, Sudanese and Egyptian waters, as they sailed up the Red Sea. We had taken any warnings very seriously and had done our best to avoid the Hanish Islands. In fact the British Admiralty Chart we had been using, only showed the Eritrean coastline, it did not reach as far as the Hanish Islands.

"Eritrea hasn't figured much in the BBC news lately," Peter continued. "Other countries have problems too, including our own. The Colombo bomb exploded two days before we left Sri Lanka. Bombs have exploded at home in London at Canary Wharf and the Aldwych. Bosnia and Rwanda have major conflicts and I'm afraid they have been in the news, not Eritrea's problems."

Mr. Immanuel left abruptly saying we could dine in the hotel dining room. Hooray!

That evening we first met Etienne and Monique Forget, the owners of PEEWIT, who had already been held for ten days. Etienne's English was about the same as my school French. It was possible to communicate, with Peter adding his quite extensive vocabulary. Everything was translated for Monique who had less English, which gave us another opportunity to comprehend that we were actually understanding each other.

They had been treated more roughly than us at first, but now they were allowed to go out for a walk each day. Why couldn't we?

They gave us a letter from Linda and Don of GREEN DOLPHIN who had been to the Khartoum hotel during the afternoon looking for us, but had been told we were not there. Linda and Don had given them a letter for us, just in case we were able to contact each other. Etienne and Monique hadn't known that we were in the hotel either.

"How did they know you were here?" we asked

"You had told them on the radio about no-one being on board PEEWIT in Baraisole Bay and our friend Hans heard. Evidently the crew from his boat were exploring Asmara yesterday and happened to see us sitting on our bedroom balcony which faces the street. They told Hans, and he and GREEN DOLPHIN travelled to Asmara immediately to see us."

Etienne pointed out that we were always watched.

We hadn't noticed that there was always a man lounging near us and a door-keeper downstairs.

In heavily accented English they told us their story.

On March 16th they had anchored PEEWIT to rest after a

hair-raising sail up from Djibouti, needing to sleep before continuing to Massawa to book in. A military launch had come alongside, armed soldiers had climbed on board, taken their passports and arrested them. They were immediately forced on board the gunboat without time to pack a change of clothes, their toilet things or pick up any money. They had been driven directly to Assab and because no senior officer was available, the driver locked them in a concrete room with no carpeting or furniture. They were very afraid.

In the morning Mr Achmed had arrived. He apologised and escorted them immediately to a hotel and sent someone to buy toiletries for them. They were flown to Asmara the next day just before we arrived in Assab. They had been lent jackets by Mr. Achmed and tee shirts and a skirt had been bought for them.

Our dinner together was an excited mixture of 'Franglais' at top speed, with pauses for us all to digest or translate the information we had for each other. We were all grandparents, they too had circumnavigated and even sailed the length of the Red Sea twice before with their children. Through the French Consul, who had been allowed to see them, they had contacted their son in Paris. He had informed the French press and through a family friend a question would be raised in the French National House of Representatives. They were hoping to be released any day. Their son had also written to Amnesty International and the International Red Cross.

If the French Consul had visited them, why hadn't the British Consul come to see us?

In our bedroom we had much to talk about before we climbed into bed, happy to know that at least we had friends in the same situation.

"I can't understand why we didn't hear Linda's voice." Peter mused. "On the radio it comes over so clearly."

I read her letter again.

> *26th March ASMARA.*
>
> **Hi Guys**
>
> *Just want you to know we're all thinking of you and hoping within days we'll be talking and seeing you. We've all kept on top of what's happening daily via Rod Hicks, the British Consul.*
>
> *MARA will be in Massawa by Tuesday 27th if north winds cease and will wait here for you, or if you choose to by-pass Massawa - small wonder - they'll rendevous as you pass. Ourselves and KULAROO will probably leave here (Massawa) Wed. Believe us when we say we've all thought up "Dirty Dozen" rescue operations.*
>
> *When we hear you've been released we'll have our radio on hourly until we hear from you - until then 7:30 a.m. - 2 p.m. and 6 p.m. The whole Red Sea yachting group are rooting for you as well as Etienne and Monique on PEEWIT.*
>
> *If any delays we will be calling our own embassies in hopes some pressure will help. Our hearts, prayers and thoughts are with you. Keep smiling and don't let them get you down.*
>
> *Don and Linda. Bill, Karen, Brian and Lorraine send their love.*

I put it under my pillow. What wonderful friends we have, if they could get a note to us why couldn't the British Authorities? Had the Irishman managed to see the Consul and passed on our message?

At midnight a gentle knock on the door woke us. I pulled a bath towel around me and opened the door a crack.

David, the Irishman, was standing outside.

"Let me in," he whispered.

I opened the door and quickly closed it behind him.

"Here, take this." He handed me a bottle in a brown paper bag.

Peter pulled on his trousers and joined us and shook his hand vigorously.

David whispered "I saw the Consul this morning. He was pleased to know where you are. Your sailing friends have been phoning him every day. He hasn't officially been informed that you have been detained. He is going to play it very cool in case the authorities take you and hide you somewhere inaccessible and nobody will know where you are."

"What is he going to do? Does London know? When is he coming to see us?" Peter asked.

"He has informed the British Embassy. He can't come and see you until he is officially informed of your whereabouts. Must go."

"Thank you so much David. You have given us hope. It is good to know somebody is doing something." I pulled out the bottle. "Wow! Brandy. Thank you very much." We opened the door and David slid out into the black hall.

Much happier, we lay close and discussed the day's happenings.

Our sailing
friends:
GREEN
DOLPHIN.....

......and MARA.

CHAPTER FOURTEEN

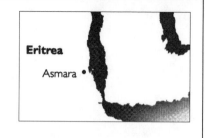

Eritrea

Asmara •

Asmara - Day 9

A bright sunny day in Asmara, perhaps they will allow us to go for a walk?
No.

After breakfast, I stood by the dining room window watching the people of Asmara going about their daily business in the clear white sunlight. The laundry opposite had more customers than the small stationery shop. A couple of cars and a few donkey carts ambled by with vegetables piled high. The donkey's tall upright ears twitched as the drivers nonchalantly whacked their dusty brown rumps.

As I passed through the reception area on my way back to our room I said good morning to a smiling, mature, local lady we had seen before. She appeared to be a member of the staff, or perhaps she was the office manageress for the fleet of hire cars? She had a little office off the reception area with two telephones and pictures of smart new cars around the walls.

We learned later from Monique and Etienne that she was the wife of the hotel owner and her name was Azib. She did manage the fleet of cars shown in the photographs. Her daughter Semira was the charming young woman who had been summoned from downstairs to interpret occasionally and had loaned us the Stephen King novel.

Azib was talking to a man who looked like a salesman by the way he was gesturing to her. He held a large cardboard box. Azib motioned me to approach with down-turned fingers as is the custom in Asia.

"Choose two," she gestured holding up two fingers.

I peered into the box and it was full of assorted ladies' underwear - knickers in fact.

"Thank you, thank you," I smiled. "Yes, they would be very useful." I was getting tired of washing undies in cold water every night.

I stirred the silky pants around in the box trying discreetly to see if there were any of cotton or large enough for my substantial rear end. Eventually I selected two pretty pairs.

"Two pairs please," I asked and "How much will they be?"

"No, no. Me to you." She pointed at her chest and then at mine. "French lady now."

"Thank you, thank you. How kind." I ran upstairs and knocked on Monique's door.

"Viens-toi. Les panties, les knickers. Venez-vous."

Monique looked at me as though I was out of my mind.

"Qu'est ce que?"

"Azib, downstairs, elle vous voire, maintenant. Venez. Azib, she wants to see you. C'mon."

Monique 'venezed' looking mystified.

By sign language Monique soon got the message and she too chose a couple of pairs of panties.

How kind of Azib, how thoughtful! We were both so impressed with her generosity and empathy. It re-affirmed how kind women usually are to each other. We don't have to compete all the time like men; women do seem to be able to just appreciate each other without having to decide who is best. It was the first of many kindly gestures which Azib made to us.

After lunch we were standing in the reception area talking to Monique and Etienne when a slim middle-aged man, in grey flannels and a sports coat, went to Peter and demanded our passports. Peter went to get them, but before he handed them over, insisted on having a receipt for them. This caused a fair amount of confusion and needed the Receptionist wearing a red tunic, to intervene. After she had made a phone call (to a familiar remembered number, she did not have to look it up) she confirmed all was in order and Peter handed over our precious passports to the man who evidently was a messenger from a government department.

Just after the messenger left with our passports and we were still standing discussing the situation with the Forgets, an elegant and business-like entourage of six Frenchmen climbed up the stairs and presented themselves. It was the French Ambassador from Djibouti who happened to be in Asmara and had come to see the Forgets without asking permission from the Eritreans. He indicated to the Receptionist that he would be taking over the dining room and invited us to join their discussion.

"Parce que vous êtes dans le même bateau, n'est ce pas?" (because you are in the same boat, are you not?) He laughed with his distinctive French "Hee haw, hee haw, hee haw!"

Monsieur Jean-Marie Monal gave us great hope that we would be released and promised to telephone our son Noel when he returned to Djibouti in a few days time. M. Monal would pass on our request for him to get in touch with Basil, one of our more influential friends in England. He introduced his troupe of diplomats and under-Secretaries and also a lean and business-like army colonel. They mentioned that they had flown up in their own plane.

"What a pity we cannot offer it to fly you to Djibouti immediately. Unfortunately we have more appointments and need the plane to complete our schedule. Quel dommage, n'est ce pas?" M. Monal sympathised.

When nothing more of importance could be exchanged, the Frenchmen departed with promises of action soon.

No sooner had they left than a very angry Mr. Immanuel bounded up the steps and quivering with indignation ordered us to our room. He questioned us harshly and wanted to know why we had refused to give our passports to his assistant and why had we spoken to the French Ambassador.

Peter countered "We didn't refuse to give our passports but we did want a receipt for them. We don't give our passports to people we don't know. We talked with the French Ambassador because he invited us to. We hope to be released soon, we do not like being detained."

"Detained? You should be grateful. I was in prison for four years."

"We are very sorry to hear that, but you were at war. We are not," Peter retorted.

He ordered us to stay in our room again and said angrily "DO NOT make contact with anybody."

As he opened our door to let himself out, he turned and sneered at us venomously:

"We know everything. Do not underestimate us!"

What did they know? What had we done? Had we been framed? What was happening? Where was the British Consul? We were really frightened, as we realised we had no idea what was happening in diplomatic circles - if anything.

Perhaps Mr. Immanuel, who was obviously in charge of us, was deranged? Perhaps his years in prison had given him an evil chip on his shoulder?

Our evening meal was brought to our room by a very stone-faced waitress who did not offer the usual cheery greeting.

The situation seemed bad. Our elation at seeing the French Ambassador had turned to fear of reprisal. We whispered about M. Monal's suggestion of their plane flying us out. Perhaps he would be able to arrange it. The Army Colonel had looked very SAS.

"Perhaps the French SAS will spring us?" I suggested.

Peter told me not to be ridiculous, saying I must have read too many spy stories. Nevertheless I opened the window and peered out. On further inspection the gutter pipe didn't look solid enough to climb down. I examined the sheets to see if they were strong enough to tie together to let ourselves out of the window and decided the bed frame would hold us. We were only one floor up and could lower ourselves into the courtyard below. I packed our bags and put everything ready in the bottom of the wardrobe - just in case.

We went to bed early very depressed. I twitched and turned waiting for a whistle or an 'owl cry' signal. It was so cold I got up and unpacked a pair of Peter's socks and put them on.

No happy remembrances of our voyaging this night, just miserable and afraid, turning questions about our future over and over in our minds. Why hadn't the British Consul, or the British Ambassador in Ethiopia been to see us, or send us a message? After all it was ten days now.

No rescuers came, nothing disturbed the night. The cathedral clock struck every hour until eventually the cold light of dawn crept into the bedroom.

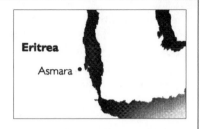

Eritrea

Asmara •

CHAPTER FIFTEEN

Asmara - Day 10

The sun rose and the morning warmed up. Unhappily we washed, still in cold water, dressed and waited for our breakfast to appear.

Smiling Mulu brought in a tray of scrambled eggs, and taught us Eritrean for the rolls - bani and honey - marmalita. I asked for hot water to wash my hair.

Half an hour later the waiter arrived with a bucket of hot water. I poured a third of it into the hand basin and with a cup, saved from breakfast, scooped water over my head and lathered in the shampoo that fortunately I had brought in my toilet bag. While my hair dried I made a 'thank-you' card for Azib, with an edging of frilly party flags.

We started an unenthusiastic game of our paper Boggle, discussing whether Mara had arrived in Massawa by now. Perhaps they would try to visit us? No, it was too much to expect them to come today; they must have all sorts of jobs to do after being at sea for twelve or so days since their last port of Aden. If they had any sense they wouldn't get involved anyway. But, we know Australians, they have a reputation of being loyal friends in times of trouble. In our hearts we knew Lorraine and Brian wouldn't desert us.

We were very depressed. Now, when we flushed the toilet, the effluent bubbled up into the shower tray. Nasty! We pressed the bell and told the unsmiling red-tuniced receptionist when she came.

We waited for Mr. Immanuel. Would he come back today? Why had he been so vicious yesterday? Had the French Ambassador's undiplomatic visit caused further problems? Were Monique and Etienne confined to their room also, or had they been able to go out for their daily walk? Why were they allowed to go out for a walk anyway and not us?

I washed my scarves and hung them out of the window to dry as a signal to Lorraine, just in case they came looking for us. When we had explored Oman and the Yemen together it had been necessary to cover our heads, as well as wear loose clothing from our elbows to our knees, so I knew she would recognise my scarves and notice which room we were in if they approached the hotel from the right direction. We sat and watched the road, just in case.

Lunch was brought. I didn't write in my journal what we ate. I didn't want to write, nothing made sense anymore. What was going to happen to us? We still hadn't been charged with any offence. In the front of my diary I doodled a sketch of CLYPEUS.

I wish I had some plain paper.

We kept watch out of the window and, lo and behold, just after two-thirty; there they were. Brian and Lorraine were walking towards the hotel. They looked up and acknowledged discreetly that they had seen us and booked themselves into the Khartoum Hotel as ordinary Australian tourists.

A few minutes later we opened our door a crack and saw them look at a room opposite ours. However they ignored us and asked the red-tuniced receptionist to show them what else was available. Lorraine winked at us as they followed her upstairs. With our ears to our door we heard them come down again and Brian say,

"Yes, this room will be fine if you don't have one with a private bathroom."

When he went with the Receptionist to sign the guest book, Lorraine, on her way to their shared bathroom, threw a plastic bag across the smooth marble floor towards our door. We surreptitiously pulled their 'care' parcel in and found it contained some paperbacks, writing pager, chocolate biscuits, a pack of cards and a caring note. Also a decorated tee shirt with a map of Eritrea and 'FREE ERITREA' emblazoned across the chest - the Eritrea was crossed through and 'CLYPEUS' was written instead. It made us smile. We immediately hid everything carefully away just in case anybody came into our room. We put Lorraine's note inside a book so that we could read it but closed the book quickly to hide it.

It was a wise precaution as the hotel staff kept a close watch on us in case we tried to contact the Australians. Unasked for cups of tea arrived; waitresses came in with feeble excuses to see what we were doing. Fortunately we were always innocently employed.

Lorraine's note to us: and our responses:

"Do you know when you may be back on the boat? **(No)**

Brian is going to phone the British Consulate later on. Linda has been calling him each day to check on the progress." **(Good)**

"We don't intend telling him where we are". **(Good)**

"Perhaps we may be able to talk with you later on tonight."

"Any ideas?"

(When you see everybody else has gone to bed. p.s. Don't trust the hotel staff, some are working for Security - The little dark receptionist wearing red pinafore tunic)

We wrote the above responses on their note. Peter decided to also write them a more comprehensive letter that read:

Dear B & L,

We are confined to our room and you should not be seen speaking to us.

We had a long interview on Tuesday with a guy from Immigration, so he said! He wanted our cruising life story and why we came to anchor in Baraisole Bay. Just south of Marsa Dudo. He did not really believe anything we said and has no comprehension of small boat life/management. He cannot believe that over 50 yachts have anchored in their waters overnight or longer, in the last two months. The French couple, Etienne and Monique FORGET off yacht PEEWIT (which is alongside us at Baraisole) are here also, next floor up.

Yesterday afternoon the French Ambassador in Djibouti, who happened to be visiting Asmara, came in with a contingent of five Frenchmen from the Djibouti Consulate in Asmara, and reassured PEEWIT and us - we were included - that the wheels were turning. A very imposing gentleman. About half an hour after the party had left, our persecutor arrived in a great rush and hopping angry and forbade us to leave our rooms. Story so far.

He is called Immanuel, we believe. He may be normal but behaves in a paranoid way about National Security. We can't decide whether he is actually in charge or just making our lives a misery until the Minister of Defence returns to the country. His parting words yesterday were

"WE KNOW EVERYTHING. DO NOT UNDERESTIMATE US!"

All you can really do is raise six kinds of hell with the British Consul and get him to contact London. Our passport numbers are Peter James Billing B397386 and Shirley C. Billing 700774982.

Please don't jeopardise your safety. We don't know when we will be released and flown/driven/boated back to CLYPEUS.

Don't wait for us. Thanks for coming."

Despite the staff's constant vigilance, we were able to slip our notes back to them undetected. In the hallway outside our door an unused semi-circular bar was stored. We opened our door a crack, Lorraine and Brian were unpacking with their door open. Peter caught Lorraine's eye, slipped out and laid the note and his letter on the bar top and Lorraine immediately walked to their bathroom, picking it up on the way. The situation was getting more like a spy movie every minute.

When 7pm came we rang the bell and asked the waiter to bring us a Coke each with ice and glasses. When it arrived we poured in some of our brandy and had a good drink. After dinner in our room, we didn't get undressed but played Boggle, then sat on our bed and read waiting for a knock on the door. It was a very long evening.

After midnight when all was quiet, a light knock and Brian slipped into our room. "You go and chat to Lorraine in our room," he whispered to me.

Patches of light from the stairway and reception area beamed thinly into the dark corridor. Furtively I stole across the wide hallway to the crack of light which was their bedroom. What would happen to us all if we were caught?

Would they arrest Lorraine and Brian?

Lorraine and I hugged each other and sat on the bed. She whispered telling me about their voyage. The day our passports were taken, a military launch had come alongside MARA while they were sailing and armed soldiers had jumped on board. After examining their passports the soldiers had returned to their launch without comment and roared away.

MARA had taken a leisurely cruise up the Eritrean coast and anchored at many islands with no further hassles. She told us how persistent Linda had been in telephoning the British and French Consul every day and trying to get some action. Now they with KULAROO had left for Safaga to meet their visitors who would be arriving in Cairo in a few weeks time.

Mara had taken a leisurely cruise up the Eritrean coast and anchored at many islands with no further hassles.

Linda had started a 'Save CLYPEUS fund' on the radio and donations were coming from or pledged by yachts who didn't even know us.

"Everybody says something like 'there but for the grace of God...' We could easily have pulled in there.'"

Lorraine whispered. "It is really good to know so many people care. The Fund is to compensate us for telephone calls, harbour dues and visa extensions. It looks as though there may be some left over for you," she grinned.

I told her how we were alternately scared out of our wits, and then bored to death.

"If they really do think we are spies, they're not doing a very good job guarding us are they?" I whispered. "We really can't understand why the British Consul hasn't even sent us a note. After all, it is ten days since we were arrested and we know he knows about us from both Linda and David." I explained to her about the Irishman. "It was absolutely devastating when he was given the note and turned his back on us. I didn't realise being 'sent to Coventry' was such a powerful weapon."

While Lorraine and I were talking Brian was telling Peter that they had been surprised at how frightened we seemed when they had arrived. They had imagined us 'living it up' in a hotel with few worries. Now they had seen more of the situation they understood, and had spent the whole evening until 11pm chasing Rod Hicks, the British Consul. Brian told Peter how scared he had been when walking to the public telephone box numerous times during the evening, as he didn't want to talk on the hotel public phone. He had found walking along the quiet street in the dark quite frightening. Men in raincoats stood hidden in doorways and lurked behind trees. One time he had heard the crackle of a walkie talkie, and had wondered if he was under observation.

Eventually he contacted Rod Hicks who had agreed to meet him after attending a function. During a long conversation sitting in Rod's car, Brian had directed him to the Khartoum Hotel, which he didn't know, to show him where we were being kept.

Rod Hicks had explained that he was playing the situation very gently. "The Eritreans are stubborn people and if they think they are being pushed around by a big power they will stick their heels in. Then they may move both couples somewhere far less accessible. At least we know where they are now and that they are being well looked after."

Brian made it clear that it was considered that progress arranging our release was not fast enough. He explained some of the sailing difficulties; that we will have to fight stronger northerly winds as the season progresses, that we would be left without the companionship and weather warnings from other yachts sailing ahead of us. He also explained that we would not want to be flown home direct to London. CLYPEUS was our home and we would only wish to be returned to her.

Brian also showed him photographs of CLYPEUS and ourselves to prove we were decent, normal, un-spy-like, sixty-plus year olds.

Rod was surprised and said "In this type of situation the safety of British subjects is first priority and flying them out of the country is the usual procedure. However, I now understand the situation more thoroughly."

Brian also showed him photographs of CLYPEUS and ourselves to prove we were decent, normal, un-spy-like, sixty-plus year olds.

Rod expressed suprise at our ages, and kept the photographs, but was still adamant that he could not move until officially informed. He would again contact London and ask them to send a note to the Eritrean Ambassador in London. He would also contact the British Embassy in Addis Ababa.

As Peter and Brian whispered in the bedroom, Brian made notes of our worries and what Peter considered essential to convey to our Consul when Brian met him again tomorrow morning.

These points were:

1. Peter is concerned they may be flown back to Britain instead of continuing their journey.

2. If and when returned to CLYPEUS they must have their charts back on board or they will not be able to proceed. (charts from Red Sea to U.K. have been taken - a very large roll).

3. We will have communication problems when we leave Massawa.

4. Shirley's medication - for hypertension
    ATENOLOL BP 50mg (generic name)
    NORMATEN or TENORMINAL are brand names)
    Her preference is: INDERAL L.A. (brand name)
    Hotel staff have been able to obtain INDERAL standard.

5. CLYPEUS's official number is O/N 397464.
    Port of registration is Portsmouth.

6. Noel 's (our son in England) phone number,
    and address were written. Please arrange
    for Noel to contact Basil.

7. Concerned about security of CLYPEUS.

8. Could they have some reading material?

Brian slid back into their room and after a hug from both, I crept back across the dark hall and through the door Peter was holding open for me into our unlit bedroom.

We sat on the bed and swopped information. We were so grateful for everyone's efforts. MARA had promised to stay in Massawa Harbour until we were released and wait for us to catch up. I told him about Linda starting the "Save CLYPEUS Fund" as so many yacht crews had asked how they could help. Donations were flowing in. Now we knew many people were praying for us and sending us loving thoughts, as well as contributions to the fund.

Brian and Lorraine's courage in waiting for us and perhaps being implicated couldn't be underestimated. Nobody would know that Brian, during his RAAF Officer days, was actually a missiles expert! Or would they?

How lucky we are to have such friends.

When we eventually got to bed I lay remembering how we had first met Lorraine and Brian in Malaysia on Langkawi Island in 1995. We had bought kebabs and murtabak (a meaty omelette) in Kuah's Muslim night food market and taken our picnic to the beachside. Sitting on the grass under the palm trees we struck up a conversation with nearby Australians who were also enjoying a spicy hot picnic. Lorraine and I had found we had many common interests: families (we were one of three daughters with a younger sister called Hilary; we both had three grown children), reading, swimming, Keep Fit and dance. Brian and Peter were both engineers and had boat maintenance, PCs, computer programs, constellation charts and tide tables to discuss.

We had met at various anchorages up and down the Malay and Thai coast as they hadn't quite decided yet whether they were going to sail to Europe or not.

How far away those carefree days of last year seemed now. However, sleep was no problem tonight, we were warm in the glow of true friendship.

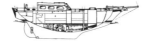

Eritrea

Asmara •

CHAPTER SIXTEEN

Asmara - Day 11

Lorraine and Brian left at lunchtime the next day without further contact. They did turn as they walked away to discreetly take a photograph. We were sorry not to talk or even smile at them, but they were sensibly ignoring us.

I tucked into "Secrets" by Danielle Steel, but couldn't remember the characters or story line, the words didn't lift me out of our situation. On the new green-lined writing pad (all Lorraine could find - there isn't much of a choice of writing paper in Eritrea) I wrote letters to our children.

After the usual lonely lunch, I tried the other book Lorraine had brought me, "Daughter of Arabia". It was an eye-opener to the restricted and cruel life many women suffer in Arabia. It made me realise how lucky I was, as I read of the treatment meeted out to many Muslim wives and daughters: confinement to their home, female circumcision, the absolute dominance of their men. It helped put our situation in proportion as I thought about the women we had met in Oman and the Yemen.

A knock on the door. The receptionist came and told us we could have our evening meal in the dining room again. Hooray!

We immediately went to the TV area. Mr Achmed, the Naval Commander had arrived from Assab. He smiled and we greeted him and asked if he knew when we would be released? How was CLYPEUS? He was very non-committal. We asked if we could go for a walk. He shook his head in refusal.

But we were full of hope that we might be released, now that this sensible and educated man had arrived. After all, he seemed so reasonable and seemed to have great integrity. However, he excused himself and left.

I wanted to be in the sun again so, clutching my book, I explored up the stairs to the roof. The staff chalets were here on the flat rooftop, together with the lines of laundry drying in the brilliant sunshine. The untidy flat rooftops of Asmara were not beautiful. Satellite dishes, old bedsteads and house-hold junk littered the flat roofs. Beyond the city, the dry plain stretched towards a hazy mountain ridge.

I sat on a spare bedspring and tried to read, but the sunlight was just too bright, it made my eyes water uncontrollably, and I had to retreat back downstairs.

Azib was waiting in the reception area with some cake and fruit drinks which she had brought into the hotel for us, at her own expense. With Monique and Etienne we had a little party. They too had been confined to their room by Mr. Immanuel.

Before dinner we went to the TV room anticipating seeing some news. What was happening in the rest of the world? But no! The hotel owner still hadn't got used to his new toy and just couldn't leave the remote-control buttons alone. Three seconds only for each programme which didn't particularly interest him, just long enough for our eyes to focus on the screen, then off "Buttons" would go again. Basketball from the U.S.A. warranted a few minutes and our eyes and ears had time to adjust to the echoing reception in the tiled room. We did see CNN news but Bosnia and Herzegovina were still dominating the headlines.

Monique and Etienne joined us for dinner. We ordered a glass of beer and were given salad and some breaded fried fish with chips for our meal - a very pleasant change. We sat in the lounge to watch TV with about six Eritrean men all

We watched, with our hearts in our mouths, as our home was lifted and swung towards the lorry, the slings slipped and 'oops' she hit the yacht alongside, bounced off and hit another on the other side.

watching the screen and chatting. I started talking to an Eritrean guest sitting beside me when he asked me which country I was from. The receptionist, whom we suspected of reporting on all our actions to Security, frowned and Peter came over and suggested we went to our room. I followed him, still completely unaware that I was doing anything wrong.

"You mustn't talk to anybody," he scolded.

"But I was only answering a perfectly normal question."

"It doesn't matter," he said. "Let's not do anything that might jeopardise our position."

"We had better stay in here then," I grumbled. "It doesn't seem right, not to answer and be friendly."

Once again there was a long evening and night ahead. I snuggled down thinking about our happy shake down cruise when we explored the East Malaysian islands.

Preparing CLYPEUS to resume our circumnavigation was hot, hard work in Singapore only 2° north of the Equator. Just before Christmas '93, at the appointed time a flat bed lorry and crane rolled into the yard. Peter showed the crane driver a photo of CLYPEUS's underwater shape and where the slings had previously been placed successfully The driver took little notice - he knew it all!

We watched, with our hearts in our mouths, as our home was lifted and swung towards the lorry, the slings slipped and 'oops' she hit the yacht alongside, bounced off and hit another on the other side. Both neighbours rocked but fortunately stayed upright. Odd pieces of wood clattered to the ground. CLYPEUS swung through the air slipping further and further out of the slings. Peter turned his back on the scene and sat on the ground hugging his knees, he couldn't bear to watch.

Eventually she was safely chocked onto the flat bed and slowly, slowly, rolled the 300 yards to the quay. This time the slings were placed where suggested and she was gently lowered into the water. With the help of Paul, the marina manager, shouting instructions in Chinese to the crane driver, the masts were stepped and the rigging tightened.

It was wonderful to be back on the water and feel our boat rocking beneath our feet.

We lived on board at Changi Sailing Club mooring for six months while preparing her for sea and fitted a mosquito net over the cockpit so that we could sleep outside. We enjoyed the Club facilities and made friends with other yachts who would be heading to Europe in October, SAIORSE, MITHRA and

SUNSHINE, all from Fremantle Sailing Club. We planned to keep in close radio contact and be close enough to discourage the pirates in Malacca Strait.

Lightning struck and destroyed the VHF aerial and blew the masthead tri-colour light to pieces. The disturbing wakes of major ships churning up to the container port at Johore Baharu prevented Peter working up the mast so our first voyage was for two miles to hide behind Pulau Ubin in calm water. We slowly motored to the ancient Chinese fuel barge and took on diesel. CLYPEUS was sluggish, the propellor had obviously grown verdant weed and barnacles in the warm polluted water.

Peter goes up.........

Behind Ubin Island was still and quiet. Peter, in his harness, clipped to the main halyard, climbed the mast while I tightened the halyard around the winch so that he couldn't fall. With only a few gentle mast-top sways he completed his task. Enough for one day, I could do the propellor tomorrow. Enjoying the warm late afternoon, we sat in the cockpit sipping a cocktail. Peter touched my arm, "Look," he pointed to the beach. A four foot grey and brown monitor lizard was walking down to the water, his forked tongue flicking forward, his bandy legs one-by-one ponderously stepping forward. He picked up something delicately and carefully in his mouth and slowly walked back into the jungle.

Cicadas sang, mynah birds hopped and squawked, a pair of sea eagles with white heads and light brown bodies and wings circled overhead. After four years on land, at last, we were back together in our real world, of peace, with time to watch and think. What contentment the cruising life brings. It restores our souls.

.......I go down. My task, to scrape the propellor clean, filled me with horror.

Perhaps it wasn't going to be so difficult after all to re-adjust to life in a small boat.

The most difficult adjustment in the tropics would be having no fridge or air conditioning.

In the morning the romance of that quiet night was forgotten. Now it was my turn. Peter goes up, I go down. My task, to scrape the propellor clean, filled me with horror. The water was filthy and what creatures lived in the black muddy slime below? Donning long-sleeved shirt and trousers, snorkel, mask and fins and thick kitchen gloves, I clutched a paint scraper and lowered myself into the brown sticky water thinking, 'I must remember to keep my mouth shut, I'm more likely to die from poisoning than drowning.'

There was no reason to be so frightened. There was only about five feet of water under the propellor but I just couldn't bear the thought of putting my feet down into the mud. With my fingers I had to feel the substantial growth on the blades as I couldn't see the scraper in my hand, the water was too murky, just a little brown light filtered down for the first six inches. It was like trying to work submerged in a giant bowl of brown windsor soup.

Eventually, with many dives down, the job was done. After a cold shower on deck we raced back to the Club where I stood under the lovely hot, hard shower and let clean water flow through my hair.

We treated each other to a good meal that night on the Club verandah. Where palm tree fronds whisper in the warm breeze, rigging tinkles against metal masts as moored boats rock in the wake of brilliantly lit giant container ships as they pass through the channel. Fishing boats and small ferries chug across to Pulau Ubin disturbing the calm water and rippling the moon's silver reflection. We would miss our friends at Changi.

Before setting sail on the 20th July 1994 to explore the East Coast of Malaysia for a six week shake-down cruise, Peter purchased and fitted a Philips GPS. He spent many hours familiarising himself with it and programming it and then taught me how to use it. It was four years since we had last raised sail. Would we remember what to do? Was CLYPEUS really ocean worthy?

We headed out through the Fairway weaving our way through the eastern big ship anchorage in Singapore Strait, one of the busiest shipping areas in the world. We anchored close to the Malay shore until the tide was with us then motored between dozens of floating monsters which towered above us; bright lights shining from their lonely decks as their generators throbbed on.

At 07.00 we turned the corner and hoisted the main, yankee and staysail. With the wind on the beam we flew through the turbulent Lima Channel into the South China Sea.

A Sumatra hit us in the afternoon, gusting fifty knots with spume and heavy rain which flattened the sea a little. Fortunately we saw the squall line approaching and were able to take down the jibs and reef the main in time. We hung on as CLYPEUS heeled and raced, plunging through the waves, clear and free at last. It was exhilarating but scarey. Was this what we really wanted, the thrill of strong winds thrusting us forward? White water foaming past as our clipper bow cut cleanly through the dark blue sea? Always the apprehension that we might hit a log, a whale, a semi-sunk container, or that something might break? Would our dear old boat pass the test?

The storm passed with no problems and we raised more sail again. Through the night our three hours on, three hours off watch keeping worked well. At 07.00 the sun broke through the mist, we put up the awning, and with the yankee poled out one side and the mainsail out the other, CLYPEUS danced, wing and wing, northwards. We gradually resumed our voyaging routine, baking bread, sprouting beans, refilling water tanks with rainwater and generally getting our survival systems into gear.

Dinner was excellent in the elegant surroundings of the Bali Hai Restaurant.

Over a sparkling sea in bright sunshine we sailed up the west coast of Tioman Island. Waterfalls glistened between the jungle green hills. The Asses Ears, twin mountain peaks, confirmed we were in the right place. At six in the evening we anchored off romantic Tioman Resort and sipped a cool beer in the sunset's glow. We would explore tomorrow.

Tioman Island is where Arab traders and Chinese junks have called for thousands of years. It was the last place to pick up fresh water before Canton. Later, East India Company galleons and Portuguese trading ships were regular visitors. The high mountain streams and waterfalls make it verdant and cool.

Windsurfers weaving between the yachts provided good breakfast entertainment as we sat in the cockpit drinking coffee. One young Englishman approached and noticing our British flag stopped to talk. We invited him on board for coffee. He introduced himself as Graham and told us he was holidaying with his recently widowed mother Sheila. We agreed to look out for each other.

We rowed ashore and walked a mile or so along the yellow, pink and red hibiscus-lined road to Malay Customs and Immigration. We booked in. No problems, no fee. A delightful swim and a cold beer at the Resort made us feel we were in Paradise. We actually were. This was where the film South Pacific was made.

The next day was our 40th wedding anniversary. I felt so lonely, even in paradise, home and family call very strongly. I

wanted to see my children. My sister Sheila and husband Tony, with whom we had shared a double wedding in 1954 were having a big party, surrounded by friends, at home in Wales. I wanted to be there too, to celebrate.

I sat in the cockpit, trying hard to appreciate how lucky we were and that in this life you have to make choices and you can't have everything, when Graham whizzed up on his board.

"We're coming to the Resort for dinner tonight," I told him. "It's our 40th Anniversary. Would you and your Mother like to join us?"

"Yes, that would be great. Come and have a swim in the pool first and then shower and dress in our suite."

It worked well. We all got on famously. Gin and tonics on their balcony watching the sunset was perfect while the voice of the Imam wailed from the mosque.

Dinner was excellent in the elegant surroundings of the Bali Hai Restaurant. When discussing desserts, the head waiter entered bearing a sparkling candle-lit cake with "Happy 40th Anniversary Peter and Shirley" on it. We were so delighted. Tears of gratitude came to my eyes and I couldn't speak. We WERE having a party and celebrating with friends after all. Thank you Graham. Thank you God.

We saw them off in the morning to take their flight home, feeling as though we had

Tourists were enjoying the clear water and varied coral

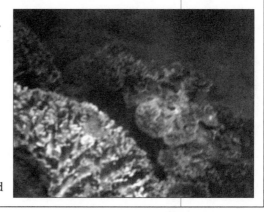

known each other for years. Hopefully we will meet again one day.

While Peter made some adjustments to the GPS, I scrubbed the propellor and hull. In this warm clear water it was a delight. Colourful little fish surrounded my hand

holding the scraper, and poked their noses close to the blade to catch any tasty morsel I scraped off. It was wonderful to swim and snorkel over and around the pristine coral close to the beach and the boat. Some mussels clinging to the underside of the keel, where anti-fouling hadn't been applied, were over 5" long and we had them for supper!

The staff of the little post office were helpful although they had run out of stamps and phone cards. This was the life! This was how I remembered our five years cruising the Pacific.

After ten days of heaven we set sail across to Pulau Talai- 'Coral Island' the tourist boats aptly called it. We anchored in a west facing bay where about ten dive boats with life-jacketed tourists were enjoying the clear water and varied coral. At 4pm they all left and we had the bay to ourselves. We rowed ashore and explored the white sand beach and mangrove shoreline. Carrying on with our maintenance plan Peter replaced a seal in the gear box.

At dusk, big wooden fishing boats began to arrive until we counted eleven in all. It was a bit intimidating to be completely surrounded by foreign fishing boats. Some of the fish-

ermen were ferried ashore, but one climbed aboard CLYPEUS, smiling, but without invitation.

"Raja Ken", he pointed to himself as he sat up on the cockpit corner seat.

"Er, Peter and my wife Shirley," Peter faltered.

"Hello", I shook his hand. "Would you like some tea? coffee?"

"Water please." I got him a

glass of water and we all sat looking at each other.

"Which is your boat?" I asked.

He pointed, "My boat."

We tried to make conversation and learned he had three children 12, 10 and 6 and that he came from the Malaysian mainland. A long hour later he was picked up by his friends.

"Goodbye. Thank you," he said as he climbed down into the dugout canoe. Although we were startled at having someone just make himself comfortable on board we were pleased to have a friend amongst the fleet.

In the gathering darkness many of the fishermen climbed on their upper decks to pray to Allah. On every boat, the little white caps rose and fell as they knelt and prostrated themselves. Indian music wavered across the bay.

Jean Phillipe was despondent with their present position.

"My boat!" he said, "my boat! I am a slave to zis boat.".

In the evening next day Raja Ken climbed aboard again hugging a big green coconut for us. This time he tried some of our orange squash but obviously wasn't over keen and left half of it. We gave him a packet of biscuits and some cigarettes. He was delighted but only stayed half an hour.

Next day we sailed to Salang Bay and dropped the anchor into crystal clear aquamarine water over white sand near a big traditional Indonesian wooden lugger 'Besok Lagi' (tomorrow will wait). We made friends with the young French owners Isobelle and Jean-Phillipe, who had had her built on Bone Rate Island and were now unofficially chartering and finding it very hard work.

After spending the day re-covering our saloon upholstery I invited them over for a meal. Jean Phillipe was despondent with their present position. "But," I said encouragingly, "many people would envy you your freedom, your life and your boat."

"My boat!" he said, "my boat! I am a slave to zis boat. Everyday somesing needs mending. Never is zer time or money to do anysing new."

Indeed, when we went on board for supper a few days later we understood. The inside was a huge dark cavern floored with wooden planks which were cut out around a giant Chinese diesel engine. Isobelle cooked in large pots on primus stoves on the floor and we sat on cushions to eat our meal. The young back-packing charterers thought it a great adventure to sleep on mattresses or hammocks on deck and use "bucket and chuck it" sanitation.

I looked at Isobelle's well scrubbed and pretty mien with even greater admiration, "You lived on Bone Rate for a whole year? When we were there we were always crowded, the children and women just wouldn't leave us alone. How did you manage?"

She smiled ruefully "I just got used to being watched all ze time, eating, sleeping, bathing, everysing, absolutment everysing."

We had been appalled at the beach on Bone Rate which was used as the village bathroom and toilet. I could imagine her distaste.

"I did make zem build me a door so that I could lock myself in the shower," she continued, "I just couldn't bear all zose eyes watching me shower."

Peter interrupted, shouting down from the deck. "All the fishing boats and ferries are leaving," he called. "Yes, come and look, there's a squall coming. Quick," he shouted. "Thank you for supper, we must go. We have heard that the swell breaks a long way out in this corner of the bay. I think we should all get out to sea."

"Au revoir, merci beaucoup pour le bon diner," I called as I scrambled up on deck.

"Au revoir, merci pour le vin. We will leave also," we heard as we let ourselves down into our dinghy.

On CLYPEUS we hastily stowed the awning, closed the hatches, switched on the navigation lights, started the engine and pulled up the anchor, leaving the stern anchor buoyed where it was. Already its little upright white fender buoy was being rolled by breaking waves. We motored out to find shelter in the lee of Coral Island.

BESOK LAGI was a long time following. What was the matter? But we had our own problems in the rising sea; the fan belt broke and the engine overheated. Urgently Peter turned off the engine. We hoisted sail in the increasing wind, which we expected to develop into a Sumatra, headed north west trying to get a safe distance from land. Some bottle-nosed dolphins played across our bows for a while. They weren't worried. As soon as we were far enough offshore we hove-to and Peter found and fitted a spare fan belt. In a few minutes he turned the key and the motor fired first time. Hooray!

The Sumatra didn't develop so we stood watch all night drifting gently. At dawn we headed back into Salang Bay, dropped the anchor and fell back onto our stern anchor buoy. We pulled the line taut so that CLYPEUS faced the incoming slight swell and had a good breakfast.

BESOK LAGI limped in. Over coffee they told us of their panic. At first their motor wouldn't start, then the propellor caught around the stern anchor line, but Xavier, one of their charterers, had been standing on the beach watching, realised their predicament, and had bravely swum out and freed the rope.

"Pouff! I am not sure how long we will continue with zis life in paradise," said Jean Phillipe. "Perhaps we will go home and work for some more money, our budget is too tight." They left to mingle on the beach to find more customers. We hope all is going well for them now.

One of the fascinations of cruising is the extremes of income and ages of different owners, yet we all have many things in common and have something to learn from each other. We chatted and shopped with the owners of a handsome Petersen 44 from Australia. Jane and John both play the international stock market for their income. A colour TV monitor in the cockpit displayed teletext Malay Stock Market Exchange prices. John made phone calls to Hong Kong, New York, Singapore.

"If you can't afford to lose $300,000 in an afternoon don't play," he warned us. He had to fly off to Kuala Lumpur as their broker hadn't performed correctly and the only way to get money there was to take cash! Their boat had a water-maker, four fridges, and luxurious accommodation. Their 16 year old son Mark was with them and studying ten hours a day for his "A" levels by a Queensland correspondence course. So their cruising is a tightrope of decisions and hightech. Not the laid back image expected when cruising.

Spear fishing has never been allowed on this coast so the fish are quite unafraid. Snorkelling across a deep channel to a little island a large turtle swam ahead of me. I followed trying to get close but he always stayed four to five feet in front, until he dived into dark-blue depths and I wasn't prepared to follow. Large yellow and black angel fish hovered in pairs. Smug looking, smiling, brown and blue surgeon and trigger fish floated by in shoals, multi-coloured parrot fish grazed on the coral. A family of eight to ten large bull-foreheaded emperor wrasse joined me, the big old man leader being at least five feet long and thick and heavy. His blue and green coloured scales were like Roman armour plates. They let me swim along with them, completely unconcerned at my presence.

Crossing back across the deep channel I saw an eight foot

black-tipped shark skulking along the bottom. I don't think black-tips attack humans, but nevertheless I swam for home as discreetly as I could and he went his own way.

We sailed back to Tekok Bay so we could celebrate my 60th birthday at the friendly Barbura Beach Restaurant. The day was spent ashore lazing on the beach, having a real holiday. We asked if we could bring a bottle of wine to have with our celebration dinner tonight, as being in a Muslim country, no alcohol is sold on the island, except at the International Resort. Peter had thoughtfully bought a bottle of our favourite Australian Wolfe Blass Yellow Label red wine in Singapore and stowed it away for today.

Dressed for the occasion, Peter rowed us ashore in the evening calm. I sat in the stern hugging the wine and my crystal goblet which I carefully keep for my usual evening drink.

The prawns in garlic butter, then chilli crab were delicious. Because we had a bottle of wine on the table, other diners came and asked "Where did you buy it?" "How much?" "Could we get some?" We explained each time that it was my birthday and we had asked permission. It was fun to speak to so many people. One couple asked us to join them when we had finished eating. We did so, and the young Australians produced a bottle of champagne from their travel bag under the table.

Later the Malaysian waiter who had earlier befriended us, came and invited us to join his 26th birthday party, which would start as soon as the restaurant closed. The restaurant didn't actually close, the diners all stayed on and became guests at the party: Germans, Swedes, Malays, Singaporeans, Australians and us.

So once again, what I was afraid was going to be a rather forlorn occasion without my family, turned out to be a happy international evening. How lucky we have been. During all our voyaging, on a one-to-one basis, everybody has been so kind.

But what about now? I shut my eyes tight, found Peter's hand to hold, and willed myself to sleep.

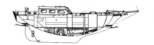

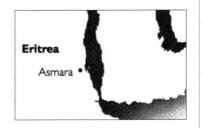

Eritrea

Asmara •

CHAPTER
SEVENTEEN

Asmara - Day 12

Very depressed. All I wrote in my journal the next day was: 'No news. Mr Achmed has left'.
Kindly Azib brought us fruit drinks and ice cream and arranged a traditional coffee ceremony in our room.
But still no news.

We did our best to be cheerful, but were so dejected. When were we going to be freed? When could we go for a walk? When would the British Consul be in touch with us himself?

Lorraine had given me some local coins and we tried surreptitiously to telephone Rod Hicks from the pay phone in the corridor, but he wasn't there. We left a message.

We still had our cameras. Nobody had asked for them or taken the films for investigation. What was our arrest all about?

Azib's gesture, to organise the maid Mulu to make the traditional coffee ceremony for us, was appreciated. Azib, Monique and Etienne joined us in our room and we sat around and watched as Mulu brought in a blazing charcoal brazier. She placed the hot metal container on the bedroom

Azib's gesture, to organise the maid Mulu to make the traditional coffee ceremony for us, was appreciated.

We watched Semira having her hair plaited by four hairdressers. They were extending the length of her shoulder-length black hair into longer thin braids in the traditional hairstyle with at least a hundred plaits.

carpet! Then she poured some popcorn into a little tin saucepan. As soon as it started popping and bursting out of the pan, she poured it into a bowl and then, to our astonishment scattered some handfuls over the carpet. I presume an Eritrean gesture of generosity and abundance?

Next she roasted the beans - the smell was delicious. Mulu performed the ceremony exactly as Worku had done in the army hut, except Mulu used an electric bean grinder, rather than an old axle shaft and hollow tree bole, to grind the coffee. Azib, who had a terrible cold, sat with us and sniffed between smiles. She should have been at home in bed. I asked her if it would be OK to take some photos.

"No problem," she said.

When the ceremony finished Azib motioned for us to leave the room so that it could be cleared up. She gestured to Monique and I to follow her downstairs. We did so, mystified. Next door was a hairdressers' salon and she wanted us to come with her. We were frightened. We didn't want to do anything wrong.

Monique returned upstairs in spite of Azib's "Come, come, no problem, no problem". I went with her and we watched Semira having her hair plaited by four hairdressers. They were extending the length of her shoulder-length black hair into longer thin braids in the traditional hairstyle with at least a hundred plaits.

"Salam", I greeted them. "Wow! It looks so complicated and time consuming. How long does it take?" I asked, looking at my watch.

"Oh! Four hours, maybe five." was the nonchalant reply. They chatted amongst themselves. I was really worried about being out of the hotel.

"Take me back please Azib."

"No problem. Come and see my house."

"No. No. not today. Please later, when it is OK."

"OK."

I rushed back upstairs, but nobody seemed to be worried about my little expedition.

After dinner Peter asked to see the BBC news on TV. It was arranged, everybody on the screen looked bright red and there was no significant information that applied to us.

The in depth interviews seemed long and boring to the Eritreans after the snappy, snap, snap, of the no detail style of CNN news items. At the first opportunity the programme was switched to something more interesting.

We retired early, lying in the dark, once again remembering our lovely time in Thailand took our minds off our present situation. However we were not always happy and managed a big step in our relationship towards togetherness last year.

At that time on board I was miserable, thinking about my elderly father at death's door in Australia. Usually my cheerfulness has kept us buoyant throughout our marriage. If I was ill or low, Peter would always sympathise with me and perhaps hold my hand, but never offer any positive encouragement: a joke, flowers, a happy card or poem. It was always up to me to pull myself together and get the family, or just us, going again. However at last we were coming to terms with our different personalities.

When miserable, he likes to be left alone; I like to be cheered up.

Clypeus anchored beneath a karst in Phang Nga Bay, Phuket.

We remember our paradise in Thailand.

This time he asked what he could do to please me. As on most yachts the navigation table was the skipper's domain and unless actually navigating or using the radios it was not my place. He spent some hours making me a little let-down desk in the forward cabin for my computer so that I could leave everything set up at mealtimes. It made such a difference to have my own space where I could listen to tapes of Beethoven, Bruch or pops, while I wrote, embroidered, painted, or sorted photographs into albums.

Earlier last year we had had an interesting discussion with a couple who both used computers for their respective careers. One day in town, she had suddenly burst into tears. She couldn't explain her depression at first. Then over a good lunch with a bottle of wine she confessed to her husband that she was crying because she had no space of her own. He then made her a let-down desk in the forward cabin for her computer so that she didn't have to clear everything away each mealtime. Passing on their experience had helped us too.

Thoughts of that serene country of temples and bells warmed me in my cold Eritrean bed.

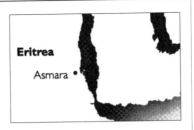

Eritrea

Asmara •

CHAPTER EIGHTEEN

Asmara - Day 13

Boring morning. Nothing happened. I thought about asking to go to church but decided not to make waves. After lunch at 2.30, the receptionist came to the bedroom and said to Peter:

"Mr. Billing, telephone." He jumped up and followed her. I hurried along behind wondering if it was news of our release, or were we to be charged and sent for trial?

It was neither, but a wonderful suprise! It was our son Noel phoning from his home in England. His first words were of anger that we had got ourselves into such a stupid position. After making sure his wife Rosemary and daughters, and the rest of our family were all well, and he had reassured us that they did still love us, he told us that Rosemary had received a telephone call last Friday, it was from the French Ambassador asking to speak to him, but he had already left for work. M. Monal told Rosemary that he had met us in a hotel the previous evening and that we were OK and there was 'no emergency'. She assumed it had been at a social function and that he was passing on our good wishes!

At 5.00pm the same day she had received a call from the Foreign Office in London from David Rowe, the desk officer for Africa, confirming that we had been held in a hotel in Asmara since the 20th March and denied consular access. They were working hard to remedy this and had contacted Dr Rod Hicks, the British Consul, to try and get things moving. The Foreign Office then passed on our message:" Tell Noel and Rosemary to contact Basil."

Rosemary telephoned Noel at work, who was obviously shocked and disbelieving. She then phoned our friend Basil D'Oliveira (not the cricketer, but a former Royal Air Force Officer, a recognised expert on navigation who moves in government and press circles, and is also a yachtsman and influential journalist.) She gave him all the details and asked if he could do something to help obtain our release.

Basil immediately set about getting names and fax numbers of all hotels in Asmara and filled her in on details about the place as he had been stationed in Khartoum many years ago. The pilots used to fly to Asmara for Italian ice-cream! Evidently the Khartoum Hotel was not listed, but he managed to obtain the number somehow.

Basil phoned us as soon as possible and we told him our story.

Later on he phoned us back again and let us know that he had made ambassadorial enquiries and that diplomatic notes had been sent from the British Ambassador to the Eritrean Ambassador in London.

Evidently we are now allowed to receive calls but cannot make them.

Peter and I sat on the bed and talked over all our news from England.

At last at 7.00pm, Rod Hicks, the part-time honorary British Consul came to see us, a handsome, tall man with floppy hair, dressed in an open-necked shirt and sports jacket.

He apologised for not being able to visit us before and explained that he had now been officially informed by the Eritreans that we were under arrest and being held at the Khartoum Hotel.

He handed over some magazines he had brought and we had a useful talk. He explained his position, that although Honorary British Consul, he was actually employed as an educator by the Eritrean Government. He emphasised that his authority was limited and that he was in no position to over-step that authority. It would only lead to bad feeling and more resistance if he pushed too hard.

"The Eritreans are a very ethical, but stubborn, people. If they think a major power is trying to push them around, they will stick their heels in and perhaps move you to some unknown place where you may not be looked after as well as you are here. Then we wouldn't know where you were or what could be happening to you either. So just sit tight and wait."

As far as Rod knew, no charges had been formulated against us. He looked at us and grinned. "Of course, they think you are spies!"

He told us of the persistence of our yachting friends in telephoning him every day to ask for progress reports.

"Yes," we affirmed. "We have the best of friends, please thank them for us next time they telephone."

After joining us for a glass of beer he left to return to his wife and family, promising to come and see us the next day.

Monique and Etienne joined us in the dining room for dinner. The French Consul had been to see them too but had no news of any charges or release. We watched TV for a while but couldn't keep up with the ever-changing programmes and retired to bed reasonably sure that things were moving, but not realising all that had gone on in England over the weekend.

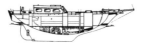

Rosemary kept notes of what happened at their end:

As soon as Noel returned from work on Friday he immediately phoned brother Paul (in the U.S.A.) and sister Andrea in Hereford, and Shirley's sisters in England, Wales and Australia. He told them all he knew and asked if they had any suggestions or useful contacts.

Later on Friday evening the French Consul phoned again and told them that Shirley and Peter were OK. but anxious at being detained for such a long time without any charges being made. He wondered whether his unannounced visit to the hotel to see the French couple had exacerbated the situation.

On Saturday 30th March.

The telephone rang all day.

Hilary phoned from Australia to let us know that money was no problem should a ransom or fines be demanded. She was Executor of Shirley's estate and was willing to use that money. Noel passed the message on to the Foreign Office that we should not be held up due to money problems.

All the family, who were extremely worried, phoned again.

After several calls to the Foreign Office they finally phoned us late to say that Dr Hicks should be coming to see you on Sunday.

On Sunday 31st March.

On the advice of Basil, the Foreign Office and family members, it was decided not to inform the press at this point in the hope that it would allow the Eritreans to extricate themselves from the situation without too much loss of face. The Foreign Office closed at 5.30 with no news from Dr. Hicks.

However something was happening outside down in the street. Forty to fifty ladies in white robes were moaning and keening and crying.

CHAPTER NINETEEN

Eritrea

Asmara •

Asmara - Day 14

At 5.00am we were woken by strange noises in the street outside, it sounded like crying and moaning. I got up to look but could see nothing.

We rose, very chirpy in the morning. Things were happening at last. We went along to the dining room for breakfast and I asked for eggs. Three soft and luscious fried eggs were placed in front of me. With tomato sauce, hot rolls, then butter and honey and 'long tea' (poured from on high into a tall glass); it was going to be a happy feast.

However, something was happening outside down in the street. Forty to fifty ladies in white robes were moaning and keening and crying. Some were dancing a slow mournful stamp around. Semira came in with tears in her eyes.

"What's happened?" we asked.

"The lady opposite, she died in the night," she sobbed. "She was our friend. Azib will not be with you today, she is going with the coffin to our friend's father's village. I'm going too."

I put my arm around her and murmured our sympathy.

"Oh!" she said. "Mother made an appointment for you and Monique to have your hair done today downstairs with Mr Abdul. It's at 10 o'clock. Don't forget."

"Thank you. How kind of her. No, we won't forget."

Our feast didn't taste so good with all the grief around us. I looked out of the window and watched a coffin wrapped in white being loaded onto the roof of a minibus. The grieving became louder and there appeared to be anger as well as sorrow in the way some older white robed women were stamping on the ground. Four men came out of the apartment building and silence descended. The men got into a car which slowly followed the mini bus, the inside of which was crammed with ladies beneath the coffin.

The other mourners stood silently outside the apartment building.

Monique and I went to have our hair done. Peter accompanied us and for a while chatted to Abdul who volunteered the information that the lady opposite had taken her own life because "her husband loved another."

"Oh dear!" That explained the hostility towards the men,

Abdul had formerly been a hairdresser at the court of Emperor Haile Selassie. With great patience and flair he gently did my long blonde hair so that I was ready to go to a ball - hardly a 'yachty' style, but it made me feel good.

one of which must have been the husband. The mourners did not disperse all day, they stayed filling the pavement and road and softy sang and murmured.

Abdul had formerly been a hairdresser at the court of Emperor Haile Selassie. With great patience and flair he gently did my long blonde hair so that I was ready to go to a ball - hardly a 'yachty' style, but it made me feel good. I think he enjoyed the change of having fair hair to deal with rather than always the dark hair of the Eritrean ladies.

Rod Hicks called again, but with no news. We asked him to see if he could arrange for us to go out for a walk.

My sister Sheila telephoned and sounded low - how difficult long distance telephone conversations are, so often you feel so much is unsaid that you are really no better off for having been in touch. Our son Paul telephoned from America too. A committed Christian, he assured us that God will look after us.

Rosemary's Notes.

Monday 1st April.

David Rowe of the Foreign office informs us that Dr Hicks has seen you and that you are fine and may be released on Tuesday. He is cautiously optimistic. They confirm you are staying in the Hotel Khartoum, which does not appear on any lists, but say they have no phone number and that you are not allowed any calls. Basil works on his contacts to obtain the number and we speak to you. We do not inform the press as we do not want to jeopardise your release. All family and friends have to be informed every time we speak to the Foreign Office including Paul and Alice in U.S.A. Paul has considered flying to Eritrea to assist, but decided there wasn't much he could do when he got there.

Monique and Etienne Forget owners of PEEWIT *and our fellow prisoners.*

Eritrea

Asmara •

CHAPTER TWENTY

Asmara - Day 15

At the hotel, nobody had come to repair the plumbing and when I got up during the night, my toes squelched into a cold, soggy carpet. Water was leaking from somewhere. We traced it to the bathroom wall and immediately rang the service bell. It was 1am and it took many minutes for the young waiter to come. He examined the carpet and went for the night watchman who waited with us while the waiter phoned somebody else for instructions.

Eventually we were led upstairs to continue our sleep in room 11. At 7am we were woken and asked to move to room 12. Pulling on some clothes and bundling up our overnight belongings we obliged. It was another large and lofty room, furnished in a similar fashion to our original room. A queen sized double bed with a shiny satin flowered bedspread; a dark wood wardrobe; a card table and two chairs, and in the corner, a child's wooden barred cot which gave it a welcome homely touch. Best of all, when we pulled back the curtains, and wound up the metal shutters, it had a balcony overlooking the street.

Now we were on the same floor as Monique and Etienne and could share the same bathrooms. Which meant that even if we were confined again we could leave messages for each other.

After breakfast Etienne spoke for twenty minutes on the telephone. "C'est un journaliste," he said with a smile of satisfaction. "Our son saw our Parliamentary Representative, and also wrote to Amnesty International and the International Red Cross. A question is to be asked in the Paris House of Representatives. Enfin quelque chose!" (At last something.)

Why hadn't we heard anything? Wasn't anybody except our family interested in us? Before leaving the dining room I looked out of the window and saw busses full of sad white-robed mourners leaving for the funeral, including Azib and Semira.

We went to our old room and transferred all our possessions up to Room 12. It was good to be able to sit out on the balcony. Fresh air at last.

Peter examined round holes in the metal shutters.

"These are bullet holes you know," he said conversationally, "imploding into the bedroom. Look, if you line them up with these gouges out of the balcony rail you can see where the sniper crouched behind that corner."

I came and followed his line of sight and it did indicate exactly where someone could have fired three shots from the far corner of the opposite building. The Eritreans fight for independence from Ethiopia was still close in time and bullet holes in the shutters were very ordinary to the staff.

It was good to sit out on the balcony and watch what happened in this small side street of Asmara - not a lot! It was a lovely spring day and I enjoyed reading in the sunshine.

Peter sat in the bedroom fretting about CLYPEUS. Was she still afloat? Had she been damaged? Were we going to meet constant head winds when we did get back on board? It was getting so late in the season. How were other boats faring?

Day 16, Wednesday 3rd April

During the morning Rosemary telephoned from England and told us that as no useful action was being taken, the family had decided to inform the press. She was going to talk to Basil for advice. She had already spoken to the secretary of our Conservative Member of Parliament, Mr John Redwood, to ask him to press the Foreign Secretary for action. She had also asked Andrea and Sheila to talk to their respective Members of Parliament in Hereford and Haverfordwest.

Colin Mitchell, a freelance journalist telephoned to talk to us. He said he had been alerted of our plight by Basil and wanted to know what was happening. It took thirty minutes to tell him. He understood the situation well as he had sailed down the Red Sea last year with yachting author Rod Heikel.

When we finished talking to him, another journalist alerted by Basil, Stephen Farrell of the London Times phoned for 50 minutes and we told him our story adding "please, please, say nothing to upset the Eritreans. They have treated us honourably but are very touchy and in 'a loss of face' situation, anything could still happen to us."

We were surprised that with all these phone calls from the press there was still no contact from the Eritrean authorities. Rod Hicks didn't come and see us or send a message. Were we newsworthy? Would the press set out our position in a sympathetic manner for us and the Eritreans? Should we have spoken to the media at all? Was there any alternative?

A grave Semira came and sat with us for a while. She taught us some Eritrean words: hello - *salaam*, goodbye -

In bed I remembered just three months ago one of our happiest times. On the 4th December we booked out of Malaysia, really for the very last time, and set off for a last few days at OUR paradise by the uninhabited Thai island of Ao Dong.

selama, thank you - *yefanelay,* please - *porabrad qui,* yes - *awa,* no - *no,* good - *tsebuk,* fish - *asa,* chicken - *dorho,* stew - *zigini*

Before dinner we had Coca Colas brought to our room and enjoyed some more of David's brandy. At 10 p.m. Paul phoned again from the U.S.A. It was wonderful to have the support of our family, but no news from Rod Hicks or from the Eritreans about letting us go. How much longer? Were we going to be held for years like Terry Waite and Terry Alexander in Beirut? They had had plenty of publicity but it hadn't secured their release. Surely Peter and I were not worth holding as hostages.

It might have been a romantic setting high on the cool plateau in this sparkling city, as it was, our predicament took all such thoughts from us. Holding hands and a comforting cuddle appeared the most our bodies wanted to give. We were so grateful to be together.

In bed I remembered just three months ago one of our happiest times. On the 4th December we booked out of Malaysia, really for the very last time, and set off for a last few days at OUR paradise by the uninhabited Thai island of Ao Dong. As we sailed through the aquamarine pass between the islands, a big blue wooden local fishing boat circled CLYPEUS and offered us lobsters and fish. The lobsters were too expensive but we bought some prawns and fish and carried on. Our special anchorage was as we remembered;

Sunshine greeted that first day of leisure and peace.
The tiare blossom again beckoned us with its fragrance in the evening and we barbecued our fish on the beach.

calm in the shelter of the mountainous island, the sand soft and white and the water warm and clear. We seemed to be the only people on earth.

Sunshine greeted that first day of leisure and peace. The tiare blossom again beckoned us with its fragrance in the evening and we barbecued our fish on the beach. We sat and sipped our wine in the firelight with the moon shining on the water as it lapped the sand by our feet. The grey green fronds of the iron bark trees whispered behind us. We talked about remembering this day and this place for the rest of our lives and vowed then that, whatever happened to us, it had been worth it.

Rosemary's notes.

Wednesday 3rd April.

I phone you this morning and you are despondent.
We decide to inform the press. I also phone my Member of Parliament
John Redwood, who is away, but his secretary takes it in hand. I phone
Andrea, Sheila and Liz and ask them to do the same i.e. try to get their
MP to press the Foreign Secretary in the House of Commons. Andrea
is offered an interview with her M.P. on Thursday afternoon.
I ask Basil to use his contacts and he phones the Times, the
Evening Standard and Meridian Television. The phone doesn't
stop ringing. I understand it is the same at Andrea's. Constant
messages from journalists to call back.
Meridian ask to come and interview Noel for TV - this is
half an hour of torture for him after work, but they do a nice piece.
The Times take our photos of you which will now appear in
practically every daily.
Andrea and I both give phone accounts of what has happened to you.

Peter and Shirley Billing aboard their yacht on an earlier trip to the States. "We're not really spy material," says Mrs Billing

Free us, plead couple held as 'spies'

A BRITISH couple arrested on suspicion of spying and held prisoner in Eritrea for the past 17 days spoke of their ordeal today and appealed: "Help get us free."

Peter Billing and his wife Shirley were on a round-the-world yacht trip when they were arrested by Eritrean soldiers who claimed they had moored their 35ft ketch Clypeus in a restricted military zone near the Hanish islands in the Red Sea. The

by BARBARA McMAHON

couple, who have six grandchildren, have been interrogated at a military camp in the desert and are now confined to a hotel in the capital Asmera, unable to leave the building.

Speaking from the only telephone in the Khartoum Hotel, Mrs Billing, 61, said: "We're not really spy material. If anybody shouts at me I cry. We

are just typical English people who have been caught up in something beyond our control and who don't know how to react except to smile a lot and be polite."

The Billings from Wokingham, Berkshire, say they consulted other yachtsmen before passing through the area from Aden. They received no warning that it was dangerous to

Continued on Page 2 Col 1

ENTERTAINMENT GUIDE 52   LETTERS 49   STARS 50   SPORT STARTS 74

The media had begun to tell the world about our arrest.

Retired couple on 13-year voyage are held captive after yacht is boarded by Eritrea

Round-the-world pair arrested in Red Sea swoop

By STEPHEN FARRELL

BRITISH couple appealed to be reunited yesterday after the Royal Navy interrupted their 13-year circumnavigation of the globe by boarding their yacht and putting them under house arrest.

Peter Billing, 65, and his wife Shirley, 61, have been prisoner for 16 days. The navy claim that their 35ft Clypeus strayed into a restricted zone near the Hanish islands in the Red Sea. They are the subject of a trial dispute with Ye. The crews of a naval

patrol vessel boarded the maneuvring boat at a bar at sunset two days out of Aden, and took the couple to a desert military camp. They were questioned and flown to the capital, Asmera, with a French couple arrested in similar circumstances. They are now being held at an hotel but cannot leave their room or make outgoing calls.

The Billings, who are experienced navigators from Wokingham, Berkshire, say that they had consulted other yachtsmen before passing

through the area and had consulted the warning when they left Aden, and said the crew to a desert military camp. They were questioned and yesterday that they had been warned by armed men who forced them to navigate dangerous shallow waters at night, then took their passports, charts and cameras.

She and her husband, an electronics engineer, were kept in a state-owned bar of gunpoint. "We were in fear of our lives for the first three days. We just had no idea what was going on and were not allowed to speak to anybody," Mrs Billing said. "They accused us of being spies, which is ridiculous. We are grandparents and so are the French couple.

"The problem seems to be that it is difficult to explain to people who have been at war for 30 years that you have enough leisure time to go off and cruise around the world on your own. They just do not understand it and they probably think we are mad."

The couple set off around the world on March 16, 1983, after selling their house. Their voyage has taken them via the

Peter and Shirley Billing, who are both in their 60s, were interrogated in a desert camp on suspicion o

the South Pacific, South-East Asia, China and Yemen. They spent four years in Taiwan and Singapore where Mr Billing worked for the engineering firm of which he was formerly a director.

On Sunday, after nearly a fortnight in captivity, they were given access to the hotel phone. "I rather they are about to be released. This should have taken place on Tuesday, but it has not yet."

thinks it is better to play the thing quietly, but the softly softly approach has gone on long enough," Mrs Billing said.

Haitsem Yohannesmail Consul-General at the Eritrean Consulate in London, said last night: "It will be sorted out. I rather they are about to be released. They should have taken place on Tuesday, but it has not yet."

feared last night that outside the Eritreans had been reluctant to grant access, but had allowed the honorary consul to visit after officials in Addis Ababa 'underlining' our concern" by letter. "The crossed reports they are in good spirits and we understand there is a likelihood they may be released very shortly," a spokesman said last night.

The couple's three children

and Friday. D Andrew Lound said she had left until she talked telephone at the righ... "They are not... I'm sure they... right. Knowing exhibit parents a have tough synchronised i here to reach forcing house

---

CHAPTER TWENTY-ONE

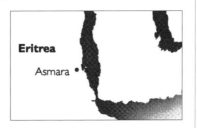

Eritrea

Asmara •

Asmara - Day 17

Another bright sunny day, so I sat on the balcony and watched the people of Asmara go by. Life in the street appears to have returned to normal, no white-robed mourners stand on the sidewalk. Donkeys clip clop by, pulling carts piled high with vegetables.

Men were unloading heavy sacks from the back of a flatbed truck. Each fifty kilo brown sack had 'SUGAR - Product of BRAZIL' stencilled on it. The Eritrean men chanted as they worked - real African sounding chanting, a melodious human worksong. Two men up on the flatbed dragged the sacks to the edge of the truck, a constant stream of bent backs leaned against it, settled their load comfortably, lifted, then staggered into a doorway and climbed up some stairs out of sight.

I looked out for friends or visitors who might be coming to see us, but nobody came. No one came from Eritrean Security, but at 10am we were called to the telephone. It was Brian from Massawa but he had no news for us and was surprised that we still haven't been released. They will come to Asmara again on Saturday. They told us that the U.K. Yacht Radio Net now knew of our plight and something may happen from that. They offered to buy food for us to supplement our stores when we rendezvoused at sea.

Our good friends Lois and James phoned from Wokingham. They had choked on their porridge while listening to Sarah Kennedy on the BBC's Breakfast Show as she read the day's newspaper headlines "British Couple on 13th year of circumnavigation held in Eritrea." They had immediately telephoned Noel and Rosemary for our phone number and managed to get through to us. It was so good to hear them.

Basil phoned to tell us that the London Times had given us half a page. He faxed the article to us but it was immediately confiscated by Eritrean Security so that we didn't see it. Oh dear! Have we messed up our chances of release again?

We received phone calls from Meridian TV in Newbury who recorded our voices. The line was very busy all day, now that our story had been released:

The Daily Express wanted an article.

BBC Southern TV recorded our voices telling our story.

The Times, Stephen Farrell wanted more details again.

Wokingham Times, Christine Cooper phoned for a special message for Wokingham readers.

The Daily Mail called, Tim Knowles, then Rebecca Hardy. She wanted to meet us for an interview and talked of helicoptering to see us and paying £5,000 for our story. We pointed out her suggestions were impractical but said we would be pleased to meet her in Cairo and would be in touch as soon as we got to Suez. We started to dream about what we would do with the £5,000: a radar to help us cope with Channel fog; a cabin heater for when we reached cooler waters, as our old paraffin heater has just about rusted away.

Rod Hicks came with some books and magazines, but no news of our release. He told us to be patient and cautioned us about the Press not upsetting the Eritreans.

We received another FAX from Basil which included the comment:

'For your information to the best of my knowledge there are no marine navigational warnings in existence for the Eritrea mainland, warning about restricted areas, nor do British Admiralty charts contain warnings in the area covering the mainland north of Assab and including Baraisole Bay. I have spoken to our Hydrographic Office about this.'

So we hadn't ignored any warnings or done anything unethical after all!

The BBC phoned and we were interviewed by Chris Lowe. Peter spoke first and while he was talking I asked our 'minder':

"Is it O.K. for Peter to speak to the BBC?" I only got a grunt for a reply, he obviously wasn't listening to me, and Peter carried on. The telephone was handed to me for the female version and after I had been speaking for about twenty minutes Peter wrote a note saying:

"Tell the BBC to clear everything with the Foreign Office first."

As he was passing the note to me our minder grabbed it, realised what was happening, jumped into the air and snatched the phone from my hand. Peter shouted down the phone

"Don't use this interview, it may hold up our release." (The BBC are very ethical. It was never used).

Our minder was extremely angry and ordered us to go to our room and said that we could receive no further telephone calls.

Actually we felt exhausted and were ready to comply. We undressed and climbed into bed, numb with worry again.

Had we messed up our chances of release? If they didn't want us to talk to the BBC why didn't they ask "Who is calling?"

The excitement of the day had got our adrenalin going though, and we couldn't sleep. Had we seriously offended anybody? What would be published? Had we said anything out of turn? When would they let us see the Times article? What would happen next? Our minds were in a turmoil as I heard the cathedral clock strike 10, then 11, 12, 1, 2, 3, and 4. At least our consciences were now clear, thanks to Basil's fax, we knew that we hadn't actually done anything wrong or ignored any warnings .

Rosemary's Notes.

Thursday 4th April

Article appears in the Times, which opens floodgates of journalists. Andrea is upset as the quote they printed from her seemed rather facile. She asks me not to give her number to any other journalists. I speak to Telegraph, Standard, Wokingham Times, BBC South. We feel unable to do any more TV interviews, who want to play up the pathos/human drama too much. I also speak to the Press Association. In the afternoon I receive phone-calls from my father and other friends working in the City of London to say that you are the billboard heading for the London Evening Standard. At one point you are front-page news, but beef BSC crisis bumps you inside on later editions.

I phone the Foreign Office who says that they hope you may be released the following day and intimate that they dislike the Standard's billboards. I phone all relatives and friends with all the news. Later that evening GMTV phone to ask if Noel will do their mainstream morning program - he says no. Then at 9.00pm he speaks to Sky radio stations (audio tape of Virgin news). Your phone communications have been cut - we are either told you are asleep or that the government is coming tomorrow and you must not have any calls (this has been the situation since just after lunch).

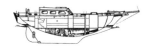

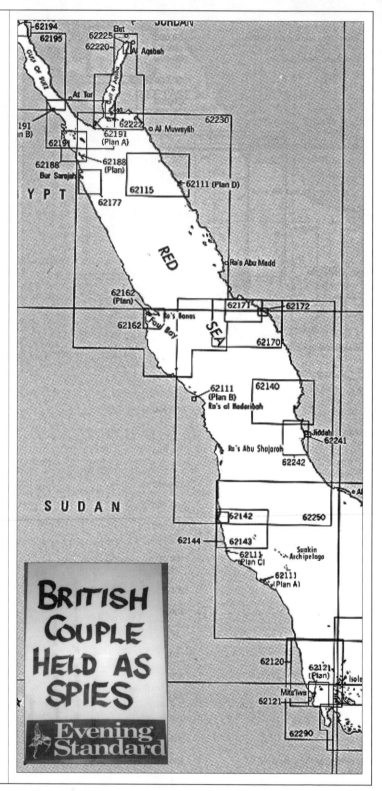

CHAPTER TWENTY-TWO

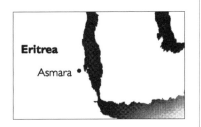

Eritrea

Asmara •

Asmara - Day 18

We decided to stay in our room, to save Security the pleasure of telling us to go back to it. We were getting less frightened and more bolshy. Why can't they make up their minds? If we are supposed to be spies why are they letting us talk to the press and our families? We ordered a substantial breakfast: Peter had tasty scrambled eggs with chopped tomato and onion mixed in, and I was given three fried eggs with rolls, marmalata and shahi abbi (honey and long tea).

Semira brought us a copy of the fax of yesterday's article in the London Times about our situation. We sat and read it and considered how well, non-provoking and accurately, it had been written by Stephen Farrell. All the details were correct and the comment from our daughter that

"They are bored silly, but I'm sure they will cope all right. Knowing them, Dad will have mended all the mobile phones and Mum will have taught them all synchronised swimming and how to teach English as a foreign language." eased any tension (she had no idea of the type of hotel we were in and that there probably wasn't a mobile phone or swimming pool in Eritrea). We were pleased we had played down our dangerous situation sufficiently for them to be able to joke about it. We hoped the practice we have had during our sailing lives to put forward that thin veneer of courage, to hide our panic from our children, still worked.

The Receptionist called Peter to the telephone. I went with him.

Retired couple on 13-year voyage are held captive after yacht is boarded by Eritrean

Round-the-world pair arrested in Red Sea swoop

Semira brought us a copy of the fax of yesterday's article in the London Times about our situation.

Mr. Immanuel was on the line. "Please be ready to see the Foreign Minister at 3pm." He didn't say what for. Was it good or bad news? Were we to be released or sent for trial?

We lunched with Monique and Etienne in a state of nervous alarm.

I asked the hotelier, 'Buttons', "The Foreign Minister is to see us this afternoon. Should we wear ordinary clothes or smart clothes?"

"Smart clothes," he replied without expression.

We dressed and I made up with care. Peter wore his tie, blazer and grey flannels. I wore my black trouser suit with a white collar and dressed my hair high with black velvet ribbon around the bun.

Mr Immanuel was smiling when he came to collect us at 2.30. Unfortunately Peter's nervous stomach had decided to go into spasm and we kept him waiting. How different Mr Immanuel's manner was from our last encounter ten days ago when he had hissed "We know everything. Do not underestimate us." Was it ten days? It seemed like a year.

He drove us to the Ministry. Through the impressive wooden doors we followed him along polished corridors to a large room with a long, highly polished elegant table and 30 leather chairs arranged around it. Rod Hicks was waiting for us. He was wearing a tie too. My! This was a formal occasion!

Rod smiled and said everything was OK and he was pleased how smart we looked.

A secretary asked us to sit and if we would like tea? The Minister would not keep us long. We sat and waited.

As the immaculately suited, smiling Minister entered, we stood up. Rod introduced us and we all shook hands, sat down and nervously sipped our tea. The Minister stood and formally apologised for keeping us at the Khartoum Hotel for so long. He handed Peter our passports and told us we were now free, and hoped we would enjoy Eritrea. We would be returned to our boat as soon as possible.

Peter stood and thanked the Minister for our passports and freedom, and apologised for the trouble we had caused.

Rod stood up and thanked everyone that the affair was concluded.

It was suggested that we move out of the Khartoum Hotel. We were also told that we would now be responsible for our own expenses.

While waiting for visas to be organised, Mr. Immanuel took us on a tour by car. First, to the British Cemetery, kept in manicured condition by the War Graves Commission. Lines of sad white headstones marked the graves of British soldiers who had been killed in this part of Africa in two World Wars "far from those green hills, hills of home."

The scenery from the edge of the plateau was spectacular. We drove to the rim of the escarpment and stood on a bluff and looked to the east over rocky valleys and mountain peaks wreathed in cloud. Had Lorraine and Brian really travelled up that tortuous mountain road from Massawa to see us? It looked an exciting ride. Swirls of white mist backed up against the edge of the 6,000' plateau and billowed in white folds over the cliff tops. Below, terraced mountain sides stepped down into the valley.

We asked Mr. Immanuel, "What is grown on the terraces?"

"Cactus, prickly pears," he replied.

We were surprised it was a crop worthy of such extensive building work.

The zoo was small but interesting: Ethiopian lions, a tiger, monkeys, gibbons, wild boar, deer, snakes. Ostriches sprinted over ponderous tortoises in the same caged run. Eagles, hawks and buzzards peered down at us from the high perches and shrieked.

We held hands and wandered between the exhibits, breathing in the cool air and feeling free, free, free. It was our first walk outside in seventeen days.

On returning to the Ministry we were given, not a visa stamped in our passports, but a letter, in Eritrean, which the Immigration Officer told us, would allow us to leave from Baraisole Bay. Then Mr Immanuel took us back to the Khartoum Hotel.

We had to explain to Etienne and a tearful Monique that yes, we had been released, and no, nobody had said when they would be. It was hard for all of us. They retired to their room extremely downcast.

Azib took Peter and I for a drink to celebrate at her City Park open air restaurant. Seated in the small triangular park placed at the junction of two main roads, we rejoiced in our freedom but worried for Monique and Etienne. We were given a whisky and water each and introduced to Azib's staff. It seemed a very successful little enterprise but she told us that Government Officials came around every month for licence fees which varied enormously, depending on who the collecting officer was. She said it was not good policy to argue "just pay up."

We returned to the Khartoum Hotel to pack our clothes. As we packed our bags we felt terrible about leaving our French friends. They didn't come to wish us goodbye.

Rod picked us up and took us to find another hotel. Most were full, but the Ambassador Hotel, opposite the cathedral on the main street, had a room and we booked in and left our cases.

He then took us to his home so we could telephone Rosemary and Noel. He introduced his tall and elegant Masai wife Beatrice and beautiful 16 year old daughter Christina. Beatrice had been a headmistress in a school in Africa when Rod had a teaching post there. They were a very attractive couple. We also found out that Rod had attended the same school: Bluecoat in Sonning, as our son Paul. They had shared the same mathematics master.

His two under-ten sons were much too busy with their game to worry about visitors, until it was suggested we all went out for pizza! Christina, who was usually at school in England, was very interested to meet this peculiar couple, whose friends had kept their telephone in perpetual motion.

Phone lines out of Eritrea are few and difficult to obtain, but we eventually got a line to England. We telephoned Noel and Rosemary and told them of our release and thanked them for their part in it. We were sure the Times article was responsible for our freedom, the day after it was published. Rod had warned us that international calls from Eritrea were difficult and expensive. It was; it cost over 25 pounds for five minutes which of course we refunded to him. He also warned us that we may not be on Saturday's flight, and even if we did manage to book seats on

We walked to the People's Bank where we had been told we could cash travellers' cheques. It looked nothing like a bank at all.

Tuesday, one in four flights out of Asmara was cancelled.

He took us all out to the Expo Hotel for a pizza dinner and then back to his house for coffee. At the Ambassador Hotel we tried to ascend to the third floor in the small lift, but it didn't work. We climbed the stairs to our bedroom - Room 303 immediately opposite the cathedral striking clock. But who cared on this night of nights!

Asmara - Day 19

After breakfast in the Ambassador dining room and a telephone call confirming we would not be on today's plane to Assab, we wandered around Asmara enjoying looking in the shop windows and mingling with the friendly people. The ladies were mostly dressed in white robes but most men were in western trousers and open-necked shirts.

Now we had some local money.

We walked to the People's Bank where we had been told we could cash travellers' cheques. It looked nothing like a bank at all. There were no signs. We walked around to the back of the building and found an open door leading to a staircase alongside a forlorn and dirty lift shaft where an elevator had once taken customers up to the bank. Evidently when the occupying Ethiopians had taken over, they had sold every piece of machinery they could extract including lift cages, cables and motors. We climbed up to the 6th floor overtaking aged ladies and gentlemen slowing ascending, leaning on their walking sticks for a breather. Peter cashed some travellers cheques.

Now we had some local money. We walked until we found a good delicatessen shop and bought Italian wine and cheeses and some oranges for Monique and Etienne and took them round to the Khartoum Hotel. They were not available so we just left the bag of goodies outside their bedroom door. Poor Monique and Etienne! Why hadn't they been released too?

From the Ambassador Hotel we sent a fax off to Basil telling

Azib came in and took us all out to a splendid lunch at El Castello where Princess Anne had eaten on her visit to Eritrea. Azib had reserved a special private room so there was no security problem.

of our release and the circumstances. A message arrived that we may be able to fly to Assab on Tuesday's plane.

Back at The Khartoum a distressed Monique and Etienne came down. They thanked us for our gifts and we sat in the dining room and talked and tried to encourage them. Azib came in and took us all out to a splendid lunch at El Castello where Princess Anne had eaten on her visit to Eritrea. Azib had reserved a special private room so there was no security problem.

We went back to the Ambassador to rest and received many phone calls including one from Brian who said:

"We'll come tomorrow. Please book a room for us at the Khartoum Hotel. We are sure the Forgets would appreciate some moral support."

The Daily Express wanted a 2,000 word article for £600 as soon as possible. The Daily Mail were very pushy and again offered £5,000 if we would forego our agreement to The Express. We said "No" and explained we had already committed ourselves, but agreed to see them in Cairo.

Rod Hicks came round and we were pleased to be able to offer him a beer and chatted for a while. We enjoyed a picnic in our room of fresh bread, cheese and tomato with a bottle of Italian wine, before wandering back to the Khartoum Hotel, to reserve a room for Lorraine and Brian.

There was no TV in our new bedroom, just 'the bells, the bells', donging every count for each hour just outside our bedroom window. It was just like the scene in that marvellous old British film 'Genevieve' where the main characters' romantic night is spoiled by a nearby church clock chiming.

Rosemary's notes.

Saturday 6th April

We go out to buy some double-glazing and a woman buying a conservatory hears us addressed as Mr and Mrs Billing. She asks if we are related to you and expresses her sympathy for your ordeal! Unbelievable. More messages from papers on answer phone trying to find your whereabouts.

CHAPTER TWENTY-THREE

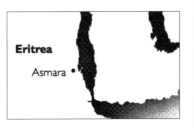

Eritrea

Asmara •

Asmara - Day 20

W e were woken by 'the bells, the bells' of the cathedral clock resonating in our ears. After breakfast I took the bus to Rod Hick's house. He had offered me the use of his computer to type out my article for The Daily Express. Beatrice and Christina had gone to play tennis but their Eritrean maid looked after me. Peter sat in the hotel and, while waiting for Lorraine and Brian to arrive, wrote thank you letters to Basil and the journalists who had covered our story so sympathetically. He took another call from Rebecca Hardy from the Daily Mail who phoned again, very persistently. "Yes," we would meet her at the Cairo Hilton. We would fax them as soon as we arrived in Egypt. "No," we wouldn't talk to any other media people after the present article for the Daily Express.

When I returned to the Ambassador Hotel at 10.30 we decided to amble around this cool town of boulevard cafes with cappuccino coffee and pastries for sale. In the side streets, some houses had Romeo and Juliet type balconies beneath Florentine and Venetian arches. The purple jacaranda and orange flame trees were almost over, but pink and purple bougainvillea cascaded over stone garden walls. The ladies in white robes and men, either robed, or in slacks and sweaters, strolled and mingled. A pleasant and peaceful ambience pervaded. The country seemed full of hope for a better life.

At noon we met Lorraine and Brian and Monique and Etienne at the Khartoum Hotel and sat and chatted. Nobody knew how CLYPEUS and PEEWIT were faring in the 40 knot winds. On the radio Linda had warned all the yachts who were following us to keep well away from the area so nobody had been close enough to see them. We prayed both boats were still floating. Brian brought us all up to date on which yachts had passed through Massawa and who was holed up in the marsas waiting for the strong winds to drop.

When lunch was served to Monique and Etienne we wandered out to find somewhere ethnic for our meal and found a 'private home' restaurant. The two front rooms of the Victorian type house had been converted into a snack bar on one side of the front door and a restaurant on the other.

Probably the snack bar was open in the evenings as well, but by the look of the television in the corner, the ornaments and easy chairs scattered on the marble tiled floor, this was obviously the family room in the evenings. A rotund pinafored house-

wife offered us injerra or curry and rice (they were the only items we understood). We all had the curry but couldn't decide what meat we were eating - probably goat.

Lorraine and I wanted to look around the town and visit the cathedral, but Peter and Brian went back to the Ambassador Hotel to discuss our route up the Red Sea: where we should rendezvous, and where we should stop to pick up water and diesel. The Minister had warned us not to stop in Sudan or Egypt. He said Sudan was about to explode in civil war and tourists were not safe in Egypt. He obviously didn't understand that we couldn't carry enough fuel for over 1,000 miles of motoring without replenishing our tanks. To stray across to the eastern shore to Saudi Arabia was not an option, unless in dire, dire straits.

Lorraine and I climbed the bell tower of the cathedral. Two teenage boys unlocked the door and pointed the way up the steep rickety wooden staircase. Some of the pigeon-poop covered steps had holes drilled through them for the bell ropes to hang down to ground level.

Nobody knew how to ring a carillon of bells any more, but the clock hours pealed automatically. Plump grey birds cooed and fluttered around our heads. The view from the top of the tower was magnificent across the shining plain and we could see Peter and Brian through the open window of our room where they sat chatting, but couldn't attract their attention.

Suddenly there was a clang from downstairs, the dear boys had locked us in. The bells started their chimes for four o'clock. It was deafening. We just cowered with our hands over our ears and thought of Quasimodo. We cautiously hurried down to the foot of the stairs. I beat on the metal door with my fists and shouted and tried not to panic.

Suddenly there was a clang from downstairs, the dear boys had locked us in. The bells started their chimes for four o'clock

Lorraine covered her head while the pigeons fluttered wildly around because of the unusual noise I was making. An elderly gentleman let us out. I was gasping to be free again.

After telling our men what had happened, it was decided a gelato would be a good idea. We walked to a spacious boulevard restaurant with wrought iron and marble topped tables and ordered coffees and ice creams. The ambience was very European.

For a celebration dinner that evening Milanos Italian Restaurant had been recommended as a good place to eat and it was! Their canneloni was out of this world; soft, tasty, meaty, creamy; and the salad with crisp lettuce, black olives, chopped tomatoes and basil was a joy. A bottle of red Italian wine made it the occasion it deserved to be. Back at the Khartoum we finished the evening with coffee and a whisky and an extra bonus: Andrea telephoned to congratulate us on our freedom and confirm that all was well with the family.

Asmara - Day 21

After spending Monday morning with Monique and Etienne, Brian and Lorraine came round to our hotel. We decided to stroll along Asmara's wide boulevards again for a coffee. As we walked along the crowded main street we

The market was exciting with a good and colourful fruit and vegetable display, and never have I seen so many types of pulses and grains for sale.

Lorraine and I shopped and both bought white muslin stoles with gold embroidered ends.

realised somebody was calling "Mr Peter, Mr Peter."

A man rushed towards us waving papers in the air. It was one of our former 'minders'.

"Mr Peter, Mr Peter," he gasped. "Your airline tickets for Tuesday." He thrust them into Peter's hand; beamed, and rushed on out of sight. We were intrigued to know how he had found us in the middle of a crowded city street. Maybe there were spies everywhere?

We immediately checked to make sure they were made out in our correct names. They were.

Relaxing over our cappuccinos, we watched Eritrean gentlemen sipping and discussing the world's business over their tiny cups of coffee - no ladies - no alcohol.

We decided lunch and a cool beer beneath the shade of trees and umbrellas at Azib's 'City Park Al Fresco Restaurant' would be pleasant. But on ordering, heard: "sorry no beer, out of stock." Then we asked for beef burgers. - but, "no meat today!" We began to realise how well we had actually been treated in the Khartoum Hotel in relation to the rest of the country.

Asmara Museum was supposed to be special, but it was closed. The market was exciting with a good and colourful fruit and vegetable display, and never have I seen so many types of pulses and grains for sale. As we wandered along beneath the arched pavement walkways lined with patient donkeys, we looked in at some of the flour mills, their wide dusty doors

open to the street. Ladies in robes and covered heads, were waiting for their grain to be ground. Young women attendants poured the cereal into a hopper on one side of the room, it was sucked through a pipe and delivered into their sack, milled ready for cooking, on the other side.

Young women attendants poured the cereal into a hopper on one side of the room, it was sucked through a pipe and delivered into their sack, milled ready for cooking, on the other side.

Lorraine and I shopped and both bought white muslin stoles with gold embroidered ends. The breeze was constantly blowing and we understood why the local ladies traditional wear included a stole over hair and face when the hot winds blew. For my grandchildren, I bought bracelets woven from giraffe tail hair, and cartoon pictures of Eritrean life painted on leather - I was only just beginning to realise that animal skin was more easily available than paper.

This time we said goodbye to Lorraine and Brian with glee as they boarded the ramshackle bus back to Massawa. "See you in a couple of days, talk to you on the radio tomorrow night," we called. Actually it took another nine days before we caught up with them. However we didn't know that then.

In the evening we had the pleasure of saying thank you to Rod Hicks, Beatrice and Christina by taking them to Milanos for another celebration dinner. They steered us into the "Eritrean Room" decorated to resemble the inside of a Bedouin tent with colourful red and blue rugs and wall hangings, huge embroidered cushions and camel seats. We had the traditional injerra meal with many tasty side dishes and maz to drink - a honeyed wine. It was a very jolly evening.

Rosemary's Notes

Easter Monday.

Telephone rings at 8.30a.m. It is the Daily Express again checking that it is OK to come round and go through albums. We say we don't have any photos and it is a Bank Holiday etc. They finally give up. We try on 5 separate occasions throughout the day to get in touch but you are always on the phone or "outside". Shame we couldn't say goodbye!

Despondently, still worrying how CLYPEUS was faring, we walked on to the British Council where we knew there would be a good library. I researched some history of Eritrea, which in the Bible is referred to as Kush or Cush. The language they speak is Ge'ez.

The country, originally Tigrinya Ertra, is the plateau escarpment up to Ethiopia consisting of the Denakil Alps and includes the Denakil Depression, reputedly the hottest place on earth. The Kobar Sink is 116m below sea level.

The Ethiopian dynasty was founded in the Second Century by Menalik the legendary son of King Solomon and the Queen of Sheba. The Queen is supposed to have rested on her journey and drunk water from a lake near Asmara.

In 1885 the Italians occupied the ports of Assab and Massawa on the Red Sea. A Prince Menelik was crowned King of Kings in 1889. From 1890 - 1941 Eritrea was an Italian colony. Back in the early 1930's, Emperor Haile Selassie 'The Lion of Ethiopia' came to the throne but was deposed in 1974 by a military coup d'etat and the monarchy was abolished.

Isais Aferwarki led the thirty year Eritrean revolution against the Ethiopians and became President. The Civil Service is composed, almost exclusively, of former freedom fighters who started in 1993 without salaries and less than seven pounds a month allowance. Russia and Cuba poured economic help into Ethiopia. Now Mengitsu Haile Mariam has emerged as Head of State.

The Tigri tribe are still the largest ethnic group in Eritrea and many live the same nomadic life as their ancestors. Female circumcision is still practised and I read in the local paper of the Tigri rituals, and in 'The Price of Honour' by Jan Goodwin, of how drastic surgery is still performed under primitive conditions in their tents by mothers and aunts. Coptic Christians in Ethiopia, Egypt and animist tribes in Africa as well as Muslims, undergo the ritual. More than 90 percent of Sudanese women undergo the most severe form of circumcision, known as "pharaonic," or infibulation, at the age of seven or eight.

During this primitive yet major surgery, it is not uncommon for girls, who are held down by female relatives, to die from shock or haemorrhaging. Internal organs may be damaged and walking made difficult for the rest of their lives. Scar tissue obstructs normal married life and giving birth requires more surgery. The tradition of female circumcision in many countries is so strong that circumcised women even in the United States usually request re-infibulation after each delivery.

What can be done to help these poor women? Why must they endure such pain and mental anguish? Perhaps doing military service together will help young men and girls understand each other more and eventually eliminate these terrible practices. It may be one of the few good things that emerge from war.

As we were not going to visit Massawa, I read avidly and learnt that it had been a pleasant resort town which had been devastated during the revolution. A macabre display of the skulls and bones of soldiers rests on ammunition boxes as a war memorial. It was renowned for being the hottest town on earth with an average temperature of 30.2° C. Brian, however, had told us that didn't actually seem all that hot living on the boat in the harbour, but it was only springtime. I was sorry to have missed the spectacular bus descent down the hairpin bends, but later heard, that the day after Brian and Lorraine's return, a bus careered over the edge and three people lost their lives.

The Debr Bizen Monastery sounded fascinating. No women are allowed to enter its gates. A three hour climb leads up to this ancient Coptic Monastery founded by Aburna Philipos in 1361. He is reputed to have said he preferred the roar of lions to the distraction of women's faces. The Ethiopian Coptic Church was founded in 4th Century AD and they worship the Ark of the Covenant.

In the library it was interesting to find out that injerra is made from teff, a cereal grass. An article described it as "a large bitter tasting pancake of unappetising grey appearance with the consistency of damp foam rubber." Yes, I can't improve on that description but it had seemed perfectly OK to us when we were held in the shed on the beach. Just the fact that we were allowed to share the soldiers' food seemed a bonus then.

Now we were tourists and not frightened to take photographs. The hotel staff loved having their photos taken as nobody owned cameras themselves.

Azib asked if we could help to organise that their second son, who was now fifteen, came to England to study. We made enquiries at The British Council, but found there was no point in trying to organise sponsorship or accommodation for him yet, as first he had to be accepted on a definite course in a specified college. We promised to keep in touch and when he has achieved the necessary grades, will do our best.

Asmara - Day 22

We went out for breakfast and just wandered the streets until we found a likely looking cafe. The smell of hot fresh bread rolls and coffee enticed us into The Parma Bar. Lotte, the dark vivacious proprietress, came and introduced herself and sat and talked with us while we ate our breakfast.

After calling at the airline office to see if we are on tomorrow's flight, which they couldn't tell us; we strolled on through the wide tree lined boulevards to The People's Bank again. We needed more Eritrean birr to pay our hotel bill.

At Azib's Park Bar we sat beneath the umbrellas and enjoyed a cold beer, then returned to our room to picnic on cheese, salami, fresh rolls and a bottle of wine. An afternoon nap helped fill the waiting time until our films would be processed.

We ambled up the main boulevard in the shade of the royal palms. The shops had a wide variety of finely knitted sweaters, cashmere, angora, camel hair, both in men and women's wear. I bought some posters of attractive young African girls I thought would appeal to our grand-daughters and would give them an idea of where we were. The helpful assistant rolled and packed them for us and I took them to the post office.

Rod Hicks came and confirmed that we would be on tomorrow's flight to Assab. We spent the evening in the Khartoum Hotel with Monique and Etienne.

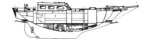

We were up at 6 am to to prepare for our 9.30 flight.

ERITREAN AIRLINES

passenger ticket
& baggage check

L–CH № 35259

ISSUED BY: ERITREAN AIRLINES. P.O. BOX 222 ASMARA - ERITREA

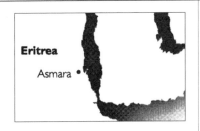

Eritrea

Asmara •

CHAPTER TWENTY-FOUR

Asmara - Day 23

We were up at 6 am to prepare for our 9.30 flight. We wrote our last letters, I went out and bought some hand-worked silver Coptic pendants and chains for our daughter in law and daughter to thank them for all the hassle and trouble they had gone through dealing with the press on our behalf. The Post Office was neat and efficient and the girls received their presents safely.

Mr Immanuel came to shake hands and say goodbye and to introduce our driver who would take us to the airport. We explained that Mr. Hicks had offered to take us.

"Never mind, our driver will follow behind." They obviously wanted to make sure we left Asmara.

At 8.30am Rod and Blaney, his diminutive Eritrean assistant, arrived in their white Land Rover to take us to the airport. We all stood outside the airport for twenty minutes until the doors opened, booked our bag in and then stood around waiting. 9.30 came and went. We were taken for coffee in the airport restaurant. Blaney went for information but came back shaking his head.

"Nobody knows" he said.

At 11 o'clock an announcement was made confirming the cancellation of today's flight.

At 11 o'clock an announcement was made confirming the cancellation of today's flight.

After retrieving our bag, Rod drove us back to the Khartoum Hotel - we decided we preferred it to the Ambassador and we could be with Monique and Etienne. It would give them heart to know that we were still in Asmara, free or not. We lunched with them, but not as lavishly, as we were paying our own bills now.

Dispiritedly we unpacked again in room 12 and re-examined the bullet holes in the shutters.

At the Eritrean Airlines office they told us, "Sorry for the delay - yes there may be a flight on Thursday but we can't be sure of seats for you. We will let you know."
Wednesday came and went.

Asmara - Day 24/25

Our farewell from the Khartoum Hotel on Thursday morning was almost tearful. Azib, Semira, the maids Varroy, Mulu and Gannet, and Monique and Etienne were all pleased with their photographs, but saying goodbye was difficult. Monique and Etienne retired to their room immediately after we had breakfasted together and didn't appear again before we left.

At 8.15 Rod and Blaney came again to pick us up ready for take-off at 9.30am. Once again we booked in our bags and were given embarkation cards. A flight delay was announced until 2.30. Rod took us to his home for coffee. Peter stayed there to mend their Apple Mac computer while I went back to the British Council Library for some more research. At mid-day Rod picked us up and took us to lunch and then to the airport. A flight delay was announced again and we insisted he went back to his office. We would 'phone him if the flight was cancelled.

It took a long time to get into the departure lounge. Firstly, because I hadn't realised I had scissors in the bottom of my haversack. Everything had to be tipped out and examined. Secondly, when we presented our passports to the Immigration Official, of course there were no entry visas. He was about to press a bell when Peter passed across our letter from the Foreign Affairs department. The Officer read it carefully then quickly pushed our passports, and the letter, back to us as though he was afraid it may bite him. We have always wondered what it said, to have such an effect.

We sat with the other friendly passengers and tried to make conversation while we waited in spite of the language difficulties. An announcement interrupted "We regret the delay. The flight for Addis Ababa calling at Assab will take off at 4.30." It did seem we were actually going to take off this time.

Suddenly a call came over the loudspeakers. "Will Mr and Mrs. Billing come to the Security Gate."

"Oh no!" we looked at each other. Were we going to be taken back into custody? As we approached the gate we could recognise three men from Security. We held hands in terror as we walked towards them.

"Who paid your departure tax?" One of them demanded brusquely.

"I did" Peter faltered.

"Well you must not do that. How much was it?"

"26 Birr" he replied.

"The Ministry wish to pay that. Have you the receipts?"

"Yes, here they are." He fumbled for them in his wallet.

"Here is the 26 Birr" (about $US 3.50) "Good day." They turned and left.

Peter pocketed the 26 Birr and we sat down and collected our wits. Next problem - will they let us through without a receipt for departure tax on our tickets? They did.

The flight was uneventful over the bare mountains and desert, down to the white salt-encrusted coast. What an arid mountainous country! At 6.30 when our lone plane landed in Assab's desert airport, there was nobody to meet us. After their 30 years' guerilla war with Ethiopia there is no road or telephone line between Asmara and Assab, the second port in the country, and the Assab officials obviously had not been told that we were coming.

Gradually all passengers and employees departed from the airport building and in desperation we asked a local businessman if we could share the last taxi. He took us to his hotel about twenty miles away, where we booked a room and fortunately found, in the bottom of my purse, the crumpled telephone number of the Naval Commander, Mr. Achmed. We managed to get through to his home and he said he would see us at 10pm. He and Mr Goulliard arrived just after ten and insisted on buying us both another beer.

We sat in the hotel garden, listening to the Red Sea waves crashing on the shore.

The maids Varroy, Mulu and Gannet, were all pleased with their photographs.

"When can we go to CLYPEUS?" Peter asked.

"When would you like to go?" was the reply. They were in no hurry and had no idea of our anguish as to whether our home was still floating and our worry about the month's delay affecting our weather window.

"As soon as possible," we said in unison.

"OK. I will arrange for you to be returned to Baraisole Bay in the morning. But where are Monsieur and Madame Forget? Why have they not returned with you?"

It seemed incredible that they didn't know what was going on.

This 'best hotel' in Assab was well sited on a sandy peninsula, but the facilities left much to be desired. Our $US40 a night room had no hot water, a dribble of a shower and a broken shard of mirror propped behind the taps on the washbasin. However the beds were clean and the air conditioning worked.

Now we were closer to home I started thinking about the practical problems. Would CLYPEUS be infested with cockroaches? Could any mice or rats have got on board with the soldiers? What sort of mess would the month old vegetables be in? How bad will the smell be? Would weevils have developed in the rice, biscuits, flour and pasta? It was a month since the drinking water had been left in this hot climate. What sort of bugs and algae would have grown in it?

Assab - Day 25

I got up early and went for a walk along the sandy beach hoping to find some unusual shells but found nothing significant for my collection. After breakfast Mr. Gouillard drove us to the house by the harbour. Once again we sat down on the couch and were given a glass of tea. Mr. Achmed asked Peter to go through our charts with a naval officer and give him any relating to the Eritrean coast. The Navy obviously didn't have charts themselves. Our charts had not been inspected or even touched!

What had this incident been about? All our route was marked on the charts with dates, times and GPS fixes. If they had really thought we were spies, surely somebody would have checked them? Peter gave them two charts but explained we needed all those to the north as we would be using them ourselves. There was no photo-copying machine in Assab.

While Peter went through the charts, a now smiling Ibraham drove me to the market to shop for meat, bread, vegetables and fruit for our voyage. All there was to buy in the dusty, meagre market were a few potatoes, tomatoes, chillies, onions and forlorn pale cabbages. Dispirited donkeys with bowed heads stood between the shafts of flat wooden carts with small parcels of vegetables laid out on them. Sacks of pulses were displayed, but few people were around to buy. There was no fruit, apart from a few black spotted bananas. What did these people live on?

Ibraham drove me around the town to try and find some fruit, and I wanted candy for the school children at Baraisole. I thought the soldiers would appreciate an orange each too. We couldn't buy fruit but I bought some lollipops. A bakery provided lovely crusty bread and some fresh eggs. But there was no butter, milk or cheese to be bought. Fortunately, I had tinned butter on board.

After another glass of shahi and saying goodbye to Mr Achmed, at 10.30 we left for Baraisole Bay. At last! Hooray! We were so excited to be going back to our home. Peter and I sat in the cab of the Toyota with a competent young driver in a pale blue shirt who introduced himself as David. A mature man in a similar blue shirt stood in the back looking over the cab. Soldiers loaded bags of flour and grain on to the truck then climbed up and sat on the sacks with their guns resting across their legs. We passed the desolate airport with the derelict MIG fighters still lined up against the perimeter. Abandoned rusting tanks and armoured cars glinted between the sand hills. The desert shimmered ahead and the mountains rose up into the cobalt sky on our left. We left the asphalt behind and bumped over the stony track.

As we drove further from civilisation we chased a herd of wild camels who didn't seem to have the sense to gallop off the edges of the path.

As we drove further from civilisation, we chased a herd of wild camels who didn't seem to have the sense to gallop off the edges of the path. Peter and I discussed how quickly we could get going. It would probably take time to stow all our gear and check things out but we should be able to pull up the anchor and go first thing tomorrow morning. We were full of hope and enthusiasm.

When we arrived at the roadhouse shack made of cardboard and straw, David stopped the truck and we all went for a Coca Cola, which we were advised to drink from the bottle and not ask for a glass. Robed and turbaned camel and goat herders sat around and eyed us curiously. Two well built pretty girls served us, but there was no banter or chat between the military and the customers. Nobody spoke until a young man came and introduced himself to Peter and I, and asked if we were English. When we said "Yes", he continued; "Do you know the song 'We are sailing'?"

"Yes. It is one of our our favourites."

"Good, I shall sing it for you," and he did.

"We are sailing, we are sailing, far away, across the sea,
We are sailing, stormy water, to be near you, to be free".

What a coincidence, if it happened in a play or novel, it would seem contrived. He went on through all three verses in good English. We clapped when he had finished.

He was in full flow now and said "I teach it to my girlfriend so that she will sing it and remember me. I also know 'Don't it make your brown eyes blue.'

There was obviously no stopping him.

Peter took a quick photo of our songbird and his friend standing beside me outside the shack.

"Good, that is another favourite of ours. Is your teacher Ursula Head?" Rod had told us how this English teacher was doing such a great job teaching English and giving confidence to teenage Eritreans in Assab.

"Yes, my teacher is Miss Ursula. She teaches us good songs and we learn English from songs." He closed his eyes and

launched into a very creditable performance of 'Don't it make your brown eyes blue.'

"May I take photographs?" I asked the senior man who had been standing in the back of our truck.

"OK." he said "We go now." and started walking towards the Toyota. Peter took a quick photo of our songbird and his friends standing beside me outside the shack.

On and on we bumped past the village and the wells, the donkeys were still pulling the wooden shafts around in a never ending circle. We began to recognise the salt flats. The pink flamingoes were still standing with their heads beneath the water. As we climbed the brow of the last hill we peered into the haze of the bay. Was she there? Was she still floating?

Yes!!

CLYPEUS was still laying to her anchors, her golden masts glistening in the sun as she pitched in the rough water.

Thank you God. We felt like weeping with gratitude.

When the Toyota stopped beside the army hut, the soldiers crowded round. We received handshakes and a great welcome. The senior man who had stood up on the truck for all three hours was covered in sand. He sat on a camp bed and the soldiers brought him bowls of water. He poured the jugs of water over his head to try and de-sand himself.

Semir was pleased to see us. Mahamir and all the same soldiers were still there but they were expecting to move out the following day.

I found Wurku and she gave me seven shoulder thumps, I felt honoured as she rushed off to make a coffee ceremony. I saw her collecting the tin brazier and jabena, but I also saw Mahamir go across and obviously tell her there wasn't time. She had to provide lunch for us all.

Guess what it was? Injerra and foul and a tall glass of shahi with shukra.

The military launch wasn't to be seen, but eventually a fishing boat with an outboard motor came to take us out. Our senior naval man took the helm. I must admit I didn't have much faith in him and was very nervous with all our charts and cameras being piled into the low-sided smelly fishing boat in the surf. However, he knew what he was doing and managed to get us to CLYPEUS, soaking wet from the spray, but with only a little water in the bilges and just wet vegetables and soggy bread.

Peter asked to circle PEEWIT so that we could see her condition. She seemed OK. One of her dodgers was splitting, but the soldiers had put the inflatable dinghy on deck and all seemed well. She was floating well above her water line.

Superficially CLYPEUS seemed fine. Nobody had been inside

Peter asked to circle PEEWIT so that we could see her condition. She seemed OK.

her and as we went below to check her out, the soldiers started raising the extra anchor they had laid.

The naval officer followed us down into the cabin. He asked if everything was OK and would Peter please write a report stating this fact. As Peter wrote a report, I scribbled a letter and wrote a cheque to Noel to help pay for all the telephone calls they must have made. I gave the sealed letter to the officer with enough birr for the stamp. (He seemed to understand what I was saying but the letter never arrived.) As soon as Peter gave his report the officer rose to depart, he was evidently hoping to get back to Assab that day.

"One moment" Peter said, "I wish to make sure the engine works." It started first turn of the key.

"One more moment" I said, " I wish to make sure our water is still drinkable." I pumped a glass of water and examined it. Nothing big was floating around in it, and it tasted OK. "No problem. Thank you."

Everybody got off our boat except us. We waved goodbye with an arm around each other's waist.

Home at last. Our sanctuary! We sat together and said a silent prayer of thanksgiving.

When we walked around the deck slowly looking for any problems we saw that one of the stainless steel lifelines had been broken and superficially repaired. One stanchion was broken and more were bent, there were some gouges out of the hull, but nothing serious, nothing that a few hours of tender loving care couldn't put right.

All the snorkelling equipment was still in the unlocked lockers, nothing had been taken or spoilt. We felt so lucky. The Eritreans are honorable people. Sand was everywhere, especially in the folds of the uncovered mainsail.

Inspecting the sack of potatoes on the floor of the forward cabin I found they were crawling with maggots.

"Quick, quick, Peter, help me take this sack outside, it's alive."

I turned the stinking potatoes out on deck and recovered a few which were still intact. Then I tipped the rest over the side, they bobbed away free in the wind and waves.

When I returned to the forward cabin to sweep up any bits, there were cocoons embedded in the carpet.

Peter had the saloon floor up and was inspecting the batteries and engine.

"Quick, let me pass with this bug ridden carpet." I tiptoed over the engine and out into the cockpit.

All the fresh vegetables and fruit we had bought in Aden a month ago had to be thrown away, only the onions had semi-survived. When the outer skins were peeled off, a slimy layer covered the core of the onions. Once that was removed the centres were OK, after being laid in the sun to dry out.

Then I looked in the flour and rice canisters. Ugh! some were crawling with weevils. The expensive packet of dates was alive with grubs, but Peter's 5 kilo chunk of dates was still fine. The other two tanks of drinking water seemed to still be sweet and clear. That was a blessing! I added some extra Chlorox into the two main tanks, just to make sure. We looked carefully for cockroaches but couldn't see any.

At 6pm we turned on the radio for the net. What a joy! Many yachts called us and congratulated us on being back aboard. It was so good to hear them all. MARA, GREEN DOLPHIN, KULAROO, DE LA MER, WIRRAWAY, SHADY LADY, THISTLEDOWN, STAR, LONE RIVAL. MARA agreed to buy us some vegetables and fruit in Massawa and bring them to us when we met up.

We had a scotch to drink, then I prepared dinner of egg and chips (from bits of salvaged potato) and tomato salad.

We sank gratefully into bed in our own dear home. Still emotionally exhausted, not ready for passion but full of love and comfort for each other and hope for the future. The hot wind still whistled and moaned from the south. Tomorrow we would be on our way again.

I discreetly took some photographs of PEEWIT and the sun setting over the mountains. We plotted our course for Marsa Dudo. Peter worked out the waypoints and punched them into the GPS.

CHAPTER TWENTY-FIVE

Eritrea
Baraisole Bay •

Homeward bound - Saturday 13th April.

We were surprised that we didn't want to get up. We didn't want to do anything. We were frightened of the Red Sea. The wind was still howling. CLYPEUS was still pitching in this relatively sheltered anchorage. What would it be like out there, with no protection?

"We must get up and we must go," I said.

"No, not yet, let's clear off all this sand and grit and make sure everything is OK first." Peter procrastinated as usual.

During the day while we cleaned up he was very touchy, I expect I was too. We grouched and grumbled at each other. The wind stayed at 25-30 knots from the south and we just didn't feel strong enough to launch ourselves into it. What had happened to us? Where had our togetherness gone now that we were back where we wanted to be?

In the afternoon we rested and listened to Beethoven's Violin Concerto in D and tried to relax and restore our equilibriums. For some reason my shoulder ached abominably. I discreetly took some photographs of PEEWIT and the sun setting over the mountains. We plotted our course for Marsa Dudo. Peter worked out the waypoints and punched them into the GPS.

"We will see how we feel tomorrow," he said.

"But I thought we wanted to get away as soon as..." I let it go, we were obviously not psychologically ready to face the Red Sea wind and waves. Perhaps we did need 36 hours to lick our mental wounds.

Peter won our game of Scrabble and we went to bed early. The wind appeared to be dying from the south.

I awoke at 4am, just as it was getting light. The sea was calm. There was no wind.

"OK. it's time to go," I whispered to Peter to wake him up. He came out and had a look.

"Come on. Come on. Let's go." I encouraged. "It's calm enough now at least to get out of the bay and between the islands."

"No, let's have breakfast first."

"No, it will be blowing again then. Come on. We've got to go sometime and it won't get better than now."

"Oh alright!" I turned the engine on with my left hand, my right arm hurt too much. Reluctantly Peter went forward to pull up the anchors.

I motored slowly away from the shore as he secured them. Gradually a breeze started from the NE - right on the nose. There was still a one metre swell from the south.

On the radio, Brian told us that he had phoned Rod Hicks to tell him that we were back on CLYPEUS and had thanked him for us. There was still no news of Monique and Etienne's release.

At lunchtime we anchored, at Marsa Dudo and I swam down to clean the propellor and wind vane rudder. Both were well encrusted with barnacles and weed, but the water was warm and clear although I was pretty apprehensive. I knew nothing of these waters and hadn't swum since Al Mukalla six weeks ago. Were there sharks or stinging jelly-fish? We set off again, but after an hour, a heavy low grey cloud was approaching from the north. Was it strong winds? Was it a dust storm? We didn't know what to expect and decided to turn back and hide behind Dudo Island again. Although we had entered the Red Sea over a month ago we only actually had four days sailing experience in it, and hadn't heard the conditions that the yachts ahead had faced.

We anchored in the channel between the island and the mainland, fearful that the soldiers may come again, but Oh! so tired. Tiredness won and we slept.

Monday 15th April

The following is a page extracted from my journal to show the difference in our characters, and how it only took two day's sailing for us to forget our joy at being at sea again. Being isolated on a boat gives you the opportunity to learn far more than just seamanship. We get to know intimately our good points and our bad, and conflicts occur with devastating ease. People think, and we like to imagine it to be so too, that just because the two of you are alone in a beautiful place you will be happy.

"Awake at 7.30, the wind was NW 5-10 almost on the nose. Will we actually make any headway to the NNW on 320° our desired course? What to do? We decide to up-anchor and motor-sail away from the island into the small but steep waves.

Peter notices that the engine cooling water was not

coming through, so we stop the motor and sail NE at 4 knots over a sparkling sea while he works on it.

I noted: CLYPEUS is going well - not exactly where we want to go but we are free to decide.

This is a typical argument I wrote down because we got so het up over making a practical decision.

P. (grumbling) "I suppose we will carry on tacking hither and thither like the Flying Dutchman."

S. (brightly) "At least we are going a bit north and it's a lovely day."

P. "We're only making, at best, 070° (almost E)."

S. "So let's tack then, we should be able to make our original course."

P. "Not yet, we can't tack, I don't know the reason for 070°. Could be the wind has dropped, or the current is against us."

S. "It will only take two minutes and little effort to tack and see."

P. "Alright, alright, if you insist. Let's tack."

S. "No, I don't necessarily want to tack, let's just talk it through."

We tacked.

P. (despairing) "I'm going to lie down."

Consequence: Before lying down, Peter checked the GPS and found we were now making 5 knots on 290° NW (only 30° from our required course instead of 110° from our required course) He had the grace to tell me!
Our life had returned to our constant problem caused by my super-optimism and Peter's cautious pessimism. While I am well, it works, but if I am ill or low, we just submerge into misery together. At least, that is what I used to think, but Peter had shown such courage and optimism while we were held captive. Is that how he really is? Is his constant pessimism just a show, in case somebody might think he was

actually happy. (Happiness was something his parents were reluctant to show, if ever) And is my super-optimism just a reflection to counteract his pessimism? Was our joint support and helpfulness to each other during this last stressful month our true selves? Perhaps we could learn something from our experience?

When he awoke, Peter sorted out the cooling system, by replacing the rubber impellor in the water pump, and we motored over a calm sea all the moonless night and all next day.

We raised the mainsail in the afternoon and caught a puff of wind. We also caught a remora sucker fish, which I cleaned and cooked then threw away! The skin is so tough and who knows what he had been eating if he had been attached to our hull! We caught three small tuna and had battered fish chunks and chips for dinner. The rest I boiled for a minute and put in the cooler to have in tomorrow's lunch-time noodles.

I read 'The Curve of Time', a fascinating story by a Canadian widow who took her children for holidays on her cabin cruiser around bays and inlets north of Vancouver. It made me thank my lucky stars I still had a husband to argue with! I also spent four hours writing about our Eritrean experience on the Toshiba laptop.

Where had the wind gone? We continued motoring all the following day and passed between Shumma Island and Massawa at dawn. We didn't seem to be going fast enough. Something seemed to be wrong. After considering all the possibilities Peter decided there must be something caught around the propellor.

"Please will you swim down and see."

No problem, I put on a tee shirt and kitchen gloves and dived down into the clear warm sea. No, nothing appeared to be fouling the prop or rudder. But there were jellyfish around which stung me. I hurriedly climbed back on board and took two Piriton anti-histamine tablets and bathed the stings in vinegar. There were no after effects.

Peter decided that cleaning the engine air filter may help our progress. The sun beamed down on a calm sea and a hot breeze swept the decks. We sailed on in ideal conditions. While Peter cleaned the air filter, I sewed the dodger hood that had suffered from the winds in Baraisole Bay. When he came up on watch I went below to make a "thank you card for MARA" ready for our rendezvous in the evening at Sheikh El Abu Reef, 30 miles north of Massawa.

It was difficult to put our thanks into words, but I tried:

> Thank you both
> FOR your courage in staying near us
> FOR the cost in time and money
> FOR your support and friendship in a time
> of fear and apprehension.
> It was an enormous comfort to know you were
> near and waiting for us.

> "But if the while we think on thee, dear friends
> All losses are restored and sorrow ends."

> *(Shakespeare sonnet)*

Then I tried to un-emotionalise it with cartoons of the 'FREE CLYPEUS' tee shirt they had given us, the books, the chocolate bars, the writing paper, and newspaper headlines of "BRITISH COUPLE HELD AS SPIES" etc. (I also put a $US100 bill to help with the expenses they must have incurred, but it was immediately returned.)

At 6.00pm on April 17th as we were approaching our rendezvous we could see MARA'S yellow hulls ahead. We were overjoyed to see them. As soon as the anchor was down we rowed over and enjoyed an emotional reunion. But Lorraine wasn't well, she had been suffering with an upset tummy for a week and couldn't eat or keep anything down. In the circumstances, we didn't stay long after agreeing on an early start.

18th April

At 0600, MARA'S anchor chain being laid on deck woke us up. By 6.15 we were underway too. We motor-sailed most of the day (Peter appeared to have cured the sluggishness problem by cleaning the air filter). I made bread. Brian caught a fine Spanish Mackerel and manoeuvred alongside to pass it across. We passed them some cheese. Lorraine was no better.

The night seemed very long. We were frightened to sail within ten miles of the coast because we were so near the Eritrean and Sudanese border which we had been warned to avoid. At 6am there were only 39 miles to go to the next recommended anchorage, Khor Narawat.

We tacked back and forth, always more than ten miles from the land, all that day and all the next night and finally arrived at Khor Narawat at 7am on 20th April in time to see

MARA disappear over the horizon ahead. (It had taken 25 hours of tacking to make the 39 miles). Peter decided we must stop here so that he could change the engine oil. He said we couldn't afford to take any chances as we had already motored way over the hours recommended between oil changes. He also thought the engine was vibrating excessively and the mountings needed tightening.

On the ham radio, we heard that Monique and Etienne had been released and the story was that the French Government had offered to fly them home for a week's rest and recuperation after they had brought PEEWIT from Baraisole Bay to Massawa Harbour.

Hooray! Now we could get on with our voyage without feeling guilty. We were out of Eritrea and they were on their way back to PEEWIT.

Peter suggested I went for a swim while he worked, and for an hour I enjoyed snorkelling in the sheltered bay. There was a profusion of seashells and birds. For the first time, the coral was covered in seaweed. Was this something to do with getting to a higher latitude? The terns and sea birds rose shrieking as I happily walked along the lonely shore.

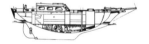

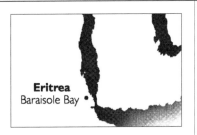

Eritrea
Baraisole Bay •

CHAPTER TWENTY-SIX

Saturday 20th April.

Now all six of us were free and homeward bound; all we had to do was get the hell out of the Red Sea! As soon as Peter was ready, we motor sailed on and reached the shelter of Raz Azis, anchored, and were in bed at 7.30pm. The nagging ache in my shoulder was worse.

At midnight we continued north through clear seas so that we could be at the entrance to the winding Subuk Channel to catch up with Mara before they left. Rounding the headland at 8.00 am we saw Mara leave Long Island about 5 miles ahead.

Acknowledging each other on the VHF, we followed them through the shallow tortuous channel's confusing beacons and gradually caught them up. It was good to be in a calm sheltered waterway where it didn't matter which way or how strongly the wind blew.

I put my arm in a sling to try and reduce the shoulder pain and took some Paracetamol. Peter brushed and plaited my hair for me. I didn't know what was wrong with my shoulder - except that it hurt.

Lorraine cooked us a delicious dinner that evening and although she didn't eat much we had a fun game of Boggle. Suakin, our only stop in Sudan, was only 16 miles ahead.

However, next day when we tried to motor sail there, we had to tack through short steep seas between the coral reefs. We actually sailed 27 miles before we anchored along-side the dramatic outline of the ruined city of Suakin. The sun was setting, giving the white coral ruins

We anchored alongside the dramatic outline of the ruined city of Suakin.

a crimson glow. Deep purple shadows lengthened between the columns and beneath arches and crumbling towers.

We were worried about our reception by the Sudanese officials. Would they accept our letter from the Eritrean Authorities? We didn't have the normal booking-out-of-Eritrea paperwork. In the dazzling white morning sunlight we surveyed the shore line. We couldn't see any people in the ruins which were all that was left of this city that had been an open slave trading city until the end of World War II. On the other side of the harbour people walked in the brown dust between little round mud brick houses. A large ferry came in with pilgrims on their way home from Mecca. By the size of their suitcases, parcels and packets they had bought a great deal there.

A launch came alongside and Mohammed, the Agent, introduced himself. He returned with the Customs and Immigration officials at 10am. They knew all about us from the other yachts and were charming and sympathetic.

The water arrived in a large metal cylinder on a cart drawn by a donkey.

"Could not happen in Sudan" they said, and did their best to make us feel welcome as they extracted $US12 each for shore passes and $US17 harbour fees. Mohammed's fee was $US20, but it would have been very difficult, if not impossible, without him. He told us we must not be ashore after dark and not travel anywhere on our own. He arranged to accompany us into Port Sudan the following morning.

Arrangements were made for diesel and water to be delivered to the causeway. The water arrived in a large metal cylinder on a cart drawn by a donkey. The man assured us that it was OK to drink, but we had our doubts. The diesel was delivered in a 200 litre drum which Peter had to siphon into plastic jerry jugs and then carry to the dinghy, then ferry out to the boat and filter as he poured it into the deck diesel filler pipes. It was exhausting for him.

Lorraine and I made for the market. and as we stepped ashore ten year old Taj introduced himself.

"You going to market?"

"Yes"

"I help you, I get you good price. Many friends in yachts."

We had heard of this little dark tousled hair "Mr Fixit" from other yachts but were still not prepared for his command of the situation. Barefooted in his tee shirt and jeans he led us to the market, chatting all the while. We looked at the produce on the stalls.

"No, you cannot buy tomatoes from that man. He does not give you a good price." Taj would wave a disdainful hand to the offending trader. "This man OK. How many you want?"

Actually it didn't always work in our favour. I wanted to buy a melon, but we never did find one at a price to suit Taj. He strode along in front of us, introducing us to shopkeepers and recommending the best bread, the price, the best

We had heard of this little dark tousled hair "Mr Fixit" from other yachts but were still not prepared for his command of the situation.

courgettes and eggplants. The market was better than Assab and much more picturesque. Camels were parked, lying down, in the middle of the market square. Tribesmen in traditional robes and turbans hunkered down with their few vegetables for sale spread on a mat before them.

Beside a shop which sold camel muzzles, saddles, carpet saddle-bags and other camel accoutrements, I saw three shallow baskets on the ground, one filled with old plastic bottles, another with glass bottles and another with used jars and containers.

"That's good, re-cycling," I said to Lorraine. But actually they were for sale - treasured kitchen containers to keep ants and insects out of food and drink!

Back on board when I went down into our cabin to stow the vegetables, strong diesel fumes rose to hit me between the eyes. The fuel tanks had been filled too full and diesel had leaked out into the food cupboards. Fortunately all the stores were in plastic containers so nothing was spoilt, but the smell!

Fortunately SAMARANG invited us on board in the evening for rum punches while we all waited for Australian ROUSEABOUT to let us know how far away she was. Their engine had failed 40 miles out near Talla Talla Islands so they were sailing in and would need help coming up the channel to Suakin. When they called on the VHF SAMARANG took their powerful dinghy out to tow them in. They were greeted with cheers and waves before they crashed out, exhausted, in no condition to party with us.

In the morning, as the local bus progressed to Port Sudan it gradually filled with all shapes and sizes of Sudanese. Fine looking nomadic tribesmen, wearing white djellabas with fair curly hair and light skins, stopped the bus by holding out their wooden shepherds' crooks. Two young tribeswomen in Rashid costume, carrying their babies, climbed in. Only their forehead, eyes and hands showed beneath their brightly embroidered veils, blouses and skirts. Were those deep furrows between their brows a sign of the pain they endured? Although we tried to make contact by smiling they were very shy and didn't wish to communicate.

Trundling along the road through the scrub we noticed grey rectangular Bedouin tents, dotting the coastal plain, their flaps held up on sticks and open to the south. Fawn rugs, with black and cream stripes, lay on the tent roofs and bushes airing in the sun. Camels and goats cropped the low grey scrub tended by wild haired girls in colourful clothes.

Once in the town we had to stay near Mohammed at first. Then as he had business to do, he told us we would be OK as long as we kept together. He would meet us in one hour at the Palace Hotel for lunch. The four of us should be perfectly safe in the market on our own.

Our first stop was to telephone home. I phoned Sheila and asked her to let the family know we were now out of Eritrea. Her unenthusiastic response made me feel even more guilty for the trouble we had caused everyone. Oh dear! How selfish we were to have unintentionally put our family through such trauma.

Port Sudan market was fantastic. A tremendous variety of good fresh vegetables and pulses were on display. Ladies sat patting high pyramids of peanut butter. They sold it by the spoonful into little plastic bags. It was cheap and tasty. Small boys crowded round trying to sell us black plastic shopping bags. They shouted "how are you?" at us. The stall holders and shoppers were very friendly, most saying "good morning, how are you?" I spoke to some tall Nubian gentlewomen in their red and orange robes. How gracious and charming they seemed.

When we returned to Suakin Harbour, a small French yacht had come in and anchored. We stopped by to see if they needed anything. The first thing they did was to pass us some fillets of fresh fish they had caught during the afternoon. They looked thin and weary and told us that they had been held at gunpoint in Assab harbour for eleven days with an

Port Sudan market was fantastic. A tremendous variety of good fresh vegetables and pulses.

The tailors' street

armed guard sitting on deck all the time. They had not been allowed off their boat, the soldiers had brought them food. Now they were just going to have one night's rest, shop for some food, and then get out of the Red Sea as fast as they possibly could. It was interesting to realise that sailing into Assab to book in would not necessarily have helped us. Everyone who stopped was suspect.

I made up some gifts for Taj and his little brother Gouray:- some flour and sugar, plastic plates, knives and spoons. They had told us that their mother lived in Massawa, but they had a father who lived with them amongst the ruins on Suakin Island, the only people actually who lived in the old town.

Lorraine, who was feeling a bit better, had some baby clothes on board as universally acceptable gifts and I had per-fumed soap and towels. We couldn't imagine anywhere that ladies would appreciate our little gifts more than here, so we walked into town looking for the hospital, hoping to donate them to the mother and children's ward. The hospital concierge obviously hadn't got a clue what we were trying to say, and in the end just let us in with a vague wave of his hand. Walking between the separate stone one-storey wards we saw no uniformed nurses, maids or porters, but waved to haggard men lying on mattresses on black metal bedsteads. The doors to the wards were wide open exposing the patients to sand, dust and mosquitoes.

We followed the sound of a baby crying and found a ward with two young women; one nursing a tiny bundle and the other holding a sick and fretful baby. We looked for nurses and found them sitting on the floor sharing injerra and foul. One tall nurse got up, wiping her hands on her skirt as we tried to explain that we wished to donate some baby clothes and mothers' needs. At last she understood and took us to the two mothers. They were so pleased with the little gifts it was pitiful.

Peter came into town in the afternoon to help carry back potatoes at 7c a pound, and onions 7c a pound, okra 50c a pound, lovely oranges 25c each. Apples were a $1.25 each - not for us, and we were suprised there was anybody in the town rich enough to buy them. Walking back to the causeway a young man introduced himself as Awad and said that he was a nurse at the hospital.

"Thank you for the clothes for the children," he bowed. "I am friends with many people from yachts for many years. I help you shop, go to Port Sudan. You ask. I help." We had to explain that we had already visited Port Sudan and would be leaving in the morning.

A crowd of men danced up the street in white djellabas and colourful turbans with long swords attached to their waists. They were thronging around a young man, obviously a bride-groom. A bus load of ladies dressed in single hued robes of orange, blue, and yellow, singing their heads off, followed behind. "Come to the wedding party tonight." Awad invited.

"Unfortunately, we leave at dawn tomorrow."

"But tonight, tonight," he said, "the full moon. There is a wedding and dancing all night in the square in the ruins of old Suakin. You must come."

"No, we cannot come ashore. It is not allowed." It was a shame. I would have loved to see traditional dancing in these

I spoke to some tall Nubian gentle-women in their red and orange robes.

ancient ruins in the moonlight. Usually I would have risked attending but now, no way were we going to break the rules and perhaps get into trouble again.

Taj and Gouray had invited us to their home (a hut made from old wood recovered from the ruins) for traditional coffee. When our eyes adjusted to the dark interior we saw they had carefully tidied up and made their beds which we sat on. A little brazier of charcoal was glowing and Taj followed the same procedure as Worku had done in Eritrea. He formally poured from the jabena, and Gouray handed round the little cups of coffee and made polite conversation. We were very impressed with their courtesy and manners. Their elderly father came in and introduced himself and did a little trick with his walking stick for our amusement.

I showed them a photograph of our Australian friends on TIMSHELL who had come up the Red Sea in 1994.

"Our friends, our friends," they cried and showed us a thick blanket. "They give this blanket to my father. Now he is warm at night."

It was good to know that Wendy and Geoff's gift was so appreciated.

Next morning we left in a rosy dawn and I have a never-to-be-forgotten picture in my mind of a white turbaned fisherman. He was flinging his circular net from his little canoe, against the backdrop of the white ruined city, while flamingoes flew overhead across the silver pink sky.

That night we anchored behind Gwiyai Reef where the cautioning metal remains of a wreck were balanced on the coral.

At 5.30 next morning we left for Marsa Fijab which, we had been told, was the loveliest anchorage along the west coast of the Red Sea. When we arrived at midday and anchored within the lagoon, we agreed. The sea hues were stunning, from the clear water lapping the white sand beach, through aquamarine over sand and coral, to turquoise then to deep, deep blue in the channels. So many beautiful shades of blues and yellows. Many sea birds and waders were pecking into the sand flats. Camels wandered, cropping the grass above the tide line. I rowed ashore to try and photograph them, but they watched my movements and as soon as I was close, galloped out of range for my little Minolta camera.

Two dive boats arrived from Port Sudan, flying German and Italian flags. Groups went off in high powered inflatables to snorkel and dive over the reefs.

I had invited Lorraine and Brian for dinner, but only he came, Lorraine was still not feeling well enough.

Sunday 28th April.

Once again an early start. We were up by 04.45 and motored and motor sailed in light NW winds that strengthened to strong NE by midday.

We anchored in the lee of three sandy islands at 3pm and went ashore. Three untidy osprey nests rested on the tip of the one metre high sand hills. The windward beach was covered with small transparent and mauve jelly fish. Lorraine came ashore but was so weak from her over-two-weeks of tummy upset that she couldn't walk far and was too tired to even sit up and talk. It was very worrying. My shoulder still hurt. Were we falling apart now that the stress was over? We were all in bed by 7.30 pm. Brian had a special bomb of a pill he was going to give Lorraine.

I awoke before dawn and sat in the cockpit listening to the noises coming from the little islands as the sleepy birds awoke - croaking, cooing, cawing, squeaking and a frumpling of feathers. Both boats left at 5 am and motored over a flat sea in a dead calm all that day and night and all the following day and night.

I read 'The Mists of Avalon' and wrote during the lazy time on watch, while the engine and autopilot did all the work. A lazy time in the hot sun was obviously what my shoulder needed and I realised it wasn't hurting anymore.

On Wednesday May 1st it was still absolutely calm. Lorraine was feeling much better and had started eating again. We were passing the most beautiful reefs with lagoons behind them. Please could we stop for just one quick snorkel? The water looked so tempting.

Brian and Peter were reluctant to stop for anything and wanted to make the most of the calm weather to get as far north and out of the Red Sea just as quickly as they could.

OK, it was decided we would stop for just half an hour. But, we couldn't find anywhere to anchor. Just a few yards from the shore the reef dropped off into deep water of over 100'. We tried four or five places and in the end decided to launch our Avon dinghy so that Lorraine and I could row into the shallow lagoon while MARA and CLYPEUS just drifted off the beach.

It was perfect snorkelling over white sand between varied lumps of corals - so many colourful fish. We indulged our-selves for half an hour, then had a walk over the sandy spit before rowing back to our dear husbands. We were very grateful for the respite. At four o'clock we were on our way again. I washed my hair in buckets of sea water as usual, and after applying a good conditioner rinsed it in a couple of pints of fresh water The wind blew it dry in a matter of minutes - the wind was as hot as an electric hair dryer.

During that night we were sliding through the mist as though on an oil slick. A distorted moon peeped from behind high silver cloud and lit up a ghostly island. It was Zabargrad where emeralds and topaz were mined for the Pharaohs. It rose out of the sea like a mist-shrouded Avalon. We didn't stop as the sea was too deep to anchor, and motored on into the afternoon. As we approached Safaga Harbour we were overtaken by the P&O cruise liner MARCO POLO out of Nassau.

It took a long time to make our way into our first port in Egypt and we didn't manage to anchor until 5am off Safaga Island and took a quick nap. At 8am we were up again to approach the jetty and book in. Karen and Bill of KULAROO and Linda and Don of GREEN DOLPHIN were waiting to greet us. They were only ten days ahead of us having had to shelter for many days from strong winds. What a great welcome. They showed us where to go for Customs and Immigration. The lofty hall was full of passengers who had just come back from Mecca. They were trying to push through Customs with large parcels and packets, trunks and cases - they must go to Mecca for much more than prayer. One chap was loading his cases and boxes onto an obviously new wheelbarrow - part of his purchases?

Our Egyptian visas, issued in Aden, which seemed a lifetime ago, were accepted without comment and we motored carefully through the coral pass to the yacht anchorage off Hotel Paradiso. There, local officials came to check our passports and visas again. However they were all friendly and smiley.

We had a celebration party dinner at the Lotus Bay Hotel that night. At last we four couples were all together again. Don made an amusing speech and then presented Peter and me with tee shirts that Linda had made for us with '007' and '0071/2'; Peter Bond and Mrs Moneypenny written on them in glitter.

Next day we all bussed into Safaga to the Police Station as we had to 'register'. All eight of us were given the run around for two and a half hours before we actually were 'registered' and then asked to return at 6pm to have the papers stamped as the official stamp was locked up in the safe and the officer with the key was off duty!

We had dinner together in a restaurant opposite the Police Station and eventually regained our officially stamped papers at 8pm. However, we all enjoyed our day together and planned to meet up again at the Suez Yacht Club.

Egpyt
Safaga Island •

CHAPTER TWENTY-SEVEN

Sunday 5th May

KULAROO and GREEN DOLPHIN sailed on to meet visitors in Cairo. Lorraine, Brian and ourselves caught a bus to Luxor. For hours we passed through an amazing terrain of stark grey cliffs and boulders, stony hills and sand, with nothing growing at all. Suddenly we dropped down into the valley of the Nile and verdant fields of waving corn greeted us. Brian had telephoned ahead from Safaga to book us into the Atlas Hotel in Luxor. At the bus terminal, 14 year old Mohammed introduced himself and took us by colourful traditional horse and buggy to the Atlas Hotel.

The hotel offered various tours and sight seeing trips. They assured us that tourists were safe at the moment. The terrorist bombs had scared most tourists away and we would have no crowds at the ancient sites. We decided to visit the Valley of Kings by donkey, rather than air conditioned bus. By telephone we also booked a taxi to take us to the Son et Lumiere show at the Karnak Temple that night, but he didn't show up, and by the time we eventually found our way there it was half over. We caught a bus back into town and wandered through streets and pavement cafes which were still busy at 10pm.

As we breakfasted on rolls, cheese, jam and tea at 4.30am. we met our guide Mohammed Ali who was going to take us on donkeys to the Valley of Kings and Valley of Queens, the Workmen's tombs and Ramses III Temple. We followed his robed, turbanned and

At the bus terminal, 14 year old Mohammed introduced himself and took us by colourful traditional horse and buggy to the Atlas Hotel.

Mounting up was a good laugh, the donkeys were so small and Lorraine, Brian and Peter are all over 6ft. tall.

sandalled, figure through the fresh, empty streets and crossed the Nile in a small felucca. On the other bank we walked again to Mohammed's house where the donkeys were kept, and stood around while the family saddled them and we mounted. I was given a grey donkey at first then changed to a brown one. Mounting up was a good laugh, the donkeys were so small and Lorraine, Brian and Peter are all over 6ft. tall. They had to lift their toes to keep them from dragging along the ground.

It was a long clip clop along the main road past the Colossus of Memnon and then up a winding trail over dazzling white sun-bleached chalk hills. Mohammed insisted on helping me in precipitous places, by holding me on my donkey - his hands always trying to become familiar. I wanted Peter near. But Peter had his own problems, he was terrified that his donkey might slip over the edge of the 200' cliff. In the end he got off and carried his donkey! Not quite, but he certainly walked almost as far as the donkey carried him.

The Valley of Kings was stupendous. Down in the tombs it

Mohammed held his umbrella over me as he 'helped' me on my donkey.

was difficult to believe that the precise wall paintings had retained their strong colours for 3,000 years. However, the burning heat which hit as you emerged from the tunnels made it impossible to think clearly. Instead of remembering the sights of a lifetime, which we saw in the tombs of Ramses 3, 6 & 9, all I could think of as we staggered out into the blazing sunlight was "Shade, shade, where's some shade?"

A few sun shelters had been erected, but not enough. The few tourists crowded into the small areas of shade made each other even hotter.

We eventually arrived at Mohammed's home. He invited us in for a cool drink. We accepted and were introduced to his beautiful Muslim wife.

In the burning heat we climbed back up the hill to the donkeys and then rode to the Valley of Queens. Nefertiti's Tomb required an extra $100 ticket so we didn't go down, but the tombs of other queens gave us an idea of their lavish domestic life. In scorching heat we rode on to the Tombs of the Nobles.

Mohammed held his umbrella over me as he 'helped' me on my donkey. Good! that meant one hand was permanently occupied. Now we were beginning to wish we were in air-conditioned coaches, but we were really getting a feel for the tomb makers, slaves and some of their problems.

In the hellish heat we started for home. On the main road, my stupid donkey decided to walk towards an oncoming car. As I pulled his head forcibly the other way, so my saddle slipped under his belly and I found myself on my back in the middle of the road.

"Yes, it does hurt, but I'm OK. No, I will walk for a bit and when I do remount I would prefer a more sensible donkey."

At the Ramses III Temple, Mohammed waited outside with the donkeys while we set off to explore the ruins. I laid down on a stone bench in the cooler arched entrance tower while the others examined pillars, walls and stones and took photographs. One of the kind, robed keepers offered me tea in his hut which I accepted. I knew he would expect baksheesh but it was nevertheless a kind gesture. The others joined me and we all sat in the shed, which, by the look of the palm woven mats and grubby blankets, must be their living quarters.

Gingerly I re-mounted and we eventually arrived at Mohammed's home. He invited us in for a cool drink. We accepted and were introduced to his beautiful Muslim wife. Dressed in a colourful long sleeved tunic and a scarf around her head, she nodded to us and indicated that we be seated.

As I looked at this serene woman I wondered was she really treated as I had been led to believe in the papers written by Nawal El-Saadawi, a 63 year old physician in Cairo who was now under permanent guard because of death threats both from the State and Islamists. Nawal argues against "state created fundamentalism, both in Egypt (Islam) and in the United States (Christian)." She writes that when she was in Cairo University in the 1950s, no women were veiled, now about 80% are veiled. She quotes an Egyptian Islamic proverb: "A woman's heaven is under the feet of her husband."

Peter thinks that this book isn't the place for the following passages about the treatment of women. But I am only me, I have no other platform. Where else can the plight of grossly under-privileged women be aired? I leave it to you, the reader, to decide whether or not you wish to read the following italicised paragraphs.

Dr Saadawi asks *"Why should a girl be a virgin, required to bleed, on her wedding night? Men are not supposed to be virgins. Why is it required of women? Why should men enjoy 'unbridled male lust'? Why is Muslim law severe on women and lax on men?"*

Dr. Saadawi's major campaign is to halt female circumcision. She writes:

"The majority of rural Egyptian women are still circumcised. Here (Egypt) they remove only the clitoris; but even so there are many problems. Infection, bleeding, damage to the urinary tract, sepsis, even death. In the villages it is performed on girls just before puberty, by untrained village midwives using any kind of knife or razor, without painkillers, and in unsanitary conditions. In the middle and upper classes, it may be carried out by a doctor. The reasons given for clitoridectomies in Egypt are 'cleanliness' and so that 'girls will not run after men'. "

There is no mention of it in the Koran and only a brief mention in the authentic hadith that states: "A woman used to perform circumcision in Medina. The Prophet said to her. 'Do not cut severely, as it is better for a woman and more desirable for a husband.'

Jan Goodwin in her book 'The Price of Honour' tells of her meeting with an Egyptian taxi driver, Abdel Wahab.

"Abdel says he knows that Cairo is a sin city, and is determined to protect his wife and daughter from any exposure. 36 years old he considers himself a "moderate conservative" and carries a Koran in his cab, which he studies between fares.

I met him on the first day of my trip and finding him helpful and honest, hired him for the remainder of my visit. Toward the end of my stay, he invited me to his home to meet his wife and family in a crowded Cairo suburb. *A narrow steep staircase, dramatically contorted by subsidence, led to the cold-water apartment consisting of four small rooms, the largest no bigger than eight feet square. Only the two front rooms had windows, which overlooked a narrow lane. Abdul lived here with his wife, Wafa aged 24, his four year old daughter, Safar, thirty month old son Ahmad, and his very elderly father and blind mother. In this dimly lighted, claustrophobic apartment where one had to step over furniture to move around, Abdel had virtually incarcerated his wife "to protect her."*

In a village, Wafa would have lived with an extended family and would have had a compound to wander through and the company of other women. Instead, she was not permitted to visit other women in her building, or to go out even to buy bread, or attend weddings, a social highlight in the lives of most women living in purdah.

Both Abdel and Wafa are college educated. He holds a degree in commerce. She was studying for a commercial diploma when they married six years ago, but Abdul refused to let her continue. *"It is better she sit home and teach the children. There are many problems in the street, and I would never let her work with men. No, no, no."* he said. *"I want to control her and my daughter wherever they go. She cannot meet other people. She has no permission to go anywhere without me, and, as a taxi driver, I work from seven a.m. until mid-night, so she must stay home. I buy the food. I do not permit her to visit the women in the building, not even for an hour. Women sitting together talking make problems - it has always been so - I have never permitted it and she must be one hundred percent obedient to me.*

Of course, I visit my male friends, we sit and talk, but men are different from ladies; they do not make problems, men are wise. The mind of a lady is not like the mind of a man. She is not equal to a man. Why? Because man is man and woman is woman. It is better my wife sit every day in the house with the children."

Jan asked Abdul how he spent his free time, particularly in the winter when there was less demand for taxis. *"In the summer I sleep, and after the tourist season in the winter, I go for picnics, for drives, to the beach. No. I never take my wife. It is not necessary. I go with my friends, all men, many times. Why should I take her? I go to such places with men. It is the same when I go to weddings. I go alone. I don't take my wife, because it is too crowded."* Similarly Abdel does not permit Wafa to attend a mosque even at Ramadan. *"She can pray at home. It is better."*

Abdel is not intentionally being harsh, he considers himself a kind man and is perceived by people that way. He is sharply critical, for example of men who beat their wives. *"There is a difference between a woman and an animal,"* he says, and he does not agree with polygamy. As far as he is concerned, he merely takes his role as guardian of his wife and children very seriously.

Wafa says. *"It is very difficult for me. I get very lonely,"* *Before, when I lived with my parents, my mother's friends visited. They were as close as relatives. When I married Abdel, we knew each other for only two weeks; there was no time to discuss how he wanted our life to be. I married him because people said he was calm and good. When he refused to let me attend weddings, my father spoke to him and tried to make him less strict, but Abdel said, "This is my character, I cannot change."*

When Jan asked the couple if they could alter anything in their lives what it would be? Abdel responded immediately, *"A new car. That is my dream."*

In front of her husband. Wafa said, *"I would change Abdel, so that I could at least go to weddings."* When Abdel stepped out to fetch sodas for his guests, Wafa gave a tight little smile and added. *"He is a good man, but if I had known his character before, I would not have married him. I guess this was my fate."*

I thanked God for my fate, and that of my mother, my sisters, my daughter and daughters-in-law.

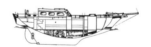

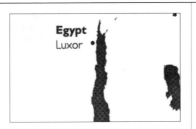

Egypt
Luxor

CHAPTER TWENTY-EIGHT

Wednesday 8th May

Before returning to our yacht we visited the new, small Luxor Museum. It was refreshing to enter a modern museum with only a few perfect exhibits; which enabled one to grasp, in an hour, some of the meaning and magnificence of the recent finds. We explored Karnak temple by day and in the evening saw the Sound and Light Show. It was a glorious evening in the open air amphitheatre with the warm breeze caressing our skins, while we listened to the story of the 3,000 year old temple. The resonant voices and clear diction of the English actors gave more meaning to this film backdrop beneath a velvet sky.

We explored Karnak temple by day and in the evening saw the Sound and Light Show.

The long desert bus trip back to Safaga was distressingly hot. A bottle of ice-cold Fanta, bought through the bus window as we passed through a town, saved us. We were pleased to be back in the small coastal town with 'normal' people - not every trader trying to rip you off, asking for baksheesh, or insisting that you buy something you didn't want.

The Karnak temple was even more than we had anticipated.

Shady Lady returned to their boat at the same time. They had splurged on a Nile cruise and seen all the sights on the way to Aswan, without the hassles we had endured. However, there was a substantial price difference. Later we heard that other yacht crews had waited until Suez, Ashkelon or Cyprus then flew to take the cruise from Cairo. Everybody we met who has taken a luxury Nile cruise, considered it excellent and money well spent.

Next morning we upped-anchor at 8am but, fortunately for me, as my bruised back from falling off my donkey was still painful, there was a 15 knot wind against us so we pulled into a sheltered bay and anchored. I slept most of the day and lowered myself down into the warm water for a relaxing swim. However pulling myself back up on board wasn't easy.

On the radio next day we heard that Peewit had arrived in Port Suez. They had made good time and obviously hadn't flown home. We motor sailed as fast as we could to make sure we saw them before they transited the Canal.

As we sailed up the Gulf of Suez on the dark blue sea, both shores were visible. The sharp outline of pale arid mountains cut into the sky. In the evening a dusty haze hid their bases and rugged crags gradually turned from white to pink to fawn, brown, mauve and then from deep purple to black, as the sun finally set.

Oil platforms glowed ahead, some brilliantly lighting the horizon with orange flares gushing from a high spout - but others! Sometimes a weak light suddenly revealed a huge dead metal structure abandoned to rust, probably a sawn-off platform. The derelict oil rigs moaned an eerie breathy clarinet whistle. We wondered who is responsible for keeping the rigs marked on the charts after the oil companies have no further use for them? The Egyptian Marine Service as both sides of the Gulf are Egyptian? Or should an international organisation be responsible? It seems that if they are not actually in the shipping channel nobody cares.

A continuous parade of lights and ships came towards us from Suez along the shipping lane. They stayed within such a tight channel it was easy to spot them and remember "red to red, go ahead". Lights coming up behind were more difficult to decipher.

On Sunday 12th May after a good calm night of motoring, a south wind blew. Hooray! we were going to be in Suez for lunch. We sailed wing and wing for an hour, then the breeze died and we motored again until we could see the channel markers for the Canal ahead. White buildings shimmered in the distance.

However the Red Sea hadn't quite finished with us. Suddenly a hot wind hit us, from the north. In minutes we were fighting to reef the sails and tack inside the buoys marking the narrow channel between the reefs and shallow water. Wrecks were strewn on either side of the beacons where unfortunate ships had been blown off course.

"Come on. Where are you? We are waiting to take your lines." KULAROO and GREEN DOLPHIN teased on the VHF. MARA had arrived in by the skin of her teeth just before the northerly started. Eventually we motor-tacked into the lee of buildings and peaceful water and our friends tied CLYPEUS to the mooring posts at the Suez Yacht Club. That northerly wind kept the more southerly yachts sheltering in bays for a further five days.

How kind the weather had been to us. It had taken us from 14th of April until the 12th of May to get from Baraisole Bay to Suez. Most other yachts had had to shelter for at least five to ten days, whereas we had been able to motor sail straight through.

Monique and Etienne dinghied over to see us. How happy they were. They looked different people, years younger. They too had never been formally charged, nor given a reason for their longer detention. Between us, we decided it had all been a political show by the Eritreans to draw attention to their new country and their independence. We concluded they were honourable people - never had bribery or baksheesh been mentioned. Nothing had been taken from our yachts. They were just politically over-enthusiastic - and who wouldn't be after thirty years of fighting for their freedom!

The story about the French government giving Monique and Etienne a free visit home was wrong. What had happened was, that a French TV station had offered to bring them

Our Suez agent - Prince of the Red Sea enjoys a pipe in his office.

home for a week for television interviews. The French Consul had said "Yes, you can go if you wish, but we cannot guarantee you will be allowed back into Eritrea to pick up PEEWIT."

They had heeded his words of warning and had sailed and motor-sailed from Massawa to Suez without stopping. It had taken them seventeen days. They were tired but happy and had just returned from a couple of days in Cairo and expected to enter the Canal the following day. As soon as they arrived in the Med, they were going to turn left and make for France and home. We made plans to visit them when we sail up through the French Canals in 2002.

In the morning our Agent, The Prince of the Red Sea brought our mail, there was very little and nothing from Andrea. We now hadn't had a letter from her since Thailand, I was very disappointed. We telephoned her and all was well, she had sent at least two letters.

At the Agent's office we telephoned The Daily Mail. "Yes," they said, "we still want to interview you. Meet us at the Nile Hilton in Cairo at 8pm of the 15th November."

"Well, we will meet you there, but will stay at somewhere less expensive."

"No. Stay at the Hilton, I am sure the Daily Mail can stand you a night."

"OK. Our fax number is .... for confirmation." (As soon as we found out about transport the next day we telephoned back to an answering machine (twice) and sent a fax confirming our appointment.)

Peter and I spent most of the morning in the Agent's office sitting on elegant embroidered chairs sipping the sweet thick black coffee, while the Prince of the Red Sea sat on the floor and then on a settee in his smart business suit, striped shirt, tie and socks, and smoked his sashi (hookah). He told us stories of his involvement with The Royal Yacht Britannia coming through the Canal, and other events and honours that had been bestowed on him.

On May 15th we travelled by local bus to Cairo with Lorraine and Brian and first went to their recommended back-packers Sun Hotel (at $40 a night for two including breakfast) and then to the Nile Hilton (at $140 a night without breakfast). We checked that the Daily Mail reporter had a reservation and then booked ourselves in.

We met Lorraine and Brian at the Cairo Museum. Fantastic - particularly the Tutankhamen Room. The funerary masks of solid gold were more beautiful than I had ever imagined, with a softness that was palpable. Like millions of other people, we were over-awed that this one young king could have been buried in such splendour. Many other objects in the museum made us once again realise what was achieved without modern technology and how we humans have lost so many skills.

A swim at the hotel refreshed us all and after a drink Peter and I dressed to receive our Daily Mail Reporter. We sat in the foyer from 8 until 10pm and then went for dinner near tables where gentlemen and a few ladies smoked their hookahs.

We stayed another night but the Reporter never did show. When we telephoned London her secretary said the interview was off as we hadn't confirmed arrangements so no expenses would be forthcoming. We were very disappointed and annoyed and could only assume that telephone messages had been wiped before being listened to, and our fax had been lost. Funny? Maddening more like!

However we would never pass this way again so there was no point in being miserable. We booked into the Sun Hotel and went off to see the Pyramids. I was apprehensive as TIMSHELL had written how, in 1994, it had been really scary and claustrophobic with so many people in the narrow tunnels down into the pyramids and I resolved not to be tempted. However, now there were so few tourists around that we were able to walk down through the tunnels into the centre of the Menkaure Pyramid without any problems. It was thrilling and I felt very privileged to be down in the cool chambers wondering how all those thousands of rocks had been placed above and around us at least 3,000 years ago.

I wish we had taken a camel ride, as at $10 for an hour, it wasn't a bad deal.

Peter climbs the pyramid of Cheops to show how large the stones are.

However, after the tourist touts in Luxor, we were so frightened of being diddled and tricked that our husbands didn't want us to indulge. Lorraine and I both regretted it and would have liked a photograph for our Christmas cards.

Now there were so few tourists around that we were able to walk down through the tunnels into the centre of the Menkaure Pyramid without any problems.

Cairo was a fascinating city and we walked ourselves to exhaustion, through the specialised markets offering a wide array of rugs, materials, tall glass hookahs, precious stones, or spices, and the various temples, and mosques. We walked in the shade of towering minarets and ornate painted balconies. On Friday, so many faithful Muslims came to pray at the mosques, tents had to be erected at the sides to accommodate all the worshipers.

One evening we wanted to see an authentic belly dance, not a tourist show - it was a poor decision. Lorraine, Brian and I (Peter was tired and not interested) took a taxi to La Palmyra. Only one other table was occupied, and that by tourists, no locals after all. We endured an amateurish male pop singer, a juggler and a six piece band and then a plump

I wish we had taken a camel ride, as at $10 for an hour, it wasn't a bad deal.

fifty-year-old belly dancer appeared. Her hips wiggled and her tummy did tremble, she was a pleasant woman, but no way was it a beautiful experience. Nothing like the Polynesian dancers of the South Pacific. An elderly Arab came in and took a front table, a waiter brought him a bottle of Black Label whisky. The dance livened up and became more erotic and suggestive.

We sat for a little longer but it wasn't a particularly enjoyable experience, so we left and walked back to the Sun Hotel. Why hadn't we taken the opportunity of seeing a more sophisticated show while we were at the Hilton?

On May 18th we bussed back to Suez and, after shopping for food, took a taxi back to our boats.

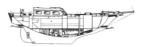

شــركة أميـر البحرالأحمر

PRINCE OF THE RED SEA Co.
(Under British & Egyptian Management)

SHIPPING AGENCY
OWNER REPRESENTATIVE
SHIPS CHANDLER
MARINE CONTRACTORS
INTERNATIONAL / DOMESTIC
TOUR OPERATOR
IMPORT / EXPORT AGENCY

Egyptian Partners :
Fathi Soukar
Ashraf Soukar
Ehab ṣoukar
British Partners :
Francis Limbrey
Dean Morris

BREAKDOWN OF SUEZ CANAL AND AGENCY FEES

Reapportioning of expenses.

- Transit fees and pilotage (SCA)	US $	114.00
- Fees per person on board (SCA)	US $	10.00
- Fiscal stamp per person on board	US $	1.50
- Fiscal stamp per Yacht (SCA)	US $	1.50
- Insurance Certificate for (SCA)	US $	5.00
- Quarantine fees	US $	7.00
- Customs forms & Fiscal stamps	US $	10.00
- Port clearance(Departure permit)	US $	16.00
- Immigration Dep/Arr Forms	US $	5.00
- Agency Fees	US $	30.00
Total US $		200.00

"The above costs is Total costs per Yacht with one person on board."

Kind Regards
Ashraf Soukar
V.Chairman

Address :
36 Gohar El-Kayed St., Port Tewfik. Suez. Egypt
P.O.Box 80, Suez, Egypt.

19 Rue Des Volubilis. 75013. Paris. France.
51 Winnham Drive. Fareham. Hants. P 016 8 QG England.

Tel.   : (20) 62 222126
Fax   : (20) 62 223825
Telex   : 66048 PRS UN
Tel./Fax : (33) 14565449ⁿ
Tel./Fax : (44) 32982677

CHAPTER TWENTY-NINE

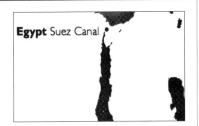

Egypt Suez Canal

Suez Canal

Back at The Suez Canal Yacht Club we found D IABLESSE, a 76' yacht, was moored next to us. The delivery crew were taking her from Australia to Florida to sell. She had been built in the south of France and was a beautiful America's Cup looking boat. The crew invited us on board for drinks and to look around. It had only taken them 39 days to sail to Suez from Perth in Western Australia.

On Sunday, when we went to pay our Canal dues and finalise the times for the pilot to arrive, the Agent again told us there was no mail for us.

Later, I was sitting in our main cabin having a little weep for my family and wanting a letter from my daughter. I tuned into the BBC World Service to cheer myself up. The morning service had just started and the cleric was talking about the 'Mappa Mundi', the oldest map of the world, which is in Hereford Cathedral from where the service was being broadcast, less than a mile from Andrea's home. It seemed to be a message from God telling me that I wasn't so far away and that I would soon see her again. The thought gave me great comfort.

We did the washing in the Club's washing machine and prepared the boat for transiting the Canal. We had been warned to leave nothing on deck that could be lifted.

Our pilot, Mohammed, was on board at 9.30am and we led the way into the Canal with M ARA following. The pilot was far more interested in asking for presents, than steering the boat or telling us details about the running of the Canal. He kept asking for a present, first for himself, then his wife and then his baby, all within the first hour. He exasperated us so much, Peter actually radioed the Prince of the Red Sea and asked him to have a word with the pilot. We would give him a $US20 present but at the end of the day, not the beginning. Mohammed looked suitably chastened as the Prince spoke to him. On arrival at Ismalia we dropped him off at the Quay with his $20, two packets of Benson and Hedges, soap and

Another pilot arrived at 9.30 - Achmed, who was dressed in white and brought us some fresh bread, for which we were very grateful.

perfume for his wife and clothes for his baby. We were pleased to be shot of him, then we relaxed and had an early night.

Foolishly, we left our sailing shoes in the cockpit and by morning they had gone, presumably stolen by the Bitter Lake fishermen - well, we had been warned!

Another pilot arrived at 9.30 - Achmed, who was dressed in white and brought us some fresh bread, for which we were very grateful. He was a very smart 37 year old, but boy didn't

he know he was handsome! He was aggressively jolly. He laid out a white towel to protect his white trousers each time before he sat down. As the day wore on he hardly took the wheel and became more and more familiar. Without invitation he followed me into the bedroom to look at photographs of our family. He asked for photographs of me!! and gifts for his wife and children. We would give him a present wouldn't we? He

Achmed insisted upon helping me and pulling the material through - too fast.

asked for cigarettes and sat in the main cabin reading magazines. He was unbearable!

After giving the men lunch I locked myself in my cabin for a couple of hours so that I didn't have to be near him. However, our Israeli courtesy ensign needed sewing so I got the sewing machine out onto the cabin table.

Achmed insisted upon helping me and pulling the material through - too fast. I realised I would actually have to be rude to him to make him stop.

As we approached Port Said he asked for "cigarettes for my friends the police. If you give them cigarettes, which I will throw to them as we pass the police jetty, you will be allowed to carry on without stopping." We wrapped up some cigarettes.

"My wife would like lipstick? or some perfume?"

In the end I told him "You have offended me. Do you walk into the homes of your Egyptian friends and demand presents? It is not our custom to ask for gifts in a home."

"But this is a boat."

"This is my home."

He pretended to be upset and put back all the gifts onto the table, and behaved like a reprimanded schoolboy. He threw the cigarettes at the police and we were allowed to carry on. When he was eventually taken off by a launch, he took the gifts and the $20 dollars!

Transiting the Suez Canal boat-wise is a doddle. It is just a ditch in the sand, nowhere nearly as complex or magnificent as the Panama Canal.

However the Egyptians hadn't finished with us yet! MARA had yet another official climb on board.

"He says you must follow us closely," Brian said over the VHF "then you will not have to have another pilot."

"We will follow you very closely," Peter replied "just get us out of here."

Once out of the main harbour and in the north-going Channel their pilot was taken off. Hooray! We were in the Med again at last. We had spent 3 glorious if apprehensive months, before our Atlantic crossing exploring the Spanish coast and Balearic Lslands in 1983 before crossing the Atlantic at the beginning of our circumnavigation. Now at last we were free of Egypt and the Red Sea. Never have I been so pleased to leave a country. Our own country's Daily Mail staff letting us down, hadn't helped our morale. Thank goodness for the integrity and kindness of our friends on MARA, which had helped us keep ourselves together.

Once in clear sea we turned right and headed on through the night towards Ashkelon Marina in Israel. A lovely sunny day was spent sailing east across the blue, dark blue Mediterranean which we had left via Gibraltar in October 1983.

After lunch, the next day the VHF suddenly crackled and a commanding voice demanded that we identify ourselves. It was the Israeli Navy who, in curt terms, demanded our

As dusk drew in we approached Ashkelon. Two miles off we called the Harbour Master and the Marina launch came and guided us in.

names, nationality, passport numbers, where we had come from and what was our destination?

Oh No! Not again, I became very anxious and for the first time in my life I took a tranquilliser to try and calm my anxiety. At 4pm a gun boat approached and circled us and again asked questions on the radio. Evidently satisfied with our replies they roared away. We hadn't realised quite how nervous our Eritrean experience had left us.

As dusk drew in we approached Ashkelon. Two miles off we called the Harbour Master and the Marina launch came and guided us in. We pulled into a space on the jetty behind MARA. CHARDEY, and MOWGLI came to welcome us and the Marina Manager, Armand and his assistant, Michael, helped us moor and told us what to expect. Brian brought us each a cold can of Fosters Lager and we sat on deck talking, waiting for the Bomb Squad to come and inspect the boat.

"Ashkelon is where Samson and Delilah had lived and where Samson pushed down the Temple pillars," we were told. "There are marble columns lying on the beach and Greek and Roman ruins everywhere."

Two pleasant, but armed, young men in navy blue bullet proof vests, went through the boat with filter papers. They rubbed the tissues on all cupboards, locker frames and sills - evidently it would detect any explosive substances. Peter had to wipe his hands on some of the same of filter paper. They asked if we had carried anything from Egypt or had any explosives on board. Peter showed them our flares and shot-gun cartridges which they accepted as a gift as we no longer have a shot gun. (We had commenced our voyage with a revolver and a shotgun, but they had caused so much hassle we left them with the Singapore Authorities in 1989.)

Next day we were taken by courtesy car to book into Israel at Ashdod Port and the chatty driver gave us a quick tour of the area. He took us along the natural vegetation of the cliff tops.

"This is how it all used to be," he said. "The land of milk and honey. You will find many trees and bushes bearing fruit." We carried on through the now irrigated farm lands; row upon row of abundant crops filled the fields. Acres of sunflowers drooped their heavy heads, shading their petals from the direct midday sun. As we returned to Ashkelon by a different route the driver pointed out large attractive apart-ment blocks with balconies and wide windows.

"They are for the 100,000 new immigrant families from Russia," he said. "Ashkelon can accommodate such a number in less than two years".

Back at the Marina we enjoyed hot showers and shampoos and after dinner on MARA relaxed, feeling safer than we had done for many weeks.

Inside the pyramid of Menkaure.

Israel

Ashkelon

We stayed a month and as our confidence and spirits returned it seemed worth all the hassles of the Red Sea to emerge into such a rich historical environment. We visited Jerusalem, Bethlehem, Masada, the Dead Sea, Tel Aviv, Jaffa, Eilat, Aqaba in Jordan and 'Petra the rose red city, half as old as time'.

CHAPTER THIRTY

Israel

Ashkelon

Modern, clean, Ashkelon marina, with space for 600 boats, would have been very peaceful if the Israel Air Force had not been flying daily supersonic sorties over the Gaza Strip fifty miles to the south, and launching missiles at the Lebanese one hundred miles to the North.

We stayed a month and as our confidence and spirits returned it seemed worth all the hassles of the Red Sea to emerge into such a rich historical environment. We visited Jerusalem, Bethlehem, Masada, the Dead Sea, Tel Aviv, Jaffa, Eilat, Aqaba in Jordan and 'Petra the rose red city, half as old as time'.

It seemed weird actually being 'on the road to Jerusalem' or Jericho, or Damascus. With Lorraine and Brian we took the local air conditioned bus to Jerusalem and stayed at a hostel inside the old city at Jaffa

Pressing my hand on the stones of the Wailing Wall was a moving experience

Gate. On the first day we walked along the top of the northern side of the ancient wall surrounding Jerusalem and decided which churches and shrines to visit and managed only a few of the many. The next day we walked the southern wall and visited more historic shrines. Pressing my hand on the stones of the Wailing Wall was a moving experience - a

warm and comforting glow seemed to be reflected back.

I hadn't realised Old Jerusalem still had a complete city wall with covered alleyways and tunnels crisscrossing the city. The pink marble Roman pavements and stone arched alleys were a surprise, as was the English organised Garden Tomb out beyond Damascus Gate. A sanctuary in a delightful garden where General Gordon had decided that Jesus may have been laid. It was certainly more peaceful, simple, and moving than the Holy Sepulchre Tomb where buildings and adornments have been built over older buildings and adornments, and Coptic, Fransciscan and Catholic priests each jealously guard their bit. I was giving thanks by the tomb of Jesus when a black robed priest entered, interrupted the four or five people praying, and in a curt voice ordered everyone out of the tomb while he changed the candles. He shattered the gentle, loving and emotional atmosphere which had pervaded.

One morning we took a tour and left Jerusalem at 3.30am to climb Masada, where the Jewish zealots had been besieged by the Romans. Lorraine and Brian forged ahead up the 1200 foot tor. We climbed more slowly and sat to watch dawn rise over the mountains of Moab to reveal a diminished Dead Sea. Mining and chemical extraction have lowered the water level. Banks of salt-streaked mud stretched to the dark water and pillars of salt rose above the surface.

We reached the top of Snake Pass and explored the hill top where Jewish patriots were besieged for three years by the Romans. Realizing it was impossible to hold out any longer, the 967 defenders committed suicide, preferring to die as free men rather than be Roman slaves. The remains of the Zealots' homes and bath houses were there, together with the oldest synagogue in the world. Herod's Hanging Palace, built on the cliff side, was an incredible achievement. How they serviced the apartments, or carried him on his palanquin up and down the steep steps, is difficult to imagine. Evidently he only visited this palace twice. We had walked down again by 8.30.

Banks of salt-streaked mud stretched to the dark water and pillars of salt rose above the surface.

in time to see the first funicular cab of tourists whisked directly to the top.

It was good to meet Cruising Association Members taking part in the East Mediterannean Rally.

Next was a fun stop to bathe in the Dead Sea. Our bodies floated so high on the water it was difficult to swim and our feet wouldn't stay down. However care had to be taken not to get the water in our eyes or mouth because it stung and felt thick and oily.

The next stop was Qmran where the Dead Sea Scrolls were found. Peter was very interested but we didn't climb up to the empty caves, just bought a book about it all.

We were already too tired to do justice to the National Park of Ein Gedi - two more hours of walking would have seen us off! We just sat outside and talked to other travellers and watched the parties of school children, escorted by their teachers with assault rifles slung over their shoulders, enter the park with their notebooks and picnic boxes.

Guns and rifles are everywhere in Israel. You get quite used to asking the soldiers, male and female, to please move their gun because it is in the way, on the bus or in the super-market. The Israelis are ready to fight NOW, not in 24 hours, or even one hour, but NOW. Young men do three years national service and the girls do two years; both then serve a month a year until the age of 45. They seem to enjoy it and don't fear that they are wasting their time. Supersonic bangs occur every day as their fighters patrol the coast.

The war-like attitude does rub off in their daily lives. They don't smile easily at strangers and are suspicious of all different ethnic groups that are now living within the country. However, when they enjoy themselves; boy! do they let go. At the Marina, two yacht rallies finished there and parties were organised. Locals and visitors danced no matter what age. It was good to meet Cruising Association members taking part in the East Mediterannean Rally.

We saw a school's dance festival which was excellent. On floodlit tennis courts the children danced exuberantly, in colourful costumes, and it was all a welcome change after no social dancing in Muslim countries. It seems the Israeli

teachers are helping to unite the immi- grant children of different ethnic and language groups in a fun way without the need of words, by the medium of dance. For one of the Marina parties we were hosted by a handsome young local Russian Jewish couple, Micki and Ramon, who had been married only seven months. They invited us to their three months' old, smart apartment. Both had been brought to Israel by their par- ents when toddlers and both were very patriotic. Micki had laid out a lavish assortment of cream cakes, cheesy croissants, dainty biscuits and good coffee. The apartment walls were all white and decorated with Salvador Dali prints. Their furniture, TV and sound system were black, modern, and could belong to any young couple in any devel- oped country. Both had parents within 50 miles whom they saw regularly at weekends, but they were hoping to ease out of that situation and develop their own friends. Micki and Ramon kept in constant touch via their mobile phones.

Travelling to Petra was a dream I had hoped to fulfil and we did it without problems, although I was again very apprehensive and wanted the safety in numbers of a tour. However our friends quite rightly suggested it would be much cheaper and more interesting to go on our own. Lorraine sorted out the logistics, she is very good with that sort of thing and organised for us to leave at 4.30am to take the modern air-conditioned bus to Eilat on the Israeli side of the Gulf of Aqaba.

From Eilat a taxi, with a lady driver, took us to the barbed wire border where we booked out of Israel. The walk across the 300 yards of no-man's-land was hot and our backpacks heavy. The Jordan officials were welcoming and helpful and the tourism agent organised for a hire car firm to come and get us. Some young Dutch and German couples waited with us, which was great, because when it came to sorting out licences for the hire car, none of us had licences which complied with the regulations. The young Dutchman kindly used his licence and drove our car for the first few hundred yards around the corner then he and Brian changed back into their own groups. It was interesting to see that the Jordanians were all small people of the same race, not like Israel where everybody is from another land.

We drove the hundred odd miles through desert and then over precipitous mountains. It was dark and eventually the lights of the village of Petra twinkled below us as we descended over a mountain pass. We booked into the Sunrise Hotel at 8.30 and had a good dinner, then sweltered in our little room with no air conditioning and no fan, until we eventually fell asleep with wet flannels on our foreheads.

We were up at 5.30 for breakfast and ready to go. Money problems clouded the first part of the morning as we had no Jordanian money and had to wait for the bank to accept our Visa cards. However by 7.30 we eventually walked towards Petra.

It was the experience of a lifetime walking though the Siq the half mile rock crevice, (as filmed in "Indiana Jones and the Jewel of the Nile") which is the only way into this

pre-Christian city of the Nabateans, Greeks, Romans, Byzantines and Egyptians. After the Crusaders left in the 12th Century it was abandoned and forgotten by all except the Bedouins, until rediscovered in 1812 by the Swiss traveller Burkhardt. Carved rock palaces and temples, homes and shrines have been sheltered from the elements by the dry air and high sandstone cliffs around them. The pink sandstone Treasury building carved from the solid rock was so finely worked it brought gasps of amazement. The vertical and horizontal walls and ceilings inside the scooped-out halls were perfect. How did they do it? What tools did they have? It really was awesome.

The pink sandstone Treasury building carved from the solid rock was so finely worked it brought gasps of amazement.

Camel Corps soldiers wandered around in their practical, yet romantic, uniform of white trousers tucked into riding boots overdraped by a khaki skirt, often tucked up into their belts. Their chests were crisscrossed with a leather bandolier of bullets held on their shoulders under their epaulettes. The headdress of red and white fringed cloth tucked into their black Arab roundel topped off their elegant garb. The faces beneath resembled younger versions of King Hussein of Jordan, handsome and well proportioned.

Camel Corps soldiers wandered around in their practical, yet romantic, uniform of white trousers tucked into riding boots overdraped by a khaki skirt.

We climbed up to the

Sacrificial Rock and lost our way in the high gorges. Scrabbling up an overgrown path we met a pleasant, blue-jeaned, sun hatted American couple descending.

The vertical and horizontal walls and ceilings inside the scooped-out halls were perfect.

"Hi, don't think anything is this aways." he said.

We shared a track down for a few minutes; they were here for just four days, on a retirement holiday from Arizona. Then our paths diverged again.

We walked down through temples and cave dwellings of coloured stone. Sheep and goat herders sat selling trinkets while they kept an eye on their stock. We stumbled down the mountain path to the 70' Arch of the Nabatean Temple, the only free standing building in the city. What a wonderful life project it would be, if one was well-educated enough, to start seeking out the social history of the dwellings and water channels.

Roman pavements led to a Colonnade, the Urn Tomb and the Roman amphitheatre; which seats 4,000 and is still used for special performances.

The only inhabitant of the ancient city was a fast-talking white-robed Arab high up on the platform outside the Urn

The only inhabitant of the ancient city was a fast-talking white-robed Arab high up on the platform outside the Urn Tomb. He chatted and joked in fourteen languages.

Tomb. He chatted and joked in fourteen languages and had a display of rugs, cards, paintings, prints, camel bags and books. He never left the City, he loved living there and talking with people from all countries as they chose souvenirs. His friends brought his food and water.

I bought a David Roberts' print and a camel hair rug and he gave us post cards and information. It was a pleasure to buy from such an erudite and amusing gentleman.

After a cup of tea back at the Sunrise we picked up our bags and started our mountainous drive back to Aqaba. Bedouin tents of the same design as those in Sudan dotted the landscape. At Aqaba we asked to be taken to the border by the car hire owner and were back in Eilat by 9.30pm where we booked into the Red Mountain Hotel. What a day!
A day of a lifetime!

CHAPTER THIRTY-ONE

Cyprus

During our time in Ashkelon Marina we talked to other crews who had experienced problems sailing up from Aden. There will probably always be disputes amongst the countries bordering the Red Sea - they won't change - yacht crews must learn how to deal with the situations. Recounting some of these incidents and how the Red Sea Class of '96 dealt with them, may help prepare future voyagers.

The first yacht to encounter bullets whizzing across their cockpit were Americans Barbara and Michael of KELLY MARIE. They left Aden on 5th December intending to day sail, taking time to snorkel and explore the fabulous Red Sea coral reefs. With strong winds, rough seas and dodging the many merchant ships, they were looking forward to a mid-morning landfall in the Great Hanish Islands.

However, as they approached what they hoped would be shelter, the winds increased to over 40 knots and each anchorage they approached looked unsafe. At last on the NW end of the Island they pulled in towards a deep bay with an inviting long white sand beach. Tiny figures walked down the hill and congregated on the shore. But 'no worries', KELLY MARIE had valid visas for Yemen for another 30 days, and port clearance to Hudaydah. However, as they came closer into the bay they could see an extensive coral reef and the wind was still howling, so they decided to try the next bay.

As they turned the boat they heard the crackle of gun fire.
"They're shooting at us!" Barbara shouted.
"But why?" Michael responded, "we're obviously leaving."
They carried on to the next bay and dropped the anchor but it wouldn't hold. There were Arab dhows on the beach and at anchor. Skiffs and tents were scattered on the foreshore. Tiny figures came running down from the hill between the bays and four men got into a skiff and paddled towards them.

Michael retrieved the anchor and while they were deciding where to try next, the skiff came alongside with four soldiers carrying automatic weapons who tried to board.

Michael, at the wheel, decided to increase speed and the skiff and soldiers were left behind.

Two and a half hours later they eyeballed their way through the reef and pulled in behind a small island off larger Zuguar. Peace at last! No wind, no people, no boats, no military! They slept for an hour, then showered and watched the prolific bird life. It was so pleasant they thought they may stay a week.

Sitting enjoying the sunset they noticed men walking along the beach. Suddenly nearby they heard commands being shouted in Arabic then a crackle crackle, and a high pitched bizz bizz just above their heads. They flattened themselves on the cockpit floor. Bullets hit the island alongside and a million birds took off in frantic flight.

Scared stiff, they crawled below, turned off all the lights, and radioed Mukha Port Control. A broken-up voice advised what they interpreted as "Proceed to Hudaydah."

Barbara sent out an "All ships" call for a radio relay to enhance their reception of the message.

A Dutch vessel responded, to whom they told the whole story. The Captain decided to contact the "International Centre for Crisis at Sea" in Norway.

As he signed off the Captain of U.S. Navy Warship # 61 MONTEREY came on the radio. He asked many questions: name and registration of boat, crew's names, where they had come from, were going to, exact position of the boat and exactly what had happened?

By this time the soldiers were still screaming at them but not shooting.

The U.S. Warship Commander came back. He had called the U.S. Embassy in Sana, the capital of North Yemen. They wanted to know "exactly what is your concern and your reason for not picking up your anchor and leaving?"

Barbara replied "It is too dark to get out of the reef,"

Michael added, "No, that is not not the main concern - I don't feel comfortable going out on deck - they might shoot at us."

The Captain laughed, "They both sound like valid concerns."

The Navy kept in touch during the evening. The soldiers limited their yelling to every five minutes or so.

At 10pm the Captain called, "The American Embassy had contacted the Yemen Military Commander who issued a strong warning that it was very dangerous right now as there is a military conflict between Yemen and Eritrea. Furthermore it could not be guaranteed they were Yemeni soldiers firing.

They could be Eritrean! They advised KELLY MARIE to attempt to leave immediately despite their concerns.

Barbara and Michael re-iterated they were sure the soldiers were Yemeni and had the Military Commander contacted them? They were assured he was contacting them now if they were Yemeni military.

At 11pm calls and whistles from the far beach recalled the trigger-happy soldiers. By 11.30 pm they had gone and all was quiet. Sleep at last.

Kelly Marie left early in the morning keeping in radio contact with U.S. Warship # 61 which they later found out was an Aegis class Missile Cruiser.

American yachts have great back-up systems!

Secondly, the story of a fleet of five yachts, including Australian VAGABOND HEART.

The yachts all left Aden on 19th of February and had passed east of Perim Island. VAGABOND HEART, Bob and Rachel with their ten year old daughter Georgia and crewman Howard on board, were sailing at the rear of the group. They heard Gary on the lead boat MISSION, say on the VHF that they were being approached by a launch carrying Yemeni soldiers with guns. A shot was fired across their bows when they didn't stop. They stopped, and were boarded and told to pull in to a nearby bay and wait. The next three yachts were all boarded and an armed guard stationed on board each one.

VAGABOND HEART thought they would make a run for it in the following wind, as with their spinnaker up and the engine on, they were making nine knots, but the launch came charging after them firing shots into the air. Five men in assorted uniforms and no papers, no authority, just one machine gun, climbed aboard and demanded they turn back. Their passports were taken and they were made to rejoin the other yachts who all had armed guards stationed on board. Then they were all forced to turn around and motor back against the wind for twenty miles in the gathering gloom.

They were questioned. Those with photocopies of their passports were only required to give up the photocopies, the other passports were checked, taken away and evidently copies made. All passports were returned that night and they were given permission to leave in the morning.

At Suez VAGABOND HEART tried to land their crewman Howard, a 52 year old Australian who had been happily on board since September. Howard wished to travel to Galipolli to meet up with his former regiment for the ANZAC Day Anniversary commemorations. Although he had all his necessary papers as an Egyptian tourist, the pilot would not allow him ashore. The pilot insisted that Bob, the owner of

VAGABOND HEART, went ashore and paid an Agent to sign Howard off. So their fond farewell finished up as a quick and upsetting cheerio.

Thirdly, not all problems occurred at sea.

When U.S. attorney, Tom Menaker of STAR went to the Eritrean Immigration Authorities in Massawa to book out, the officer stamped Tom's wife Bonnie's passport, then noticed that the entry stamp was different in Tom's passport (Tom hadn't looked at his visa or realised there was a discrepancy). He was accused of changing the dates on the visa, arrested and immediately put in jail.

When he did not return, Bonnie roamed the streets looking for him. Nobody came to tell her what had happened. She eventually returned to STAR distraught.

Tom managed to talk to the official Prosecutor and said "What do I have to do to get out of here? If I have to plead guilty and pay a fine. I'll plead guilty and pay a fine."

However the Prosecutor wouldn't let him do this, when he was obviously innocent! Tom was returned to his cell. Meanwhile another prisoner had been brought in, a foreign business man. During the night this man was so sick the police thought he might die on them so let him go. They decided to let Tom go at the same time and returned his passport. He had to sleep on the quay until Bonnie woke up, saw him and came to get him.

Next, was PEEWIT'S arrest and as they did not have an SSB/amateur radio, and were not sailing in company, nobody knew they had been arrested, until we were detained and we told on the regular radio schedule of this lone yacht at anchor with no one aboard.

The lessons we all learned were:

1. IF GOING NORTHWARDS IN THE RED SEA, BOOK INTO ERITREA AT ASSAB. OTHERWISE DO NOT ANCHOR ANYWHERE BEFORE BOOKING IN AT MASSAWA.

2. HAVE A RELIABLE LONG RANGE SSB/AMATEUR RADIO TRANSCEIVER AND KEEP IN TOUCH WITH OTHER YACHTS, NOT JUST FOR THE WEATHER AHEAD, BUT HAVE A FIXED SCHEDULE SO THAT IF YOU DISAPPEAR SOME-BODY KNOWS WHERE AND WHEN.

3. SAIL IN A GROUP, OR AT LEAST IN COMPANY.

4. CARRY PHOTOCOPIES OF YOUR PASSPORTS AND SHIP'S PAPERS.

5. CHECK THE ENTRIES IN YOUR PASSPORT BEFORE YOU LEAVE THE IMMIGRATION OFFICE. BE PATIENT, SMILE AND BE POLITE, EVEN IF IT HURTS!

6. IN THE FUTURE, A SATELLITE RADIO TELEPHONE HIDDEN IN YOUR POCKET, COULD BE YOUR MOST VALUABLE AID.

However, there are many positive aspects of the Red Sea - it may be one of the last unspoiled warm cruising grounds left in the world and with the 'Red Sea Pilot' (Imray Laurie Norie & Wilson) and a GPS, the natural hazards are not unreasonable. The clear water, excellent snorkelling, the wonders of the world at the northern end - Luxor, the tombs of the Pharaohs and Karnak Temple; the Nile Valley, the Pyramids, Cairo, then Israel, leading to the civilisations of the Mediterranean and Europe to explore, make it a fascinating route to the other side of the world. Although our initial plan had been to round the Cape of Good Hope, the natural difficulties and disasters of the treacherous East African seas seemed a greater hazard than tackling the Red Sea. Certainly, we met no dangerous weather or sea conditions. I wouldn't have missed it.

It was difficult to leave Ashkelon - not just tearing ourselves away from the clean Marina and new friends, but the Israeli Navy was exercising offshore and three times we had to deviate, on their instructions, to keep out of the way of

It was a delightful two day sail to Larnaca, in Cyprus, where CLYPEUS now rests. Snugly cocooned in her steel cradle she looks out over the harbour awaiting our return in two years time to complete our circumnavigation.

their rockets. Eventually, after dodging around all one day and night, we returned to Ashkelon Marina, put more diesel on board and had another go.

It was a delightful two day sail to Larnaca, in Cyprus, where CLYPEUS now rests. Snugly cocooned in her steel cradle she looks out over the harbour awaiting our return in two years time to complete our circumnavigation. After exploring the Coptic Monasteries, Troodos Mountains, Aphrodite's Pool, Paphos with its Roman ruins, forts and castles with Lorraine and Brian, they headed on to Turkey and left us behind. As MARA sailed out of Larnaca Harbour the tears flowed freely. How could we ever repay such trustworthy friends

Exploring
the Coptic
Monasteries
and the
Troodos
Mountains.

"Goodbye, God bless, Bon voyage!"

"We will see them again won't we?"
I sniffed in Peter's arms.
"Yes. We will make sure we do," he comforted.

A few weeks later, we too left Larnaca, but by air, excited to be returning home. It was wonderful to be back with our families in what now seems quaint, green little, free little, England. Rosemary and Noel and their daughters Laura and Emily, and Andrea and Rupert with their sons Alexander and Frederick, were well and happy and pleased to see us and we were able to thank them all for their efforts on our behalf. Rosemary had written very comprehensive notes of how things happened to them, which I have included. It is really quite amusing that the French Ambassador's first phone call was considered only a social conversation !

Now I sit in Paul and Alice's home in Sturgeon Bay, Wisconsin, U.S.A. watching the snow flutter down outside the window. Our American grandchildren Hazel and Owen are out there, bundled-up and round as snowmen themselves, working to make a snow fort. It is difficult to realise that all this has happened in just one year. Please God, our next year in Shanghai in China when Peter takes up a two year contract with his former company, will not have quite so many anxious moments.

Index

The following International Yachts
*supported us and many contributed to The Save Clypeus Fund;
there are others about whom we do not know.* **Thank you all.**

ALLEGRE, ALPINE ROSE, ANNIE'S SONG, ARGYLE, BLACK BULL, BOMBINI, BUSTER, CAPE PROVIDENCE, CHARDONAY, CHARISMA, COCKAIGNE, DE LA MER, DIABLESSE, DOUBLE M, ELEANOR, EMMA FELIX, JANE, GANNET, GENOA, GREEN DOLPHIN, HALCYON, INERTIA, INTERLUDE, JE T'AIME, KAIENA, KELLY MARIE, KHANSIN, KULAROO, LA COMPLICE, LA ROSA. LA TORTUGA, LAZYBONES, LONE RIVAL, LUDUS AMORE, MALEK, MARA, MARAKI, MITHRA, MOWGLI, NIATE, PAPA KILO, PEEWIT, PIPE DREAM, PLAIN JANE, QUALLEE OF SYDNEY, RATTLE & HUM, RESOLUTE, RAI RIVA, ROUSABOUT, RUM ADA, SAIORSE, SEMARANG, SHADY LADY, SIOUX, SIFTING BULL, STEADFAST, STAR, STARGAZY, SUNFLOWER, SUNSHINE, SWEET SURRENDER, THISTLEDOWN, TRINITY, VAGABOND HEART, WIAERE, WIRRAWAY, and of course SUTAMON our cruising buddy boat in '88 and '89 around Australia, Papua New Guinea, and on to Indonesia and Singapore.

Equipment list - Clypeus

Anchors -20 kg Bruce + 100m 10mm chain
60 lb CQR + l00m 18mm nylon
601b Fisherman
Engine - Perkins 4-108M diesel
Diesel 100 gallons. Water 125 gallons.
Avon Inflatable with Mercury 2.2 outboard
8 ft. fibreglass dinghy
Aires wind self steering
Ampair trailing generator
Auto Helm ST 3000 wheel autopilot
Phillips AP Mk6 GPS
Sestrel steering and handbearing compasses
Radios - Kenwood TS 4308, Amateur SSB Icom VHF
Grundig Satellit SW receiver
Solar Panels - 3 Solarex, 10 amps total.
Sails 7 - All Lucas of Portsmouth
Red Sea Pilot
British Admiralty Charts
Guide to Eritrea by Edward Paice
British Admiralty charts were used on board CLYPEUS

The charts used to illustrate this book
are reproduced by courtesy of Bellingham Chart Printers
PO Box 1728, Friday Harbour, WA 98250 USA.
Tel: (800) 643 3900
Fax: (360) 468 3939
E-Mail: sales@tidesend.com
Web: http//www.tidesend.com